The Mathematics
of
Personal Finance

The Mathematics
of
Personal Finance

A COMPLETE REFERENCE

Donald E. Lutz

toExcel

San Jose   New York   Lincoln   Shanghai

The Mathematics of Personal Finance

Published by toExcel

For information address:
toExcel
165 West 95th Street, Suite B-N
New York, NY 10025
www.toExcel.com

ISBN: 1-58348-378-0

LCCN: 99-64652

Printed in the United States of America

CONTENTS

Part Two
Applications of Financial Math

Planning. Are Tax-Free Municipal Bonds Appropriate for You? Tax Avoidance Planning.

Preface

My purpose in writing this book is to set forth the fundamental principles of financial mathematics and to show how to apply these principles. My goal is to help you to win in the increasingly complex financial world in which we all live. To reach that goal, information and techniques are presented to enhance your ability to:

1. Evaluate your financial options,
2. Monitor your financial progress,
3. Plan your financial life,
4. Ensure that you are not being financially exploited (ripped off), and
5. Make informed financial decisions.

We live in a financial world where we must make financial decisions almost on a daily basis. We make personal and business financial decisions whether we are investing or borrowing money. The present-day financial industry has invented a variety of borrowing, insurance, and investment options. Qualified income tax-deferred savings plans offer many new options for investments. To cope with this changing financial environment, people now need to be investors instead of just savers. Investors must sort through numerous financial options, make choices, and take control of their finances in a way never before envisioned.

The "time value of money" concept is explicit in all financial decisions and is determined by the application of financial mathematics. Without the ability to conduct financial analyses, you must rely on others to do it for you or must make uninformed decisions based on a hunch or gut feeling. Neither option is very satisfactory.

But where do you look for information to develop the analytical ability to cope with the modern financial world? Financial math and its applications are not offered in public schools. Colleges and universities only offer financial math to business finance and accounting majors. Even then, it is corporate rather than personal finance and accounting that are emphasized.

On bookstore shelves you can find many books that provide general information about budgeting, borrowing, investing, and planning your financial future. You should avail yourself of these books. You will find very few books, however, about the basics or applications of financial math. This book seeks to correct that situation.

The Mathematics of Personal Finance is a comprehensive book written as a personal study reference; it can also serve as a classroom textbook. I do not tell you what investments you should make; rather I provide the analytical tools you need to make the financial decisions you will encounter throughout your lifetime.

This book is written in two parts. The first part presents the basics of financial math. The second part shows how to apply financial math to analyze situations that most people are likely to encounter in their financial lifetimes. Throughout the book I show how financial data are gathered and analyzed to make informed financial decisions. Once you have mastered the basic math and have experienced how it is applied, you should be able to analyze any financial situation that you encounter in either your personal or business life. Moreover, the material in this book will not become antiquated because the emphasis is on mathematical methods. Changes in tax laws, investment instruments, insurance policies, mortgage types, etc. do not change the mathematical methods for analyzing these financial situations.

Because I am an engineer, I bring an engineering approach to this subject. Engineers frequently use diagrams as visual aids. I explain cash flow diagrams and use them extensively. These diagrams facilitate visualization of "time value of money" transactions. I also provide many examples, tables of data, and graphs to aid your understanding of the subject.

For your practice, I have developed problem sets entitled "Now It's Your Turn." These appear at the end of each chapter except the first. Answers are provided for each question. If you want to be sure you not only grasp but also know how to use and therefore benefit financially from the information given on this book, it will be worth your while to work these problems.

In addition to the general public, I believe the following professionals can benefit from this book:

- Bank employees who wish to hone their knowledge of simple and compound interest rate calculations
- Anyone about to take the certified financial planner's (CFP) examination
- College business alumni who did not major in finance but who need to acquire specialized knowledge of financial mathematics
- Anyone who is in business or about to go into business
- Federal Trade Commission officials who must interpret and enforce the Truth-in-Lending Act
- Real estate agents and mortgage brokers who must calculate and explain home mortgage financing to their clients

- Income tax professionals who desire more knowledge about the application of financial math when performing income tax-avoidance planning
- Engineers and other technical personnel who are about to take a state professional engineer's license examination
- Lawyers who would like to learn the financial mathematics useful for estate planning and trust investments

Finally, be aware that this book is quite comprehensive. It will require some effort to master the subject. It is for those who want to self-actualize and rise above the crowd. Those who do will be financially rewarded.

Acknowledgments

Several people provided valuable assistance and aid in the preparation of this book. My eldest son, Dr. Andrew E. Lutz, Ph.D. in engineering mathematics, reviewed the book for mathematical methods and content. My youngest son, Gregory T. Lutz, MBA in business finance and a CPA, offered valuable suggestions on the content and the approach to financial applications. Mr. Charles Shoemaker, MBA in finance and a vice president at the firm of Salomon Smith Barney, reviewed the book and offered valuable suggestions. Victoria R. M. Scott edited the manuscript. My wife, Mary Jane Lutz, encouraged me during the long hours involved in research and writing the book. I owe a debt of gratitude to each of these individuals.

Donald E. Lutz
San Jose, California

Part One

The Basics
of
Financial Math

Why You Need to Know Financial Math

All successful corporations have knowledgeable financial analysts who continuously analyze financial opportunities and supply information on which to base financial decisions. This is considered necessary in the business world. Shouldn't it also be necessary in a personal financial world? Everyone should have this same knowledge, but do most people possess it?

Let's look at how John, a 65-year old schoolteacher, made an important decision about his retirement future.

John is a 65-year old schoolteacher and has been contributing to a 403(b) *Tax-Sheltered Annuity* with an insurance company. The insurance company was selected as custodian of the 403(b) plan by the school, but upon retirement John now has the opportunity to roll his money into an IRA (Individual Retirement Account). John has an accumulated sum of $138,000 in his annuity and now elects take a monthly income. He examines two basic options: (1) annuitize with the current insurance company to receive a lifetime income, or (2) roll his annuity over to an IRA in a mutual fund family and take systematic monthly withdrawals.

John contacts an insurance agent who sends John's data to the insurance company's home office; the results come back a week later. Based on the 403(b) fund's value of $138,000, the insurance company offers John a lifetime annuity of $765 per month. John calculates the annual rate of return that the insurance company is actually offering and it turns out to be only 3%.

John finds a balanced mutual fund that has enjoyed an annual compound rate of return of 8.5% since its inception in 1927, and a rate of 15% annually over the last 10 years. If he chooses to withdraw a monthly income for 180 months (his expected lifetime) at a conservative annual interest rate of 8.5%, he calculates a monthly income of $1,359.

John decides to select the mutual fund over the lifetime guaranteed insurance annuity because the mutual fund offers the potential of a 78% higher income and has historically demonstrated a solid financial performance background.

It is not difficult to perform the calculations that John did in the above example. With the financial math presented in this book and a hand-held electronic calculator, you can perform these calculations as expeditiously as the corporate analysts can. But you must recognize the need to do so.

Do you know anyone who has calculated the rate of return of his or her insurance policies, stocks, bonds, 401(k) plans, and IRAs? Why do so many people have their investments in low paying fixed-income investments? A survey of 401(k) plans by the consulting firm of KPMG Peat Marwick found that 50% of all participants still invest in low interest bearing fixed-rate securities.

The lack of ability to analyze and continuously monitor financial options bodes ill for those who expect to retire with an adequate income. In *The Myth of Retirement*, Craig Karpel shows that many in the Baby Boomer generation will not have sufficient resources to support retirement. He states that "Our parents grew up in the first and only 'Retirement State' the world has ever known." Mr. Karpel asserts that Social Security benefits will have to be reduced, that many retirement plans are being phased out, and that many existing plans are seriously underfunded. Moreover, people are not saving nearly enough to provide a sufficient retirement income. Karpel further states that, "the end of mass retirement will be, on balance, a beneficial phenomenon. Those who do not see it coming will suffer terribly. But if we prepare for it, we'll be able to build opportunities."

What about common, everyday financial decisions in which a lack of knowledge can be expensive? Does this happen?

A young husband and wife have finally bought their dream house and now need some additional furniture. They have a relatively high combined income but very little cash on hand. After selecting $5,000 worth of furniture, the salesperson offers them four-year financing at "a *nominal* interest rate of only 1.5% per month." Their other option is to take an 8 % annual interest rate loan from the wife's company's credit union.

To save time and because it sounds reasonable, the couple decides to take the salesperson's offer. How reasonable is this offer, and what difference will it make? The table below tells the sad story.

Interest Rates	8.0% per year	1.5% per month
Loan principal	$5,000	$5,000
Effective interest rate	8.30 %	19.56 %
Term	48 months	48 months
Monthly payment	$121.26	$144.70
Total paid	$5,820.48	$6,945.60

Although a 1.5% nominal monthly interest rate sounds quite low, it is actually quite high. It is an *effective* annual interest rate of 19.56%. Not recognizing this play on words, the couple paid a $6,945–$5,820 = $1,125 penalty over just four years.

DO YOU NEED TO BRUSH UP ON FINANCIAL MATH?

Do you understand and know how to perform these personal financial tasks?

- Compute simple and compound interest transactions
- Take advantage of the "magic of compounding"
- Use present value methods for comparing financial alternatives
- Use a financial calculator and/or a computer spreadsheet for financial analysis
- Compute the rate of return on your stocks, bonds, and mutual fund investments
- Perform income-tax-avoidance planning
- Consider inflation effects in your financial and retirement planning
- Analyze and save money on your home mortgage
- Evaluate and select your company's optimum pension plan option
- Calculate the discount rates, coupon equivalent rates, and effective rates of Treasury bills
- Make informed purchase decisions by calculating the yield to maturity of bonds
- Analyze and compare term and cash-value life insurance policies
- Analyze consumer credit and loan options and select the most favorable

Are you more knowledgeable in financial analysis than the salespeople who sell you financial products? In your financial world you will encounter such terms as yield, simple and compound interest rates, discount rate, nominal and effective interest rates, total average annual rates of return, annual percentage rate (APR), annual percentage yield (APY), and rate of return. Do you know what these terms mean and how they are

applied? These are some of the topics presented in this book. You will be fully knowledgeable about them when you have finished reading it.

WHAT IS FINANCIAL MATH?

The *time value of money* forms the basis of financial math. Understanding the time value
of money is the key to financial thought. Time value of money means that the value of
money always changes over time. It does so because of factors such as the interest
charged or received for the use of money, capital gains and/or losses, dividends, and
inflation.

Intrinsic to the time value of money is *compound interest.* Albert Einstein once
remarked, "Compounding is a miracle of modern mathematics."

Compounding is something we all can use to our advantage. Compounding is often
referred to as the *magic of compounding* because your money grows more rapidly when
it earns compound interest. Compound interest rates are the measuring stick for *all*
investment or borrowing options. In this book, compound interest math is explained and
demonstrated by many examples.

WHAT IS IN THIS BOOK AND HOW TO STUDY IT

The information presented in this book is for the most part progressive. Starting with
the most basic principles, the material is introduced sequentially in detail and thus
should be easily understandable. We recommend that you start at the beginning and
study Chapters 2 through 11 in that order. After that you will have the analytical tools
and knowledge to choose to study the remaining chapters in the order of your specific
interests.

Chapter 2 presents a review of the mathematics used in the remainder of the book.
We are all probably a little rusty and can benefit from the review.

Chapters 3 through 6 present the basic fundamentals of simple and compound
interest calculations. Once you learn the time value of money methods thorough the use
of mathematical formulas and diagrams, it will be easy to understand and use a hand-
held electronic calculator to expedite calculations.

Be especially careful to understand the "present value" concepts presented in Chapter 6. Present value techniques are different from what most people have been exposed to, but are used extensively for financial analyses. The methods presented are the same as those that professionals in the financial industry use to make financial decisions.

Chapter 7 explains the contents of financial interest tables and shows how to use them. There are a few good books of compound interest tables available in book stores, but many have deficiencies. One of the better books on the market is *Realty Bluebook Financial Tables* by Robert de Heer, (Real Estate Education Company). You will find, however, that compound interest tables have only a limited usefulness in the overall techniques of financial analyses.

Chapter 8 explains the characteristics of a hand-held financial calculator and shows how it is used to solve financial problems. The Hewlett-Packard 12-C financial calculator is illustrated because it is used by almost everyone working in the industry. Other calculators on the market are also sufficient and work similarly. Many financial planners take a course in using the HP-12C financial calculator in preparation for the certified financial planner (CFP) exam. Upon completion of this book, you should be on a par with most CFPs in the field of financial analyses.

Chapter 9 presents methods for calculating the rate of return of investments, including how investment results are annualized. Don't slight this chapter. Rate of return is the bottom line on everyone's investments. Also the "modified internal rate of return" (MIRR) is introduced for those who would like to pursue an advanced concept. It is a technique that investors use to factor in stipulated reinvestment and borrowing rates.

Chapters 10 and 11, on income taxes and inflation, provide information and techniques for the more general applications that follow. It is important to understand how income taxes and inflation affect our financial well-being. Chapter 10 shows how tax-deduction savings take place and why you should use your marginal-tax-bracket value to calculate these savings. Income tax-avoidance planning is necessary to legally minimize your income tax load. Considering inflation's effects is necessary to properly monitor and plan your retirement assets.

For those who buy bonds, Chapter 12 has some very important information on the characteristics of deep discounted and premium priced bonds available on the secondary market. No one should buy bonds without a complete understanding of this chapter.

Chapter 13 addresses various types of securities sold by the US government. The government debt of approximately $5 trillion represent the one of the largest money transactions taking place continuously. Since these securities are highly interest rate sensitive, their price trends and yield curves need to be understood by successful prospective buyers.

Chapter 14 presents what you need to know about home mortgage analyses. When you get through this chapter you will be rewarded by learning how to apply a simple method to painlessly save significant amounts of interest on your home mortgage.

Chapters 15 and 16 involve analysis of insurance annuities, life insurance policies, and retirement options. It is important to understand and be able to quantify each of these items in order to make informed decisions which can significantly influence your financial future.

Chapter 17 presents methods that engineers and financial managers use to compare alternatives as a basis for making financially driven decisions. This method is called "trade-off studies" by industry. They can be very helpful in making personal financial decisions such as buy or lease a new auto.

Chapter 18 deals with various offerings of consumer credit and loans. You will see some good credit and loan options and some bad ones. Reading this chapter is a must for all of us because many times in our financial lives we will need to use credit and to secure loans. Even many financial officers and lenders do not understand these, but you will. You will be amused at how they are taken back and off guard by those who can analyze these options.

Chapter 19 introduces computer spreadsheet programs. Spreadsheets are an excellent tool for performing all types of financial analyses. With the knowledge you will have by reading previous chapters, you will readily be able to understand spreadsheet financial applications. The intent here is to show what is involved in using spreadsheets and to demonstrator their capabilities. If you should choose to use computer spreadsheets, Chapter 19 offers quick start instructions for doing so.

Finally we would like to emphasize that this is a comprehensive book not intended for idiots or dummies as some books indicate in their titles. There is no royal road to knowledge. Even though *The Mathematics of Personal Finance* is written to clearly explain the fundamentals, it will take some effort to master them. When you do, however, you will be as knowledgeable as college finance majors and professionals in the field of financial mathematics.

Let's get started. Good luck in your study.

A Little Math Goes A Long Way

LEARNING OBJECTIVES:

This chapter is a review of some basic math used in this book, including:

1. Calculating percentages
2. Solving simple algebraic formulas
3. Applying unit and ratio analysis
4. The basis point system
5. Significant digits and rounding
6. Interest rate conversions
7. Constructing and using cash flow diagrams.

The basic math needed for the financial analyses presented in this book is reviewed here because we are all probably a little rusty. We will touch on percentages and some algebra. The algebraic formulas reviewed in this chapter are necessary to perform compound interest calculations.

Also, the concepts of unit analysis and cash flow diagrams will be introduced. You will find these very helpful in applying financial math. Unit analysis is a very useful method in understanding and carrying out calculations involving units such as dollars, days, months, years, and percentages. Cash flow diagrams are necessary to visualize just how the time value of money takes place.

CALCULATING PERCENTAGES

Conversion Between Decimal and Percentage Numbers

Financial calculations require frequent conversions between the decimal equivalents and the percentage forms of numbers. All numbers must be in decimal form when performing the mathematical operations of multiplication or division.

We can demystify the notation of percentage by pointing out that a number expressed in percent is merely a decimal number that has been multiplied by 100. For example, when multiplied by 100 the number expressed as the decimal 0.50 becomes 50% (0.50×100 = 50%). Conversely, a number in percentage form is changed to decimal form by dividing it by 100 and dropping the percent sign. The term "percent" really means one part in a hundred.

When we convert from decimal to percentage form it is important to always write the percent sign "%" after the number to indicate that it is a number in percentage form. If we did not show the percent sign we would have to assume that the number was in decimal form, and then when we multiplied it by a decimal number the result would be 100 times too large.

The table below shows corresponding numbers expressed in decimal and percentage forms.

Decimal	Percent
0.05	5%
0.50	50%
5.00	500%

From the table it is obvious that a simple method to change from decimal to percent is to move the decimal point two places to the right and then add the percent sign. The converse is true when converting from percent to decimal.

Calculating Percentages

To determine the percentage of a number, simply multiply that number by the percentage number in *decimal* form. For example if we said our monthly grocery bill is 20% of our total income of $2,000, what would be the amount we spend on groceries? Determining 20% of $2,000 is done as follows: $2,000×20/100 = $2,000×0.20 = $400.

Net Amount

Net amount is the base amount plus or minus the percentage amount. Net amount is useful to determine such items as discounts on offered purchases and the net cost of the purchase.

Example 2.1:

You are considering buying a new car that lists for $15,000. The salesperson offers a discount of 10%, and you have to pay a state sales tax of 8.25%. What is the cost of the car to you and what is the net amount you must pay for it, including sales tax?

Solution:

The discount (percentage amount) is:
$15,000 × 0.10 = $1,500
The cost of the car is:
$15,000 − $1,500 = $13,500
The sales tax is:
$13,500 × 0.0825 = $1113.75
The net cost to you is:
$13,500 + $1113.75 = $14,613.75

Notice that each quoted percentage number applied in the calculations is in decimal form.

Percent Difference

Percent difference is used extensively to determine financial gains or losses. The calculation involves the change between an initial (base) number and the final number, divided by the base number.

Formula 2.1: Percent Difference

$$\frac{\text{Final Value} - \text{Base Value}}{\text{Base Value}} \times 100 = \text{Percent Difference}$$

Example 2.2:

Your favorite stock increased from an initial base value of $1,000 to a final value of $2,000 in five years. What is the percentage difference (gain)?

Solution:

$$\text{Final value} = \$2,000$$
$$\text{Initial value} = \$1,000$$

$$\text{Percent difference} = \frac{\$2,000 - \$1,000}{\$1,000} \times 100 = 100\%$$

Notice that a number doubled in value represents a 100% difference.

Now assume that your stock fell to $1,500 the sixth year. What is the percentage difference (loss) during that year?

$$\text{Initial value} = \$2,000$$
$$\text{Final value} = \$1,500$$

$$\text{Percent difference} = \frac{\$1,500 - \$2,000}{\$2,000} \times 100 = -25\%$$

Notice that for the first calculation the base was $1,000, but $2,000 becomes the base number for the next calculation starting the sixth year. Also notice that the result is negative, indicating a loss for this period.

Some other general items to notice concerning percent differences are:

- Percent difference is also referred to as *percent change, percent gain, percent loss, percent* increase, and *percent decrease.*
- The percent difference can be either positive (gain) or negative (loss). If the base number is greater than the final number, the percent difference will be negative.

Percentage Distribution

Percentage distribution is useful to determine the distribution of a group of numbers. To calculate the percentage distribution:

1. Calculate the total amount by adding the individual amounts.
2. Divide each individual amount by the total amount.

Example 2.3:

On behalf of his planning effort, a financial planner asks you for the percentage distribution of your invested assets. You have $2,000 in cash, $4,000 in stocks, and $5,000 in bonds. What do you tell him? (Round to whole numbers.)

Solution:

Total invested assets:
$2,000 + $4,000 + $5,000 = $11,000
Percentage distribution:

Cash	$2,000/$11,000 × 100 =	18%
Stocks	$4,000/$11,000 × 100 =	36%
Bonds	$5,000/$11,000 × 100 =	46%
	Total	100%

As a check on these calculations, the percentage total must equal 100%.

Why Percentage Terminology?

All this discussion may make you wonder why we use percentage terminology and functions when it is possible to operate using decimals only. But as one dictionary puts it, "The use of percent is a convenient way to express many proportions."

We can appreciate this. For instance, it is easy to say, "Your Social Security taxes each year are 7.65% of the first $51,300 you earn." Can you picture anyone saying, "Your Social Security taxes are 765 ten thousandths of the first $51,300 you earn?"

Basis Points

To be complete we will discuss basis points since this terminology pops up frequently in financial reporting. Basis points are commonly used to express the change in the yield of securities such as bonds. A *basis point* is a change of 0.01% in the quoted yield of the security.

Basis points should not be confused with the percentage difference discussed above. It is not a percent difference, but merely the difference between two numbers. The following example should clarify this.

Example 2.3:

The yield of a long term government bond is quoted as 6.50% on February the 1st and 6.55% on March 1st. What is this change in terms of basis points?

Solution:

The difference is 6.55% − 6.50% = 0.05%

This is an increase of (0.05/0.01 = 5) five basis points. In financial jargon this would be called "a five basis point movement." For comparison, the percent difference is 0.77%.

$$\text{Percent difference} = \frac{6.55\% - 6.50\%}{6.50\%} \times 100 = 0.77\%$$

SOLVING SIMPLE ALGEBRAIC EQUATIONS

Analyzing the time value of money requires solving compound interest formulas. This involves plugging some numbers into algebraic formulas and turning the crank. Hang in there, this isn't too difficult.

Using a Hand-Held Calculator

First you will need a hand held calculator. Any calculator that has a y^x function will do. You can find many inexpensive calculators with the y^x function key. If you want to go much further in financial analyses, you can do so with a financial calculator such as the Hewlett-Packard HP-12C.

Solving the yx Function

Given: $y = 3$, $x = 2$
$y^x = 3^2$
$3^2 = 9$

We know that 3 raised to the second power is 3 squared, or 9. Now if you are using a calculator, other than a Hewlett-Packard, you would solve $3^2 = 9$ by the following operations:

1. Press the number 3 key.
2. Press the y^x key.
3. Press the number 2 key.
4. Press the *equals* sign (=) key.

The number 9 should be displayed in the calculator window. But If you have a Hewlett-Packard hand-held calculator, you would solve $3^2 = 9$ as follows:

1. Press the number 3 key.
2. Press the *enter* key.
3. Press the number 2 key.
4. Press the y^x key.

Example 2.4:

Solve for z in the equation, $z = y^x$, given x and y. (The answers are in bold type in the table below.)

Solution:

Solutions for the equation $z = y^x$

x	y	z
3	5	**125**
0.5	50	**7.07**
12	1.08	**2.518**

Another form of the y^x you will use is how to solve for y when we know z and x. To do this we rearrange the equation as follows:

$z = y^x$ rearranged is $y = z^{1/x}$ This is simply done by taking the xth root of each side

Solving the equation for $z = 4$, $x = 2$:

$y = z^{1/2}$, or $y = 4^{(0.50)}$
$y = 2$

Example 2.5:

Solve the equation $z = y^x$ for y, where z and x are known. The tables below show three solution examples (The answers are in bold.)

Solution:

Solutions of the equation $y = z^{1/x}$

x	$1/x$	z	y
2	0.500	2	**1.41**
6	0.167	4	**1.26**
8	0.125	6	**1.25**

As you will see later, $y^{1/x}$ is one of the most useful forms of the equation $z = y^x$

Solving $z = y^x$ for Negative Exponents

Remember that a negative exponent in an equation such as $z = y^{-x}$ is the same as $z = 1/y^x$
This is solved as follows:

$$\text{Given: } y = 4, x = -1.5$$

$$z = 4^{-1.5} = \frac{1}{4^{1.5}} = \frac{1}{8} = 0.125$$

Using any hand-held calculator the fraction 1/8 can be reduced to a decimal easiest by pressing the 8 key, then the 1/x key.

UNIT AND RATIO ANALYSIS

A *unit* defines the physical quantity that numbers represent. For example, some units of length are inches, feet, yards, and miles; some units of time are days, months, and years.

A *ratio* is one number or unit divided by another. For example, 35 miles per hour is a ratio defining speed. For mathematical operations, this ratio is written as $\dfrac{35 \text{ Miles}}{1 \text{ Hour}}$.

Unit analysis is a very convenient way to convert units and also calculate ratios. This can be done even though we do not know the formulas for the calculations. For example, how long does it take to travel 100 miles if your speed is 35 miles per hour?

By unit analysis, we multiply 100 miles by 1 hour per 35 miles (the inverted ratio 35 miles per hour):

$$100 \text{ miles} \times \frac{1 \text{ hour}}{35 \text{ miles}} = 2.86 \text{ hours}$$

We knew how to do this calculation, but this way we have confirmation that we did it correctly and arrived at the right units. Notice that we canceled units by drawing a line through like units. Like units in the znumerator and denominator can be canceled. We multiplied 100 miles by the ratio 1 hour per 35 miles in order to get the time in the numerator. We are left with the unit of time, which is what we were seeking.

If we had multiplied the ratio 35 miles per hour times 100 miles, the units could not be canceled and the answer would obviously be wrong. For example:

$$100 \text{ miles} \times \frac{35 \text{ miles}}{\text{hour}} = 3,500 \text{ miles} \times \text{miles/hour}$$

These are not the miles per hour units set out to find.

How Many Kilometers Are There in a mile?

Let's find out how many kilometers (km) there are in 1 mile. Use the facts that 1 meter = 39.37 inches, 5,280 feet = 1 mile, 1 foot = 12 inches, and 1 kilometer (km)=1,000 meters.

$$1 \text{ mile} \times \frac{5280 \text{ feet}}{1 \text{ mile}} \times \frac{12 \text{ inches}}{1 \text{ foot}} \times \frac{1 \text{ meter}}{39.37 \text{ inches}} \times \frac{1 \text{ kilometer}}{1000 \text{ meters}} = 1.609 \text{ kilometers}$$

This seems like a complex operation, but it demonstrates the method. You can put this conversion to use if you travel to Japan or Europe. (Also automobiles now have both miles per hour and km per hour on the speedometer.) Suppose you are in Europe and it is 125 km to your destination. How many miles will you travel to reach your destination?

$$125 \text{ km} \times \frac{1 \text{ mile}}{1.609 \text{ km}} = 78 \text{ miles}$$

Time Conversions

For financial applications, we need to be concerned with various periods of time. The following are definitions of the units of time:

$$1 \text{ year} = 365 \text{ days} = 52 \text{ weeks} = 12 \text{ months}.$$

A standard term for a home mortgage is 30 years. How many months are there in 30 years?

$$30 \text{ years} \times \frac{12 \text{ months}}{1 \text{ year}} = 360 \text{ months}$$

How many days are there in 2.5 years?

$$2.5 \text{ years} \times \frac{365 \text{ days}}{1 \text{ year}} = 912.5 \text{ days}$$

Salary Conversions

John's salary last year was $25,500. He worked 230 days per year, 8 hours a day. What was John's hourly rate of pay?

$$\frac{\$25,500}{\text{year}} \times \frac{1 \text{ year}}{230 \text{ days}} \times \frac{1 \text{day}}{8 \text{ hours}} = \frac{\$13.86}{\text{hour}}$$

Interest Rate Conversions

Interest rates are usually quoted on an annual basis, but as we will see in the Chapter 3, they frequently are converted to monthly and daily rates. Convert an interest rate of 10% per year to: (1) a daily rate, and (2) a monthly rate.

Daily interest rate:

$$\frac{10\%}{\text{year}} \times \frac{1 \text{ year}}{365 \text{ days}} = \frac{0.02740\%}{\text{day}}$$

Monthly interest rate:

$$\frac{10\%}{\text{year}} \times \frac{1 \text{ year}}{12 \text{ months}} = \frac{0.8333\%}{\text{month}}$$

SIGNIFICANT DIGITS AND ROUNDING

In our financial calculations we need to reconcile the significance of decimal places needed to accurately arrive at the desired values.

Significant Digits

Significant digits of a decimal number are the digits reading from left to right from the decimal point, beginning with the first non-zero digit and ending with the last digit written. For example, the daily and monthly interest rates 0.02740% and 0.8333%, (shown at the end of the last section) have four significant digits. For the number 0.02740%, there are four numbers (2740) beginning with the number 2, which is the first non-zero digit, and ending in 0, the last digit written. For the number 0.8333%, there is no non-zero digit after the decimal point. Thus 8 is the first non-zero digit and the last digit written is 3.

A number such as 0.0000123, thus has three significant digits. The number 0.02740% has four significant digits even though there is one zero immediately after the decimal point. For the number 0.0000123, there are three significant digits even though there are four zero digits immediately after the decimal point.

For whole numbers, the number 125 would have three significant digits. However, for whole numbers ending with zeros, the position of the zeros may or may not be significant. For example if the population of a town is reported as 15,000, it impossible to determine which zeros, if any, are significant. If the population was counted to the nearest thousand, none of these numbers is significant. If counted to the nearest hundred, the first zero is significant and the last two are not.

Observe that the number of significant digits in a number does not depend on the position of the decimal point. For example, the number 10.0002450 has nine significant digits. The number 10.2450 has six. The number 0.0002450 has four significant digits.

Perhaps you have noticed that some annual interest rates are quoted to four significant digits. For example, it is not uncommon to see a mortgage loan rate of 9.875%. This number is quoted to four significant digits, but the decimal portion of this number is quoted as three significant digits. It is frequently necessary to use periodic interest rates significant to four digits. Some compound interest tables provide factors to eight significant digits or greater. The choice depends on the accuracy you are seeking. Most hand-held calculators can to show nine decimal places.

Rounding Numbers

Rounding is done to reduce the number of digits past the decimal point. Whole numbers can also be rounded. When the rounding process can lead to two numbers, each equally close to the given number, we use the arbitrary rule of rounding up if the number is 5 or greater. For example, if we had the number 310.16459412 and wanted to round it to three decimal places, the result would be 310.165. For the number 310.1645, we change the 4 to 5 since the number immediately after 4 is 5. If we round the number 310.16459412 to five decimal places, the result is 310.16459.

When rounding whole numbers, for example, the number $5,186 could be rounded to the nearest $10 as $5,190. This is frequently done when the accuracy to a dollar is not desired.

USING CASH FLOW DIAGRAMS

Textbooks in engineering economics use cash flow diagrams extensively to visualize time value of money transactions. You will find these diagrams to be very helpful, if not necessary, to understand cash flow scenarios. We will use these diagrams throughout this book.

The Time Line

Cash flow diagrams start with a time line. This is a line divided into the periods of time of a financial transaction. Suppose you had a loan with a four year term transaction. The time line would be:

Four-year time line

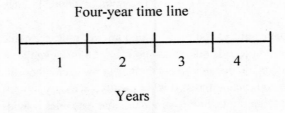

Years

The time line does not have to be drawn exactly to scale as long as it is proportional enough to visualize the process. It is sometimes desirable to divide the time line into monthly periods.

Cash Flow Arrows

Cash flows are represented by vertical arrows. Money you received is represented by an arrow pointing upward. Money you pay out is represented by an arrow pointing downward

Money received

Money paid out

The Cash Flow Diagram

Suppose you deposited $1,000 in a savings account and subsequently deposited $500 at the beginning of years 2, 3, and 4. The account pays an interest rate of 4 percent compounded yearly. At the end of four years your bank reported that the amount of money in your account was $3,581. The cash flow diagram would look like this:

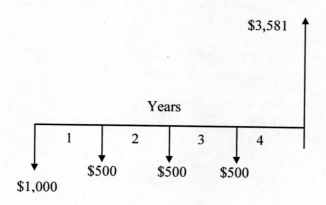

Each cash flow diagram of a complete transaction must have at least one cash flow in each direction. The arrows represent only actual cash flows at each point. For example, the deposited cash flows of $1,000, $500, $500, and $500 do not represent any accrued interest at those points in time because interest was not withdrawn at those times by the depositor. The terminal point in the time line is where the principal and accrued interest become the actual cash flow. The sum of $3,581 is cash flow accrued to the depositor at the end of the transaction under consideration.

As we progress through this book, the value of the cash flow diagrams in describing and aiding the calculational processes will become readily apparent.

Now It's Your Turn:

1. Numbers used in the arithmetic operations of multiplication and division must be in percentage form.
    a. True
    b. False

2. A number in percentage form is simply a decimal number multiplied by 100.
    a. True
    b. False

3. The easiest way to change a number expressed in percentage form to a number in decimal form is:
    a. Multiply by 100
    b. Move the decimal point two places to the left
    c. Move the decimal point two places to the right

4. Jane's personal income was $10,000 last year. She received a raise of $100 per month this year. Her percentage increase in annual income is:
    a. 10%
    b. 12%
    c. 15%

5. Your friend Bill says his mutual fund value increased 20% last year. The value of his mutual fund was $5,000 at the beginning of the year. The value of Bill's fund at the end of the year is:
   a. $7,000
   b. $8,000
   c. $6,000

6. The 1992 trade deficit with Japan was reported to be $42.5 billion. It increased to $52.3 billion in 1994. This is a percentage increase of:
   a. 32%
   b. 23%
   c. 17%

7. How many basis points did Mary's mutual fund move in one year when its annual return was 10.05% for 1993 and 11.01% for 1994?
   a. 96 basis points
   b. 50 basis points
   c. 85 basis points

8. An official of the Federal Reserve Board was recently quoted as saying, "Interest rates must still go up another 50 basis points." How many percentage points does this represent?
   a. 0.05%
   b. 0.50%
   c. 5.00%

9. Greg bought a computer at a price of $2,500 and was given a discount of 10%. He paid a state tax of 8.73%. What is his net cost?
   a. $2,250.00
   b. $2,718.75
   c. $2,446.88

10. Bob's annual salary is $50,000. He pays $9,000 in federal income taxes, $2,500 in state income taxes, and $3,825 in Social Security taxes. What percentage of his total salary does each of these items constitute?
    a. 18% federal, 5% state, and 7.65% social security
    b. 20% federal, 4% state, and 5.65% social security

11. Using a calculator, evaluate the function yx for the values of $y = 1.10$, $x = 5.00$. Round off your answer to two decimal places.
    a. 1.61
    b. 1.11
    c. 2.30

12. If $z = y^x$, what is the value of z when $y = 4$, $x = -2$? Round off to three decimal places.
    a. 0.054
    b. 0.063
    c. 0.126

13. If $z = y^x$, what is the value of y when $z = 1.15$, $x = 2.6$? Round off to two decimal places.
    a. 1.45
    b. 3.03
    c. 1.06

14. If $z = y^x$, what is the value of y when $z = 2.5$, $x = 3$? Round off to three decimal places.
    a. 2.114
    b. 1.678
    c. 1.357

15. Jason worked 36 weeks last year and earned $8,370. He worked 3 days each week, but only 5 hours per day. What was Jason's hourly rate of pay?
    a. $12.55 per hour
    b. $12.78 per hour
    c. $15.50 per hour

16. How many hours are there in a year? There are 24 hours in a day, 7 days in a week, and 52 weeks in a year, plus 1 additional day.
    a. 8,500 hours
    b. 8,736 hours
    c. 8,760 hours

17. In the Olympics there is a 400 meter race. How long is this in yards? Use the following ratios: 2.54 centimeters per inch, 100 centimeters per meter, 12 inches per foot, and 3 feet per yard.
   a. 430.00 yards
   b. 437.45 yards
   c. 462.56 yards

18. What would be the daily interest rate for an annual interest rate of 12.50%?
   a. 12.50%
   b. 0.03425%
   c. 1.04167%

19. How many significant digits are there in the number 0.002467?
   a. Five
   b. Six
   c. Four

20. If you rounded the number to 0.002546 to three significant digits, what would that number be?
   a. 0.0026
   b. 0.00255
   c. 0.010

21. How many significant digits are there in the number 1468.1230 ?
   a. Four
   b. Eight
   c. Three

22. Philip deposited $3,000 initially, and subsequently deposited $100 at the beginning of the second, fourth, and eighth months. During the year he withdrew $50 at the end of the fifth and sixth months. The bank compounds each month. At the end of year the bank reported an account value of $4,167.70 To draw a cash flow diagram, how many upward arrows and how many downward arrows would there be?
   a. Four down and three up
   b. Four down and two up
   c. Three down and two up

23. You bought an auto and financed it over two years. Auto loans compound monthly. The amount financed was $12,000 and your monthly payments were $542.72 per month. To draw a cash flow diagram how many upward and downward arrows are there?
    a. One up, 24 down
    b. One down, 24 up
    c. Two up, 23 down

ANSWERS: 1.b, 2.a, 3.b, 4.b, 5.c, 6.b, 7.a, 8.b, 9.c, 10.a, 11.a, 12.b, 13.c, 14.c, 15.c, 16.c, 17.b, 18.b, 19.c, 20.b, 21.b, 22.a, 23.a

Interest:
The Time Value of Money

LEARNING OBJECTIVES:

This chapter will help you learn:

1. How interest drives the time value of money
2. How to calculate simple and compound interest
3. The difference between simple interest and compound interest transactions
4. The meaning of ordinary and exact simple interest rates
5. Why compound interest earns more money than simple interest
6. How to apply the "Rule of 72" to estimate the compound doubling time of money

Anyone who loans, borrows, or invests money should understand interest and interest rates. Interest gives money added value over a given period of time. In a broader sense, interest is the return obtainable by the productive investment of capital.

The subtle differences between simple and compound interest transactions are rarely understood. It is quite amusing to have an auto salesperson offer a "simple interest loan of 9%," then proceed to look up the monthly payment in a book of compound interest tables. It is more disconcerting to have a bank loan officer tell you that the bank offers an 8% simple interest home-mortgage loan. Home mortgages are compound interest loans.

In many of your dealings with financial institutions you will be subjected to different approaches in describing and applying interest computations. Some of these will be aberrations of the accurate simple and compound interest computation methods.

Although you may not always be able to correct these methods, you should understand what you are dealing with in order to make wise financial decisions.

In this chapter the basic fundamentals of simple and compound interest transactions are introduced. Compound growth of money and compound interest applications are discussed further in Chapter 4.

WHAT IS INTEREST?

Interest is money paid for the use of borrowed money. If you lent $1,000 to someone and they paid you $1,050 a year later, the original $1,000 is the *principal* and $50 is the *interest* paid for use of the *principal*. In this example your original $1,000 grew to $1,050. Thus the value of your original holding changed over time. All money subject to an interest charge must change in value over time. This is how interest moves the time value of money.

Interest rate is a ratio, just as miles per hour is the ratio of the number of miles that a car travels divided by the time it takes. The rate of interest is the amount of interest expressed as a percentage of the principal earned over some *period* of time. For example, if $50 is the interest charged annually on a loan of $1000, the interest rate is $50 \div \$1,000 = 0.05$ per year. In percentage terms, this is an interest rate of 5% per year. Interest can also be computed more often then once a year for example, daily, monthly, quarterly, or semiannually. Quoted interest rates are understood to be on an annual basis unless stated otherwise. When interest calculations are performed, interest rates must always be expressed in the period commensurate with the selected interest periods. For example, if interest is to be calculated for monthly periods, the annual rate must be converted to units of percent per month. An annual interest rate of 12% is a monthly interest rate of 12% ÷ 12 months = 1% per month.

The *term* of the loan is the total time that the principal (or portions of the principal) remains with the borrower and the borrower pays interest. The term is the total sum of the interest time periods of the loan. For example, a standard home-mortgage loan has a term of 30 years. Since home-mortgage payments are made in monthly periods, the term consists of 360 months. When all of the scheduled loan payments have been made, the loan has matured.

KINDS OF INTEREST

There are two basic kinds of interest: *simple* and *compound*. The difference between these two lies in how interest is applied. When a loan transaction is initiated it is necessary to identify whether it is a simple interest or compound interest loan. The formula for calculating the amount of interest earned over any given simple interest or compounding single interest period is the same for both. However, as you will see later, the formulas for calculating the future values of simple and compound interest loans are not the same. In this chapter we present the formula for the future value of a simple interest loan.

Simple interest is interest that is earned only on the original principal. Once simple interest is earned it is *never* added to the original principal to earn interest again. When the loan matures, the interest and principal are returned to the lender. Simple interest is usually applied to relatively short-term loan transactions of one year or less.

Compound interest is interest that earns interest on interest. The term of a compound interest loan is usually made up more than one compound period. For each compound period, interest is calculated and added to the previous principal. The interest earned and the principal become the new principal for the next compounding period. For example, if $1,000 is the original principal and the interest rate per compounding period is 10%, the interest earned by the end of the first period is $1,000×0.10 = $100. The earned interest of $100 is added to the original $1,000, and the new principal becomes $1,000 + $100 = $1,100 at the beginning of the second compounding period. During the second compounding period, the depositor earns $1,100 × 0.10 = $110, and the new principal at the beginning of the third period becomes $1,100 + $110 = $1,210. The extra $10 earned during the second period is the compound interest. This process continues until the loan matures. Most present-day loans are compound interest loans.

As we will see later, annual compound interest rate is the standard measuring stick for comparing interest rates of loans and/or investments.

CALCULATING INTEREST

The formula for calculating the amount of interest earned or owed is the following:

Formula 3.1: Calculation of Interest

$$INT = PV \times i \times n$$

Where

INT = the amount of *interest* earned or paid
PV = the *present* value of money (principal)
i = the *interest* rate
n = the *number* of interest time periods in the term

(For the most part, the symbols used throughout this book are the same as you will find in financial calculator and personal computer software manuals.)

Example 3.1:

Calculate the amount of interest that will be earned by an investment of $5,000 at an interest rate of 8% per year. The term of the loan is one year.

Solution:

$$PV = \$5,000$$
$$i = 0.08 \text{ per year}$$
$$n = 1 \text{ year}$$
$$INT = PV \times i \times n$$
$$INT = \$5,000 \times \frac{0.08}{1 \text{ year}} \times 1 \text{ year}$$
$$= \$400$$

Remember, interest rate time units must always be consistent with those used for the term. An interest rate expressed in percent per day must multiplied by the total number of daily time periods in the term, etc. Selecting the number of interest periods in a year is done by one or more parties of the transaction. When the selected interest period is less than one year, it is necessary to convert the quoted annual interest rate to the appropriate fractional rate. This is true for both simple and compound interest transactions

The following is the formula for converting an annual interest rate to a fractional period rate:

Formula 3.2: Periodic Interest Rates

$$i = \frac{\text{Annual Interest Rate}}{\text{Number of Periods in a Year}} = \text{Periodic Interest Rate}$$

For example, an annual interest rate of 10% is converted to a daily rate in decimal form as follows:

$$i = \frac{0.10}{365 \text{ days}} = 0.000274 \text{ per day}$$

The 365-day year used for this example results in what is referred to as an *exact* interest rate. The financial community sometimes uses a 360-day year for simple interest transactions. This is an *ordinary* interest rate. For the 360 day year, the periods of the loan, for simplicity, are sometimes divided into to periods of 30, 90, 180, or 270 days, commensurate with monthly, quarterly, semiannually, and three-quarter time periods. For example, regardless of the actual days in the given month (such as 28 or 31 days), ordinary interest would be calculated using a 30-day month.

All this may seem a little confusing at the beginning but will become clear to you after working through a few examples. Everyone seems to apply interest rates differently. Conventions once established never seem to be changed. For institutions you deal with, it is important that you know how they calculate interest. It would be instructive to ask an officer at your bank how it is done there.

Example 3.2:

Convert an annual interest rate of 15% to various other interest rate time periods. Convert the 15% rate in decimal form.

Solution:

Daily rate (exact) 0.15/365 = 0.0004110 per day
Daily rate (ordinary) 0.15/360 = 0.0004167 per day
Monthly rate   0.15/12 = 0.01250 per month
Quarterly rate 0.15/4 = 0.03750 per quarter
Semiannual rate 0.15/2 = 0.07500 per half year

(Notice that we have rounded to four significant digits. This is sometimes desired for accuracy.)

Simple Interest Transactions

Example 3.3:

Your brother needs a loan for a down payment on an auto to tide him over until his CDs mature in three months. You lend him $4,000 at 6.50% simple interest, to be calculated on a 360-day annual basis. What is the amount of accrued interest that he will pay when the loan matures? What total amount will he return to you?

Solution:

$$PV = \$4,000$$
$$i = 0.0650 \text{ per year}$$
$$n = 90 \text{ days (represents three months, or one quarter)}$$

The daily ordinary interest rate is:

$$i = \frac{0.0650}{1 \text{ year}} \times \frac{1 \text{ year}}{360 \text{ days}} = 0.00018055 \text{ per day}$$

$$INT = PV \times i \times n$$
$$= \$4,000 \times \frac{0.00018055}{1 \text{ day}} \times 90 \text{ days}$$
$$= \$65.00$$

Total amount returned when the loan matures is the principal plus accrued interest.

$$\text{Total} = \$4,000 + \$65 = \$4,065$$

Notice that this example could also have been calculated using either monthly or quarterly interest rates and the corresponding periods. If we had chosen to use monthly periods in place of daily, the interest charged would have been calculated as INT = $4,000 × 0.065/12 × 3 months = $65.00. Using quarterly periods, the INT = $4,000 × 0.065/4 × 1 quarter = $65.00.

Example 3.4:

You have refinanced your home. The closing documents are signed, and the money is paid to the new lender on February 10. You notice a charge for interest paid to cover the remaining 19 days of February. The lender states that simple interest will be charged for the remaining days of February. Payback of principal is not involved during this period. This charge is necessary because the lender is entitled to earn interest until your regular monthly payment begins in March. Your loan principal is $150,000 and the mortgage interest rate is 7.50% per year. How much interest will you be charged for 19 days of February?

Solution:

$$PV = \$150,000$$
$$i = 0.075 \text{ per year}$$
$$n = 19 \text{ days}$$
$$i = \frac{0.0750}{1 \text{ year}} \times \frac{1 \text{ year}}{365 \text{ days}} = 0.00020548 \text{ per day}$$
$$INT = \$150,000 \times \frac{0.00020548}{1 \text{ day}} \times 19 \text{ days}$$
$$= \$585.62$$

The lender chose a simple interest loan and a 365-day year. The lender thus chose to use *exact* interest for the 19-day term loan. The U.S. Department of Housing and Urban Development (HUD) pamphlet entitled "Settlement Cost & You" uses ordinary interest in its instructional examples.

Example 3.5:

Your brother is now going into business and estimates that he will need to borrow $5,000 for a four-year term. How much interest would he pay you at the end of a four-year term loan if you charged him 7.50% *simple* interest? What is the total amount your brother would pay you at the end of the four-year term?

Solution:

Interest earned each year is:

$$PV = \$5,000$$
$$i = 0.075 \text{ per year}$$
$$n = 1 \text{ year}$$

$$INT = \$5,000 \times \frac{0.0750}{1 \text{ year}} \times 1 \text{ year} = \$375$$

Total accrued interest:

Year	Interest Earned
1	$375
2	375
3	375
4	375
Total	$1,500

At the end of four year term the total money paid is the principal and total accrued interest:

$$\$5,000 + \$1,500 = \$6,500$$

Notice that the annual interest earned is *not paid* to the lender until the term matures. Also notice that the interest earned each year earned no further interest during the remaining loan term.

Let's sketch a cash flow diagram for this transaction from the lender's perspective.

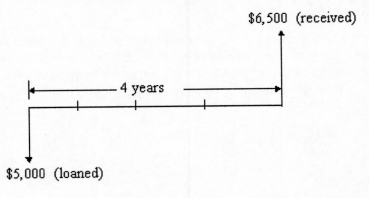

$6,500 (received)

4 years

$5,000 (loaned)

Future Value Calculation of a Simple Interest Loan

Formula 3.3: Future Value of a Simple Interest Loan

$$FV = PV\,(1 + i \times n)$$

Where

FV = the *future value* on money at the end of n periods

PV = the *present value* of money (principal) i.e., the initial amount of money at the beginning of the transaction

i = the *interest rate*

n = the *number* of interest time periods in the term

Example 3.6:

Use Formula 3.3 to calculate the future value of the loan transaction of Example 3.5

Solution:

PV = $5,000

i = 0.075 per year

n = 4 years.

FV = PV (1+i × n)

= $5,000 (1+0.075 × 4)

= $6,500

Notice that for Example 3.5 we calculated the interest earned each year and then added the four years sum of accrued interest to the original principal. To calculate Example 3.6, Formula 3.3 did it for us. You can do it either way you choose.

Compound Interest Transactions

For interest to compound, it must be calculated for *each* compounding period and then added to the principal of the previous period. The number of compounding periods within the year must be stated in order to calculate a compound interest transaction. This is necessary to determine the periodic interest rate to be applied as well as the total number of periods in the term of the transaction.

Example 3.7: Compound Interest Calculation

In Example 3.5 above suppose you changed your mind and decided to charge your brother compound interest at an interest rate of 7.50% per year. You select annual compounding periods and your brother agrees to this. How much interest will he owe at the end of the four year-term?

Solution:

$PV = \$5,000$
$i = 0.075$ per year
Compounding period n is 1 per year
Term of loan is 4 years, made up of 4 compounding periods

We will need to make four calculations in series, one for each compounding period. Interest earned by the lender each year is calculated using Formula 3.1 $INT = PV \times i \times n$ as follows:

First year:
$INT = \$5,000 \times 0.0750/\text{year} \times 1 \text{ year} = \$375.00$

Second year:
Principal at the beginning of the second year is:
$\$5,000 + \$375 = \$5,375$
$INT = \$5,375 \times 0.075 \times 1 = \$403.13$

Third year:
Principal at the beginning of the third year is:
$\$5,375 + \$403.13 = \$5,778.13$
$INT = \$5,778.13 \times 0.0750 \times 1 = \$433.36$

Fourth year:
Principal at the beginning of the forth year is:
$\$5,778.13 + \$433.36 = \$6,211.49$
$INT = \$6,211.49 \times 0.0750 \times 1 = \$465.86$

The total interest earned is:
$\$375 + \$403.13 + \$433.36 + \$465.86 = \$1,677.35$

Total end-of-term payment is:
Original Principal + Accrued Interest = Total payment
$\$5,000 + \$1,677.35 = \$6,677.35$

Let's put the results of these two loans from Examples 3.5 and 3.7 in tabular form and compare them.

Table 3.1: A Simple Interest Loan (Example 3.5)

End of Year	Principal	Interest @7.50%	Accrued Interest	Year End Payment
0	$5,000			
1	5,000	$375	$375	$0.00
2	5,000	375	750	0.00
3	5,000	375	1,125	0.00
4	5,000	375	1,500	$6,500

Table 3.2: A Compound Interest Loan (Example 3.7)

End of Year	Principal	Interest @7.5%	Accrued Interest	Year End Payment
0	$5,000			
1	5,375	$375	$375	$0.00
2	5,778	403	778	0.00
3	6,211	433	1,211	0.00
4	6,677	466	1,677	$6,677

Table 3.3: Loan Summaries

Type of Loan	Original Principal	Total Interest	Total Amount Paid
Simple interest	$5,000	$1,500	$6,500
Compound interest	$5,000	$1,677	$6,677

Notice that no year-end payments are made for either type of loan until the term is complete. For compound interest loans, the interest must remain on deposit in order to become principal to earn interest during the next period. At the end of the term, the total paid is equal to the final principal.

The annual interest shown for the simple interest loan does not become principal. Accrued interest is not realized until paid at the end of the term. If the simple interest had been paid annually to the lender, it would not be true simple interest because the lender would immediately have the opportunity to lend it again to earn interest during the next years. This would have the same effect as compounding. It is a very subtle point often misunderstood.

Since the interest earned by the compound interest loan is greater ($1,677 vs. $1,500), it is readily apparent that compound interest loans are advantageous to the lender.

Also, note that money committed to a compound interest transaction grows more rapidly when there are a greater number of compounding periods. The following example demonstrates this fact:

Example 3.8: *Comparison of Compound Interest Period*

A set of grandparents deposited $10,000 in a account for their newly born grandchild with the aim of providing money for college in 18 years. Compare the sum of money (future value) the child will have to start college if the account's interest rate of 9.00% is compounded: (1) annually, (2) monthly, or (3) daily.

Solution:

The results are shown in tabular form below. The future values are in bold type.

Table 3.4: $10,000 Invested for a Term of 18 Years @ 9.00%

Compounding Periods	Annually	Monthly	Daily
Periods per year	1	12	365
Total number of periods	18	216	6,570
Future value	**$47,171**	**$50,226**	**$50,521**

Can you verify the total number of compounding periods? The number of days resulting for an 18 year term is:

$$18 \text{ years} \times \frac{365 \text{ days}}{1 \text{ year}} = 6{,}570 \text{ days} \quad \text{(Neglecting leap years.)}$$

To illustrate a point, we have skipped ahead a bit in calculating the future values. To get the future value of daily compounding, for instance, we didn't perform 6,570 individual calculations. There is a single formula we will introduce in Chapter 4 that does it in one calculation.

Table 3.4 shows a relatively large difference in the future value between compounding annually and monthly ($50,226-$47,171 = $3,055). Between monthly and daily compounding there is a much smaller difference ($295). Because of the advantage of greater compounding periods, you should strive to get monthly compounding or better when you deposit or invest money.

THE RULE OF 72

The "Rule of 72" is a quick, handy way to estimate the time it takes to double invested money. It is a very helpful thought process. The rule applies to money invested at compound interest. We *emphasize* that it is an approximate method but accurate enough for quick and easy comparisons.

To estimate the doubling time of invested money, divide 72 by the annual interest rate expressed in percentage form:

Formula 3.4: The Rule of 72
(The doubling time of money.)

$$\frac{72}{\text{Interest Rate}} = \text{Years to Double}$$

Example 3.9:

An institution will give you 10% compound interest if you deposit a minimum of $5,000 now. About how long will it take to double this amount to $10,000?

Solution:

$$\frac{72}{10\%} = 7.2 \text{ years}$$

Notice that the interest rate is in percentage form when applied to this approximate formula. This is different from normal mathematical operations that require numbers be in decimal form. Also we reiterate that the result is an *approximation*. The exact doubling time for money deposited at 10% per year compounded annually is 7.27 years. The rule is close enough for planning purposes, but not for actual interest calculations.

Why Should You Use the Rule of 72?

The Rule of 72 is an easy approximation to use and can enhance your financial awareness. It is very important to be constantly aware of your financial options. Too many people just park money various places without realizing the potential income they are losing. The Rule of 72, if used, tends to make one continually aware of interest rate values.

For instance, an easy place to park money is in a passbook savings account earning 2% per year interest rate. This doubles your money in 36 years. Not a very exciting prospect, is it? Suppose you could get an 8% compound rate of return. Now your money doubles in 9 years. This is much better. The result is a 75% decrease in the doubling time of your money.

Take this a step further. Suppose someone started with $20,000 in an account earning 2%. This is money set aside for retirement. Compare this to having the option of an investment returning 8%. In 36 years the value of the 2 percent account is $40,000. The invested money earning 8% is $40,000 in 9 years, $80,000 in 18 years, $160,000 in 27 years, and $320,000 in 36 years.

Is the magic of compounding at larger interest rates enhancing your awareness? The person with the 2% account would probably have to depend on Social Security for most of his or her retirement income, whereas the 8% account could provide a more comfortable retirement income.

SOME FINAL REMARKS
ABOUT INTEREST CALCULATIONS

Many books on the subject of financial math used a slightly different form of Formula 3.1. Recall that Formula 3.1 is $INT = PV \times i \times n$. An alternative formula is:

$$Interest = Principal \times Rate \times Time$$

The latter is a rather inflexible generic formula in that it is applied by using the "rate" only as an annual interest rate, and the time as a whole number of years or fractions of a year. The formula does not emphasize "rate" as being a true time-dependent rate because in practice interest rates are expressed over various time periods. Most importantly, it does not provide a good transition formula to the understanding of compound interest calculations. The latter are really the basis of financial math since simple interest is not widely used.

Now Its Your Turn:

1. Bond holders receive an interest payment every six month period. Principal is paid only when the bonds mature. This type of interest payment is tantamount to:
   a. Simple interest
   b. Compound interest

2. The term of a loan consists of:
   a. One year
   b. Three months
   c. The time represented by the number of interest periods in the term

3. Compounding periods can be selected as any period of time within a year.
   a. True
   b. False

4. The value of the original principal grows more rapidly when interest is compounded because:
   a. Interest becomes principal and again earns interest
   b. Interest rates increase for each compounding period
   c. Both of the above

5. When interest compounds monthly, how many compounding periods are there in a year?
   a. 365
   b. 30
   c. 12

6. It is always necessary to match the rate of interest per period to the stated number of compounding periods per year.
   a. True
   b. False

7. What interest rate would you use when calculating the interest for a loan of 8% compounded quarterly?
   a. 8%
   b. 4%
   c. 2%

8. How much compound interest will be earned on a principal of $10,000 at the end of a three quarter term loan using the interest rate in question 7?
   a. $600.00
   b. $612.08
   c. $61.20

9. How much interest would you earn at the end of a 90 day term if you invested $5,000 at 5% ordinary simple interest?
   a. $52.50
   b. $62.50
   c. $125.00

10. How much interest would you earn on $5,000 by the end of a 90 day term using an exact simple interest rate of 5%?
    a. $62.56
    b. $63.25
    c. $61.64

11. If you borrowed $2,000 at a simple interest rate of 9% per year for a four year term, how much money would you have to return to the lender at the end of the term?
    a. $2,840
    b. $2,720
    c. $2,560

12. If you invested $4,000 in a two year CD that pays an annual interest rate of 5% compounded semiannually, how much money would you draw at the end of the term?
    a. $4,400.00
    b. $4,415.25
    c. $4315 68

13. Using the Rule of 72, about how long would it take to double your money invested at 12% compound interest?
    a. 10 years
    b. 8 years
    c. 6 years

14. For an annual inflation rate of 4%, estimate how long it takes to double the cost of living. (Hint: Use the Rule of 72.)
    a. 12 years
    b. 18 years
    c. 20 years

ANSWERS: 1.b, 2.c, 3.a, 4.a, 5.c, 6.a, 7.c, 8.b, 9.b, 10.c, 11b, 12.b, 13.c, 14.b

Compounding: A Way to Grow Money

LEARNING OBJECTIVES

From this chapter you will learn:

1. What is meant buy the "Magic of Compounding"
2. How to calculate the compound growth of money
3. The definition of nominal and effective interest rates
4. How to convert nominal interest rates to effective interest rates
5. Why you should use effective interest rates when comparing investment alternatives
6. What your bank means by the commonly used terms "Annual Percentage Rate" (APR) and "Annual Percentage Yield" (APY)

You can greatly improve your financial future by learning how to take advantage of the power of compound interest. As we saw in the Chapter 3, money invested at compound interest grows faster than it would if invested under simple interest. Your money grows exponentially when invested under compound interest.

In this chapter we introduce the compound interest power formula. This formula is very useful in your everyday financial thinking. The relationship between nominal and effective interest rates is also explained. Surprisingly enough, this simple relationship is not understood by many of those employed in the banking profession. Your understanding this relationship is vital when comparing calculating and comparing your investment opportunities.

WHAT IS THE "MAGIC OF COMPOUNDING"?

The magic of compounding is often illustrated by a rather humorous example: If your ancestors had deposited one penny in the year 1 A.D. with the bank of Jerusalem, what would that investment would be worth today if the bank paid an annual compound interest rate of 2%? The answer is: $1,500,000,000,000,000.

A more practical modern example is to follow a $10,000 investment at a compound interest rate of 10% over a 40-year term. Ten percent is the long-term annual rate of return realized by the Dow Jones Industrial stocks. The following graph depicts this growth.

Figure 4.1
How a $10,000 Investment Grows
at 10% Compound Interest Rate

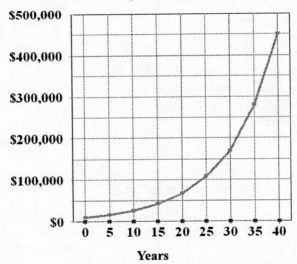

Years

Test your knowledge of compound doubling time explained in Chapter 3. Did $100,000 grow to $200,000 in 7 years? The "Rule of 72" is quite accurate here.

Notice that the curve slopes upward in a circular arc. In the vernacular of mathematics, this plot is called a power function curve. Compounded money here grows magically over time. The money value curve almost goes straight up—and the amount of your money with it—as the length of time increases. Time is a great friend to compounded investments.

HOW TO CALCULATE COMPOUND GROWTH OF MONEY

Compound growth is calculated by a simple power formula. This formula is the culmination of the method we described in Chapter 3 to calculate interest earned during each compounding period. Compound growth is expressed as the future value of an initial amount of money compounded over time.

Formula 4.1: Future value—Single Payment
(The power formula)

$$FV = PV(1 + i)^n$$

The symbols of this formula are the same as those used in Chapter 3, and the definitions are provided here for convenience as follows:

FV = the *future value* of money at the end of n periods
PV = the *present value* of money (The principal is the single payment for this mode.)
i = the *interest rate* per interest time period
n = the *number* of interest time periods in the term

The expression $(1+i)^n$ in Formula 4.1 is called the *single payment compound amount factor*. You can see that this is called a power formula because the values in the parentheses are raised to the power of n. For example, $(1+i) \times (1+i) = (1+i)^2$ is $(1+i)$ raised to the second power. Recall that in Chapter 3 we performed a calculation for each compounding period. Using the power formula you now can get the results with only one formula even though there can be many compounding periods. You will need to use your electronic calculator with the y^x key.

Cash Flow Diagrams for the Single Payment Mode

These diagrams clarify the lender's and borrower's cash flow for this type of transaction:

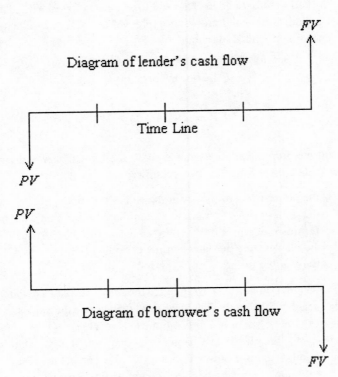

From the lender's perspective, *PV* is the initial payment loaned to the borrower. At the end of the loan term the borrower pays the *FV* to lender. This includes the *PV* principal plus the accrued interest. The opposite is true for the borrower. The borrower receives the *PV* amount of the loan and pays back the *FV* the end of the term.

Example 4.1:

What is the future value of $1,000 invested at a compound interest rate of 10% for a term of 20 years? The lender compounds interest yearly.

Solution:

Using Formula 4.1. we begin the solution by identifying the values of the known variables:

$$PV = \$1,000$$
$$n = 20 \text{ years (20 compounding periods)}$$
$$i = 10\% \text{ per year}$$
$$FV = PV (1+i)n$$
$$FV = \$1,000 (1+0.10)^{20}$$
$$= \$1,000 (1.10)^{20}$$
$$= \$6,727$$

To solve the $(1.1)^{20}$ part of this formula: using your calculator, key in 1.1 and press the y^x key. Then key in 20 and press the "=" key. You should see the number 6.727 in the calculator window. Multiply it by 1,000 to get 6,727.

Example 4.2:

Calculate the future value of $1,000 invested at an interest rate of 10% for a term of 20 years. Perform this calculation for three different compound periods: (1) daily, (2) monthly, and (3) quarterly.

Solution:

(1) Daily compounding

$$PV = \$1,000$$

$$i = \frac{0.10}{\text{year}} \times \frac{\text{year}}{365 \text{ days}} = 0.00027397 \text{ per day}$$

$$n = 20 \text{ years} \times \frac{365 \text{ days}}{\text{year}} = 7,300 \text{ days}$$

$$FV = \$1,000 (1.00027397)^{7300}$$
$$= \$1,000 \times 7.387$$
$$= \$7,387$$

We get this result by keying in 1.00027397, pressing the y^x key, keying in 7300, pressing the "=" key, and read 7.387 in the window. The calculator was set to round to three decimal places. Multiplying this by 1,000 and get 7,387. This is a matter of choice.

If we had desired greater accuracy, for example, to one cent, we could have set the calculator to found to rounded to five decimal places before multiplying by 1,000.

(2) Monthly compounding:

$PV = \$1,000$

$$i = \frac{0.10}{\text{year}} \times \frac{1 \text{ year}}{12 \text{ months}} = 0.0083333 \text{ per month}$$

$$n = 20 \text{ years} \times \frac{12 \text{ months}}{\text{year}} = 240 \text{ months}$$

$$FV = \$1,000 \ (1+0.0083333)^{240}$$
$$= \$7,328$$

(3) Quarterly compounding:

$PV = \$1,000$

$$i = \frac{0.10}{\text{year}} \times \frac{1 \text{ year}}{4 \text{ quarters}} = 0.0250 \text{ per quarter}$$

$$n = 20 \text{ years} \times \frac{4 \text{ quarters}}{\text{year}} = 80 \text{ quarters}$$

$$FV = \$1,000 \ (1+0.0250)^{80}$$
$$= \$7,210$$

To further appreciate the advantages of multiple period compounding, let's summarize and examine the results of Examples 4.1 and 4.2.

**Table 4.1: Comparison of Future Values of $1,000
Invested at 10% for 20 Years at Different Compounding Periods**

Compound Periods	Number of Periods	Future Value	Percent Difference
Annually	20	$6,727	Base
Quarterly	80	7,210	7.18%
Monthly	240	7,327	8.92
Daily	7300	7,389	9.84

Compounding daily at an annual rate of 10% produced a future value sum of money about 10% greater than that by compounding annually.

Must "n" in the Power Formula Be Expressed as a Whole Number Multiple of Years?

The answer is "no" as long as the time periods are the same as the compound interest rate time periods.

Example 4.3:

Suppose that you deposit $1,000 in a bank savings account and intend to withdraw it in 18 months. The bank compounds interest daily, as most savings accounts do. If your savings account pays an annual interest rate of 4%, how much will you withdraw in 18 months (1.5 years)?

Solution:

$$PV = \$1,000$$

$$i = \frac{0.04}{365 \text{ days}} = 0.0001096 \text{ per day}$$

$$n = 1.5 \text{ years} \times \frac{365 \text{ days}}{\text{year}} = 548 \text{ days}$$

$$FV = \$1,000(1+0.0001096)^{548}$$
$$= \$1,062$$

The power formula can be solved mathematically for any combination of interest rates and commensurate compound periods. Financial institutions, however, may not accommodate some withdrawal periods. For example, if the bank compounds annually, you might not be credited with any interest if you withdraw money between annual periods. Moreover, for certificates of deposit there is usually a penalty for early withdrawal even when your bank compounds daily.

Solving for the Present Value

It is also useful to use the power formula to solve for the present value. To use this formula it is only necessary to rearrange it as follows:

Present Value of A Future Value Amount

This is Formula 4.1 rearrange to solve for the present value given the future value. The symbols are the same as Formula 4.1.

$$PV = \frac{FV}{(1+i)^n}$$

Example 4.4:

Frank needs to replace his aging auto in five years. He would like to deposit a single sum of money now sufficient to pay for a new auto in five years. He estimates that in five years a new auto will cost $18,000. He can raise that future sum by depositing a sum of money now (PV) in a five year CD account bearing an annual interest rate of 6%. How much will he need to deposit?

Solution:

$$FV = \$18,000$$
$$i = 0.06 \text{ per year}$$
$$n = 5 \text{ years}$$
$$PV = \frac{\$18,000}{(1+0.06)^5}$$
$$= \$13,450$$

Therefore, about $13,450 invested today will provide $18,000 to buy a new car debt free, in five years.

WHAT ARE NOMINAL AND EFFECTIVE INTEREST RATES?

This is the logical place to explain the meaning of *nominal* and *effective* interest rates. These two rates are necessary adjuncts to the understanding and use of compound interest mathematics.

First, Some Definitions

Nominal annual interest rate is understood to be the interest rate quoted by the lender. Unless otherwise indicated, quoted interest rates are taken to be nominal rates. Nominal interest rates are undefined quantities *that cannot be used in calculations* until the number of compounding periods per year are known. Interest rates in nominal form must be converted to a rate per compounding period in order to be used in a compound interest formula.

Effective annual interest rate is the nominal interest rate converted to an *interest rate with a compounding period of one year*. (Sometimes the effective annual interest rate is called the "true interest rate.") To be comparable, interest rates must be effective rates. Nominal rates are not comparable because different compounding periods produce different effective yields.

Annual percentage rate (APR) means the same thing as the nominal annual interest rate. Annual rate is the terminology used by banks and many other financial institutions. It is also the term used in Regulation Z of the Federal Truth-in-Lending Act.

Annual percentage yield (APY) is the same as the effective interest rate. It is also a term quoted by banks and many other financial institutions.

Explanation of Nominal and Effective Interest Rates

Consider a loan transaction in which interest is charged at an annual rate of 12%. The lender compounds monthly. This rate should be described as a *nominal annual rate* of 12% compounded monthly. The monthly interest rate is 1%.

If you deposited $1,000 at a nominal interest an annual rate of 12% compounded monthly, the future value of this amount at the end of the first year by monthly compounding is calculated as follows:

$$n = 12 \text{ months}$$
$$PV = \$1,000$$
$$i = 0.12/12 = 0.01 \text{ per month}$$

By Formula 4.1

$$FV = \$1,000(1.01)^{12}$$
$$FV = \$1,000(1.127)$$
$$= \$1,127$$

If the same \$1,000 had been deposited at 12% per year compounded annually the FV would be:

$$i = 0.12 \text{ per year}$$
$$n = 1 \text{ period}$$
$$FV = \$1,000(1.12)^1$$
$$FV = \$1,120, \text{ or } \$7 \text{ less than that by compounding monthly}$$

Notice that monthly compounding has the same effect on the year end amount as charging a rate of 12.70% compounded annually. Thus, a nominal annual interest rate of 12% compounded monthly is equivalent to an annual interest rate of 12.7% compounded annually. The latter rate is called the *effective* annual interest rate. It *always* has a one year compounding period.

Now remember, to calculate any interest rate problem using the nominal interest rate, you must also know the number of periods in a year that compounding takes place. When calculating an interest rate problem using the effective interest rate, you already know the number of periods because it is always one per year. But when using the effective interest rate, always use *n* of Formula 4.1, in years or a fraction of years depending on the term of the loan. For example an effective interest rate loan term of 18 months would require $n = 1.5$ compounding periods in terms of years.

Converting A Nominal Interest Rate To An Effective Interest Rate

This is accomplished by the following formula:

Formula 4.2
Calculating Effective Interest Rate

$$i_E = \left(1 + \frac{i_N}{M}\right)^M - 1$$

Where:

i_N = Nominal annual interest rate.
i_E = Effective interest rate
M = number of compounding periods per year

This is simply Formula 4.1 rearranged so that the left side "*n*" is a compounding period of one per year $(1+i_E)^1$, and the right side "*n*" is compounding periods per year. *Notice that we use "M" in Formula 4.2 in place of n of Formula 4.1.* This is a subtle point that must be understood. The "*n*" of formula 4.1 is the total number of compounding periods of the transaction. Formula 4.2 is a one-year transaction and the "*M*" is the number of compounding in periods in *one* year.

Formula 4.2 is thus developed by equating it as follows:

$$\left(1 + i_E\right)^1 = \left(1 + \frac{i_N}{M}\right)^M$$

Subtracting 1 from each side produces Formula 4.2.

The number of compounding periods in a year is the choice defined by some person or some organization that offers the investment opportunity. As we have stressed, *the effective interest rate is actually the nominal compound interest rate converted to equivalent interest rate with a compounding period of one year. If the nominal interest rate is quoted with a compounding period of one year, then nominal and effective rates are equal.*

An easy way to remember the nominal-to-effective interest rate conversion process is to follow the following steps:

1. Divide the nominal annual interest rate i_N in decimal form by the number M of compounding periods in a year.
2. Add 1 to this amount and raise this sum to the power of the number of compounding periods in a year.
3. Subtract 1 from that amount.
4. Multiply by 100 to convert to percentage form.

Example 4.5:

Convert a nominal interest rate of 10% compounded monthly to an effective interest rate.

Solution:

$i_N = 0.10$ per year
$M = 12$ compounding periods per year
$i_N / M = 0.10/12 = 0.008333$ per month

$$i_E = (1 + 0.008333)^{12} - 1$$
$$i_E = 10.47\% \text{ per year}$$

Let's verify the equivalence of nominal and effective interest rates.

Example 4.5:

Calculate the future value of (1) $2,000 invested at a nominal interest rate of 10% compounded monthly for a term of 5 years, and (2) the same investment using an effective interest rate of 10.47% (equivalent to 10% nominal). Use Formula 4.1.

Solution:

1. Nominal 10% interest rate compounded monthly:
    $PV = \$2,000$
    $i = 0.010/12 = 0.008333$ per month
    $n = 5$ years $\times$ 12 months per year $= 60$ periods
    $FV = \$2,000 (1 + 0.008333)60$
    $= \$3,290$

2. Effective interest rate of 10.47%
    $PV = \$2,000$
    $i = 0.1047$ per year
    $n = 5$ years
    $FV = \$2,000 (1+0.1047)^5$
    $= \$3,290$

We reiterate that the correct way to compare interest rates is to compare the effective annual interest rates. Nominal interest rates are not comparable unless the compounding period is one year.

THE ADVANTAGE OF A GREATER NUMBER OF COMPOUNDING PERIODS

It is informative to compare the nominal and effective interest rates for various numbers of compounding periods within a year. Table 4.2 compares the effective interest rates for various compounding periods you will encounter.

Table 4.2: Comparison of Nominal and Effective Interest Rates

Compound Periods	Periods Per Year	Nominal Rate	Effective Rate
Annually	1	10.00%	10.00%
Semiannual	2	10.00	10.25
Quarterly	4	10.00	10.38
Monthly	12	10.00	10.47
Daily	365	10.00	10.52

This table demonstrates why you cannot compare nominal interest rates when considering an investment since under these conditions there is more than half of a percentage point interest-rate advantage for daily compounding compared to annual compounding.

A local Savings & Loan published the following table. Can you verify the annual percentage yields? The Savings & Loan compounds daily.

IRA Fixed-Rate Certificates		
Months	Annual Percentage Rate	Annual Percentage Yield
24 — 35	4.46%	4.56%
36 — 47	4.66	4.77
48 — 60	5.17	5.31

Now it's Your Turn

1. From the Figure 4.1 graph, the 10% interest rate is compounded annually. If the $10,000 present value is compounded daily, what would the future value of $10,000 be in 40 years?
   a. $490,000
   b. $546,000
   c. $525,000

2. For daily compounding, how many compounding periods will there be for a 10-year term loan?
   a. 3,000
   b. 3,750
   c. 3,650

3. If the nominal interest rate is 6.0% compounded monthly, what is the interest rate per compounding period?
   a. 0.30%
   b. 0.50%
   c. 0.70%

4. When $n = 8$ in the power formula, how many times is $(1 + i)$ multiplied by itself?
   a. 8
   b. 6
   c. 7

5. What is the future value of $2,000 deposited for a term of 6 years at a nominal rate of 3.5%? Assume daily compounding.
   a. $2,360
   b. $2,467
   c. $2,247

6. What would the future value be if $1,500 is deposited for a year and four months? The S & L compounds monthly and offers an annual rate of 5.50%.
   a. $1,614
   b. $1,598
   c. $1,652

7. Grandpa Jones put $10,000 in a zero coupon bond for his new grandson. How much will the young lad have to start college at the end of 18 years if the nominal interest rate of 8% compounds semiannually?
   a. $45,560
   b. $41,450
   c. $41,039

8. How much money would you have to deposit now (PV) to have $10,000 for a new auto at the end of 8 years if the account pays 8% nominal interest compounded daily?
   a. $4,569
   b. $8,340
   c. $5,273

9. How much would Rex need to deposit now if he plans to withdraw $5,000 in 3 years? The S & L compounds monthly and offers 3-year CDs at 4.00%.
   a. $4,605.76
   b. $3,950.63
   c. $4,435.49

10. Your local bank offers an annual rate of 5.25% for an IRA account if you deposit your money for a 48-month period. For daily compounding, what is the annual percentage yield?
    a. 5.39%
    b. 5.65%
    c. 5.25%

11. For question 10 the bank decided to compound monthly. What is the annual yield? Round the to two decimal places.
    a. 5.39%
    b. 5.38%
    c. 5.37%

12. Brad saw a bank advertisement offering an annual percentage yield of 8.30%. In small print the bank stated monthly compounding. Brad wondered what annual rate was. He found it was:
    a. 7.00%
    b. 7.80%
    c. 8.00%

13. Under what circumstance are the nominal and effective interest rates equal?
    a. None
    b. Interest is compounded yearly
    c. Interest is compounded monthly

14. From Table 4.2, what is the percentage difference in the effective interest rates between compounding annually and monthly?
    a. 4.70%
    b. 3.50%
    c. 5.20%

15. -For the same data in question 14 above, what is the difference in basis points between the effective interest rates of annual and monthly compounding?
    a. 45 basis points
    b. 52 basis points
    c. 47 basis points

ANSWERS: 1.b, 2.c, 3.b, 4.a, 5.b, 6.a, 7.c, 8.c, 9.c, 10.a, 11.b, 12.c, 13.b, 14.a, 15.c.

Now the Rest of the Compound Interest Formulas

LEARNING OBJECTIVES:

This chapter will teach you how to:

1. Understand the meaning of "annuity due" and "ordinary annuity" payment modes
2. Calculate a uniform series of payments
3. Calculate future and present values of a uniform series of payments
4. Avoid erroneous use of the anachronistic "sinking fund" formula
5. Use the generalized compound interest formula

The compound interest formulas introduced in Chapter 4 apply to the future or present values of a single payment or receipt of money. In this chapter we present the formulas for a series of uniform (equal amount) payments of money made at each compounding period. Home monthly mortgage payments are an example of this type of uniform payment. Another example is annual deposits to an IRA investment account to accumulate a future sum of money.

The payments referred to here can be made either to retire a loan, a debt, or to accumulate funds in savings or investment accounts. Either way, the payments represent a periodic flow of an equal sum of money, whether as disbursements or receipts.

We would like to point out here that many authors erroneously misapply some of the formulas when they calculate the future value of a uniform series of payments. Later in this chapter we explain this error and tell you how to avoid it.

THE PAYMENT MODES

Uniform payment modes are defined as annuities. Generically an *annuity* is simply a series of equal amounts of money paid at regular intervals. The insurance industry adopted the term annuities to define a policy which can be bought to secure a uniform series of income payments (an annuity). It is necessary to understand the use of annuities in the mathematics of uniform payment series.

To solve uniform series of periodic payments problems, the payment mode must be known. Payments can be made at the beginning of each compounding period: this advance type of payment is defined as an *annuity due* transaction. Payments can also be made at the end of each compounding period: this is defined as an *ordinary annuity* transaction. Once the payment mode is decided, it cannot be changed throughout the transaction. If it is changed at any point, the uniform payment formulas would not produce accurate results.

The symbol for a uniform payment is *PMT*. We use the symbol PMT_b to indicate payments made at the beginning of the compounding periods and PMT_e to indicate payments made at the end of the periods.

Cash flow diagrams showing the two payment modes for money paid are:

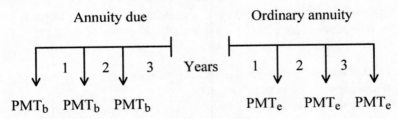

The diagrams in Figure 5.1 below show two completed payment mode transactions. Payments made by an investor are shown by arrows pointing down. In these diagrams each equal payment is made over a term composed of four compounding periods. To be a complete transaction, every cash flow diagram must have at least one cash flow arrow in each direction. Only cash flows are shown on the diagrams.

Figure 5.1: Cash Flow Diagrams of Annuity Payment Modes

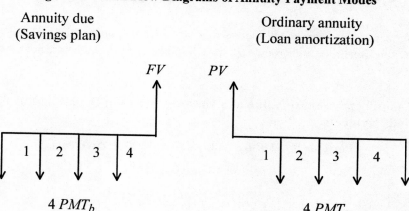

For the annuity due diagram, four payments are made, and the payments and total earned interest culminate in a future value amount of money to be received by the investor. The future value arrow points up to indicate receipt. The annuity due is typical of a savings plan where the deposits are made and each earns compound interest in each period up to the future value amount.

The ordinary annuity starts with a present value amount of money received on behalf of a borrower who in turn makes four equal payments to the lender to retire the loan. This process is termed *amortization*. A debt is reduced by regular payments, each consisting of some principal and interest sufficient to retire the debt. Home mortgage and auto loans are typical of this mode.

In applying the annuity mathematics introduced in this chapter, it must be recognized and remembered that regardless of whether payments are made at the beginning or end of the compounding periods the number of payments PMTs must always be the same as the number "n" of compounding periods. As before the interest rate "i" must always be expressed in the same time units as the compounding periods. The other symbols FV and PV are the same as those of Chapter 4.

UNIFORM PAYMENT COMPOUND INTEREST FORMULAS

Uniform payment compound interest formulas involve combinations of the same power function $(1+i)^n$ as the single payment formula. These formulas are not too difficult to solve.

Calculating the Future Value of a Uniform Series of Beginning-of-Period Payments.

Formula 5.1: Future Value of Annuity Due Payments

Find FV, given PMT_b, i, n

$$FV = PMT_b(1+i)\left[\frac{(1+i)^n - 1}{i}\right]$$

Example 5.1: Future Value of an Annuity Due

John plans to save money to buy a new car in six years. He can afford to deposit $150 a month in his savings account which pays 5% interest compounded monthly. How much money will John have at the end of the six-year term?

Solution:

$PMT_b = \$150$

$i = 0.05/12 = 0.0041666$ per month

$n = 6$ years ´ 12 months/year $= 72$ months

Using Formula 5.1, the FV is:

$$FV = \$150\ (1+0.0041666)\left[\frac{(1+0.0041666)^{72} - 1}{0.0041666}\right]$$

$$= \$150\ (1.0041666)\left[\frac{1.3490 - 1}{0.0041666}\right]$$

$$= \$12,617$$

The cash flow diagram for this annuity due transaction is: $FV = \$12,617$

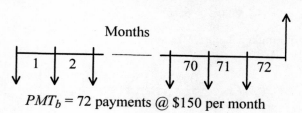

Months

$PMT_b = 72$ payments @ \$150 per month

Seventy-two beginning of month payments of \$150 are made, and at the and at the end of 72 months the future value is \$12,617.

There are a lot of numbers to keep track of, but with rounding off to five significant digits, the result we obtained with a financial calculator (\$12,617) exactly equaled the result we obtained by plugging numbers into the formula. Later on we show you how to use interest rate tables and a financial calculator for these calculations. The importance of calculating with formulas and seeing the cash flow diagrams is to learn the basics.

Calculating Annuity Due Payments to provide a Future Value Sum

Formula 5.2: Annuity Due Payments

Find PMT_b, given PV, i, n,

$$PMT_b = \frac{FV}{(1+i)}\left[\frac{i}{(1+i)^n - 1}\right]$$

Example 5.2: *Building a College Fund*

The Jones have a son who will go to college in 18 years. They estimate they will need \$200,000 at the start of his freshman year. How much will they need to deposit annually to accumulate that sum if they can realize 10% annually in the equity market?

Solution:

$$FV = \$200,000, \ i = 10\%, \ n = 18 \text{ years.}$$

Using Formula 5.2, the PMT_b is:

$$PMT_b = \frac{200,000}{(1+0.10)}\left[\frac{0.10}{(1+0.10)^{18}-1}\right]$$
$$= \$3,987 \text{ per year}$$

The configuration of the cash flow diagram for this exercise is similar to that of Example 5.1.

Calculating the End-of Period Uniform Payments (Ordinary Annuity — Amortization)

Formula 5.3: Ordinary Annuity Payments

Find PMT_e, given: $PV, i, n,$

$$PMT_e = PV\left(\frac{i(1+i)^n}{(1+i)^n-1}\right)$$

Example 5.3: Calculate Monthly Home Mortgage Payments

Keith has taken a conventional 30-year home mortgage. The loan principal is $100,000 and the nominal annual interest rate charged is 7%. What will Keith's monthly payments be?

Solution:

Keith starts making mortgage payments at the end of the first month after the principal (present value) is paid by the lender.

$$PV = \$100,000$$
$$i = 0.07/12 = 0.0058333 \text{ per month}$$
$$n = 30 \text{ years} \times 12 \text{ months/year} = 360 \text{ months}$$

Using Formula 5.3 the PMT_e is:

$$PMT_e = \$100,000\left(\frac{0.0058333(1+0.0058333)^{360}}{(1+0.0058333)^{360}-1}\right)$$

$$= \$100,000 \times 0.0066530$$

$$= \$665.30 \text{ per month}$$

The cash flow diagram for this transaction is:

$PV = \$100,000$

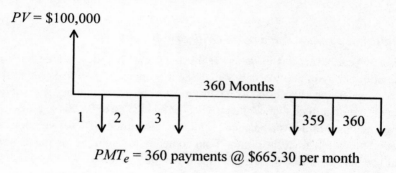

$PMT_e = 360$ payments @ $665.30 per month

Example: 5.4:

Sara bought a new car and financed $18,500 at an interest rate of 8% over a four-year term. How much are Sara's monthly payments?

Solution:

$PV = \$18,500$

$i = 0.08/12 = 0.0066667$

$n = 4 \text{ years} \times 12 \text{ months/year} = 48 \text{ months}$

Using Formula 5.3, the PMT_e is:

$$PMT_e = \$18,500\left(\frac{0.006667(1+0.0066667)^{48}}{(1+0.0066667)^{48}-1}\right)$$

$$= \$18,500 \times 0.024413$$

$$= \$451.64 \text{ per month}$$

Calculating the Present Value of a Uniform Series of End-of-Period Payments

Formula 5.4: Present Value of Ordinary Annuity Payments

Find PV, given PMT_e, i, n

$$PV = PMT_e \left(\frac{(1+i)^n - 1}{i(1+i)^n} \right)$$

Example 5.5: *Present Value of an Ordinary Annuity*

Sally is a 60 year old artist who wants to slow down a bit, but she needs a supplemental income until her main pension and Social Security incomes start in 5 years. She has received a modest inheritance and would like to know how much money she would need to invest in a mutual fund that would provide her an income of $5,000 per quarter over 5 years. The mutual fund is a balanced fund that has earned 10% per year for the last 10 years. She will instruct the mutual fund company to begin the payments immediately at the end of the first quarter after the investment date.

Solution:

$PMT_e = \$5,000$

$n = 5$ years $\times 4$ quarters per year $= 20$ quarters

$i = 0.10$ per year/4 quarters per year $= 0.025$ per quarter

Using Formula 5.4, the PV is:

$$PV = \$5,000 \left(\frac{(1+0.025)^{20} - 1}{0.02 \, (1+0.025)^{20}} \right)$$

$$= \$77,900 \quad (\text{Rounded to nearest } \$100.)$$

The cash flow diagram for this transactions is:

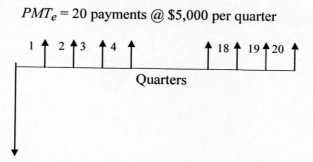

PMT_e = 20 payments @ $5,000 per quarter

Quarters

$PV = \$77,900$

Calculating the Present Value of Beginning-of-Period Uniform Payments. (Annuity Due)

This is the case where a person purchases (or sells) an annuity due type of uniform series of payments. The present value of this purchase is received (or paid) in lieu of the annuity due payments.

Formula 5.5: Present Value of Annuity Due Payments

Find PV, given PMT_b, i, n

$$PV = PMT_b(1+i)\left(\frac{(1+i)^n - 1}{i(1+i)^n}\right)$$

The cash flow diagram for this is shown below as a PV amount received for five (PMT_b) periodic payments. This is the present value of an annuity due payment mode. At time zero an annuity is purchased (or sold) by paying a present value sum of money. Notice that there are five yearly periods, but payments are made only at the beginning of the periods. This differs from an amortized loan. The payments are not retiring a loan, but are a financial obligation to provide a stream of payments for the present value paid for the annuity. In this case the buyer of the annuity would not want to wait a year to start receiving the payments.

Cash flow diagram for the present value of an discounted annuity due transaction.

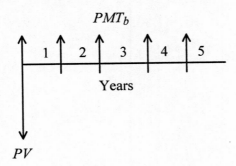

An example which can aid understanding of a series of payments discounted to a present value amount is the state lottery. Although winning the lottery is a big deal, how much does a person actually win? And how much would such winnings be worth if sold on the open financial market?

Example 5.6: The State Lottery: What is it Worth?

Mort won the state lottery. Its value was stated to be $2,000,000. Mort, however, was surprised to find that he will receive $100,000 a year for 20 years, not $2,000,000 today. Mort decided he wanted the money up front, not in annual payments. He approached a financial institution who advertises on TV that they buy annuities. They offered a 16% discount rate for annuities. (The interest rate for a present value calculation is usually called the discount rate.) Below is the calculation the buyer performed to determine the present value of the twenty $100,000 annual payments.

Solution:

$$PMT_b = \$100,000$$
$$n = 20 \text{ years}$$
$$i = 16\%$$

Using Formula 5.5, the *PV* is:

$$PV = \$100,000\,(1+0.16)\left(\frac{(1+0.16)^{20}-1}{0.16\,(1+0.16)^{20}}\right)$$

$$= \$687,746$$

In this case, Mort's two million dollar lottery has a present value only 37% of the stated value. The present value depends on the discount rate (interest rate) the buyer is willing to offer. The greater the discount rate the buyer offers, and thus the greater profit to the buyer, the less the buyer is willing to pay for it. This seems a little backward, but it will become clearer after you have read Chapter 6 on present value.

Calculating Uniform Payments Formulas When the Compounding Periods Don't Match the Payment Periods

Many times, the uniform period payments are made at periods that differ from the stated compound periods. The example below illustrates this and shows how to accommodate this difference.

Example 5.7:

Suppose Don has an IRA to which he contributes $2,000 at the beginning of each year (annuity due). He would like to know how much will have accumulated at the end of 20 years. The account pays a nominal interest rate of 7 % *compounded monthly*.

Solution:

Don has a problem in this calculation. Do you recognize it? The time units do not match: The payments are made on an annual basis, whereas interest is compounded monthly. Since Don does not want to send monthly payments, we need to make some changes to the variables.

The easiest method is to convert the nominal interest rate of 7% to an effective annual rate. Recall that the effective annual interest rate is the true annual interest rate for a compounding period always of one year (see Chapter 4). The conversion Formula 4.2 is:

$$i_E = \left(1 + \frac{i_N}{M}\right)^M - 1$$

Where:

i_N = nominal interest rate
i_E = annual yield or effective interest rate
M = the number of compound periods in a year

The effective annual percentage yield is calculated as follows:

$$i_N = 7.0\%$$
$$M = 12 \text{ per year}$$
$$(1+0.07/12)^{12} = 1 + i_E \qquad \text{Formula 4.2}$$
$$i_E = 7.2290\%$$

Now we have consistent units:
$$PMTb = \$2,000 \text{ per year}$$
$$i_E = 0.072290 \text{ per year}$$
$$n = 20 \text{ years}$$

Solving for the FV by Formula 5.1:

$$FV = \$2,000\,(1 + 0.072290)\left[\frac{(1 + 0.072290)^{20} - 1}{0.072290}\right]$$

$$= \$2,000 \times 1.072290 \times 42.035$$

$$= \$90,148$$

Example 5.8:

Suppose you want to deposit $25 a month to an account (annuity due) that pays 5% annually but compounds daily. What would be the future value of this account in five years?

Solution:

We need to determine the nominal monthly interest rate in order to match the monthly payment mode. This is solved by a three-step process:

1. Convert the annual nominal interest rate of 5% to an effective rate using daily compounding.
2. Convert that effective rate back to a monthly nominal rate.
3. Then use the monthly nominal rate to solve for the future value.

Step 1: Using formula 4.2,

$$i_E = \left(1 + \frac{0.05}{365}\right)^{365} - 1 = 0.05127$$

Step 2: Rearrange Formula 4.2 to solve for the monthly nominal rate:

$$i_N = M\left(1 + i_E\right)^{1/M} - M$$

$i_E = 0.05127$, $M = 12$ compounding periods per year.

$$i_N = 12\left(1 + 0.05127\right)^{1/12} - 12 = 0.05010 \text{ per year}$$

Step 3: Plug the values $i = 0.0501$ (0.004175 per month), $PMT_b = \$25$, and $n = 60$ months into Formula 5.1, and you should get a future value of $1,707.69.

ERRONEOUS USE OF THE SINKING FUND FORMULA

We have found that many authors of books and compound interest tables error when calculating the future value of a uniform series of annuity due payments. The common error involving the future value of a series of uniform payments stems from the erroneous use of the sinking fund formula.

A *sinking fund* is a fund set aside in a separate custodial account to which a uniform series of payments is made to accumulate a future sum for the purpose of retiring a debt. Industrial financial planners use the sinking fund concept for such purposes as securing a sum of money at the end of a term to replace worn out industrial equipment. The sinking fund established to replace equipment is a good concept. However, the sinking fund formula is antiquated. It gives erroneous results. The sinking fund payments are actually end of period payments or ordinary annuity type of payments, but are almost always confused with annuity due type of payments. It is amazing to see how prevalent the sinking fund formula is presented by those who write books and also teach finance even at the college level.

Formula 5.6: Future Value Of Sinking Fund Payments
(An erroneous formula)

$$FV = PMT_e\left[\frac{(1+i)^n - 1}{i}\right]$$

Notice that this formula is the same as Formula 5.1 except that: (1) the $(1+i)$ term in front of the brackets is missing, and (2) the uniform payment is made at the end of the compounding periods rather than the beginning. To deposit a payment at the end of a period is not a realistic situation. When a deposit is made, earning interest begins immediately, *not at the end of the period*. The sinking fund formula is an anachronism. A cash flow diagram of the sinking fund as an ordinary annuity transaction illustrates the difficulty we are explaining.

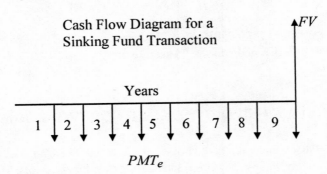

Cash Flow Diagram for a
Sinking Fund Transaction

As the diagram shows the first payment is made at the end of the first period. Thus it earns no interest during the first period. The last payment is made at the end of the last period and also does not earn interest; it is just added to the end sum to get the future value. This sinking fund type of transaction makes no sense. Any uniform cash flow would grow to a future value using the annuity due formula, not the sinking fund formula.

The following example shows the results of a series of payments made at the beginning and end of compounding periods.

Example 5.9:

A book written be two professors of finance at a major university asked the question: "What is the future value of a $250 annuity at the end of 5 years if the annual compounding rate is 10%? Their answer was $1,526. Lets compare a correct annuity due analysis to determine what the answer should have been.

Table 5.1: Comparison of the Future Values of an Annuity Due and the Sinking Fund Formulas

Year[1]	Annuity Due		Sinking Fund	
	Payment	Value[2]	Payment	Value[3]
1b	$250	$250		$0
1e		275	$250	250
2b	250	525		250
2e		578	250	525
3b	250	828		577
3e		910	250	827
4b	250	1,160		827
4e		1,276	250	1,160
5b	250	1,526		1,160
5e		1,679	250	1,526

(1) b = beginning of year, e = end of year
(2) Results calculated by Formula 5.4
(3) Results calculated by Formula 5.5

The detailed year-by-year analysis is shown in Table 5.1. The correct answer is $1,679 in place of $1,526. As the formulas of an annuity due and the sinking fund show, the future values differ by a factor of $(1+i)$. For an interest rate of 10% this is a factor of 1.10. The detailed analysis of Table 5.1 show that this is indeed correct, i.e., 1.10 × $1,526 = $1,679. Notice that sinking fund payments are made at the end of the first and fifth year periods and thus earn no interest during the first or fifth year periods. The fifth year payment of $250 is just added to the interest-principal of 1.10 × $1,160 = $1,276 to provide the end-of-five year value of $1,526.

In other words to assume that payments are made at the beginning of the period and then use the sinking fund formula for this example results in a 10% error. The absurdity here is why would someone have an annuity in which they deposit the last payment at the end of the period and then immediately withdraw it?

It is not too difficult to understand how the wrong formula was initially used in the early days of financial math, perhaps even going back to the days when it was applied in the economics of the rail road industry. The formula is derived in almost all algebra text books by finding the nth term of a geometric progression. The derivation is easily done if it is assumed that the payments are made at the end of the compounding period. The derivation is much more difficult if the payments are made at the beginning of the period. Thus it appears to have carried over for decades without recognition that it is erroneous. Overcoming a convention is difficult due to the inertia of custom. It is time to correct this error. Some authors correctly present annuity due results. The book *Realty Bluebook Financial Tables* by Robert de Heer, (Real Estate Education Company) has the correct values for annuity transactions.

In order to not repeat the above type of error, we recommend that the sinking fund formula or tables not be used for calculations involving the future value of a uniform series of payments.

THE GENERALIZED COMPOUND INTEREST FORMULA

It is possible to write a generalized formula that covers all compound interest calculations. Using a generalized formula you can solve for any one of the following: present value (*PV*), future value (*FV*), and periodic payments (*PMT*). All of the compound interest formulas we have introduced so far are included in this generalized formula. Electronic calculators such as the Hewlett-Packard 12-C financial calculator are programmed to solve this formula.

Formula 5.6: The Generalized Compound Interest Formula

$$0 = PV + (1 + iS) PMT \left[\frac{1 - (1 + i)^{-n}}{i} \right] + FV (1 + i)^{-n}$$

Where:

n = number of compounding periods
i = interest rate per compounding period
PV = present value
FV = future value
PMT = periodic payment
S = payment mode factor (0 or 1)

$S = 0$ for payments made at the *end* of a period (ordinary annuity), and $S = 1$ for payments made at the *beginning* of a period (annuity due). This feature requires judgement based on the knowledge of the payment modes under question. That is for PMT_b, $S = 1$ and for PMT_e, $S = 0$.

In using the generalized formula it is necessary to keep track of the negative and positive values of *PV, FV, and PMT*. A positive value means you receive the money, and negative means you pay it. The formula is not accurate unless the proper negative and positive sign conventions are observed. This is also true when using an electronic calculator or the formulas of a personal computer spreadsheet program. The HP-12C calculator has keys "begin" (S=1) and "end" (S=0) for period mode settings (more on that later in Chapter 8).

For this formula, if you know any two of the three variables *FV, PV*, and *PMT*, you can solve for the third variable. Interest rate tables cannot do this. In addition to knowing any two of *PV, FV*, or *PMT*, it is, of course, necessary to know the interest rate and number of compounding periods. The following example demonstrates the use of this formula.

Example 5.9: A Balloon Payment

Fred has just secured a $200,000 mortgage on his home. The term is 30 years and the interest rate is 8%. He wants to calculate two items:

1. How much will be his monthly payments
2. The remaining principal of the loan after he has made payments for 15 years

Solution:

First Fred must solve for the monthly payments.

1. Calculate Fred's monthly payments (PMT_e):

   PV = $200,000 (positive value because it was received on Fred's behalf.)
   i = 0.08/12 = 0.00666667 per month
   n = 30 years or 360 months
   S = 0 since payments are made at end of the month (ordinary annuity)
   FV = 0 because the mortgage will be completely paid in 30 years

Plugging values into the generalized formula we have:

$$0 = \$200,000 + PMT_e \left[\frac{1-(1+0.00666667)^{-360}}{0.00666667} \right]$$

$$-\$200,000 = PMT_e(136.2834)$$

$$PMT_e = -\$1,467.53$$

The monthly payment is (PMT_e) is negative because Fred makes the monthly payments. Notice that we rounded the interest rate to six significant digits in order to get six-place accuracy in the answer. The lender would calculate the monthly payments accurate to the penny.

2. Calculate the principal remaining after 15 years (Commonly called a balloon payment.)

Here we will see how to calculate FV when the PV and PMT_e are known. We plug in the following numbers to find out the remaining balance 15 years after Fred began making payments.

$$PV = \$200,000$$
$$i = 0.0066667$$
$$n = 15 \text{ years} \times 12 \text{ months} = 180 \text{ months}$$
$$PMT_e = -\$1,467.53$$

$$0 = \$200,000 - \$1,467.53 \left[\frac{1-(1+0.0066667)^{-180}}{0.0066667} \right] + FV (1+0.00666667)^{-180}$$

$$0 = \$200,000 - \$1,467.53 \times 104.6410 + FV \times 0.302394$$

$$FV = -\$153,562$$

The cash flow diagram for this transaction is:

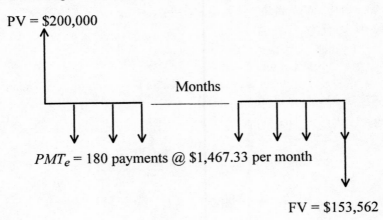

PV = \$200,000

Months

PMT_e = 180 payments @ \$1,467.33 per month

FV = \$153,562

Notice that the remaining loan principal (future value) is negative. This indicates that Fred would have to make a balloon payment of $153,562, in addition to the final monthly payment, to retire this debt.

Another type of problem that the generalized formula can solve is where four variables (*PMT*, *PV*, *n*, and *i*) are known. Let's see how this applies.

Example 5.10:

Margaret currently has $2,000 in her savings account. She now decides to deposit $500 per year over a term of five years. Her account's interest of 5% compounds annually. What will be its future value at the end of five years?

Solution:

$$PV = -\$2,000,\ PMT_b = -\$500,\ i = 5\%,\ n = 5$$
$$S = 1\ \text{(annuity due)}$$

$$0 = -\,2000 + (1+0.05)(-500)\left(\frac{1\,-\,(1+0.05)^{-5}}{0.05}\right) + FV\,(1+0.05)^{-5}$$

$$FV = \$5,454$$

PV and *PMT$_b$* are negative because they are paid by Margaret. *FV* is positive because it represents the money that can be received even though Margaret may not elect to take it five years from now.

The cash flow diagram is:

$$FV = \$5,454$$

Years

1   2   3   4   5

$$PMT_b = 5\ @\ \$500\ \text{per year}$$

$$PV = \$2,000$$

It is clear that the generalized formula offers the full range of variables (PV, FV, PMT) in the solutions of the uniform periodic payment problems. This flexibility is also available by using a financial hand held calculator.

Now It's Your Turn:

1. The meaning of uniform periodic payments is:
    a. Payments of any amounts of money made at equal time intervals.
    b. Payments of equal amounts of money made at equal intervals of time.
    c. Payments of equal amounts of money made at various time periods.

2. Payments, deposits, disbursements, and receipts are all valid terms to describe uniform series of payments.
    a. True
    b. False

3. The time periods referred to in applying the compound interest formulas always refer to the compounding periods.
    a. True
    b. False

4. To retire a debt using a uniform series of payments, payments are made:
    a. At the beginning of the periods
    b. At the end of the periods
    c. Both of the above

5. To accumulate a future sum of money using a uniform series of payments, payments are made at:
    a. The beginning of the compounding periods
    b. The end of the compounding periods
    c. Both of the above

6. When a debt is amortized, the payments are made at:
    a. The beginning of the compounding periods
    b. The end of the compounding periods
    c. Both of the above

7. For an amortized debt, the sum of the interest and principal payments made at each period is:
    a. Always an equal amount
    b. Never an equal amount
    c. Neither of the above

8. An annuity due payment mode is:
    a. Payments made at the end of the compounding periods
    b. Payments made at the beginning of the compounding periods
    c. Both of the above

9. The payment modes of an ordinary annuity and amortizing a loan are:
    a. The same
    b. Different
    c. None of the above

10. The monthly PMTe to pay a loan of $125,000 amortized over 15 years at 7.75 % is:
    a. $1,564.10
    b. $1,176.59
    c. $1,254.55

11. Mike has been offered a partnership share in a walnut farm that will pay him $100 a month for 10 years. The last payment will be made at the end of the tenth year. At that time the farm will be sold and return a single payment of $5,000 the end the tenth year. What should Mike pay for a share if he wants to realize a 12% compound annual return on his investment?
    a. $9,807
    b. $8,485
    c. $7,907

12. Charley intends to make a monthly compounded payment to an annuity due plan to accumulate a future value of $200,000 at the end of 20 years. His insurance company guarantees that he will earn a nominal annual interest rate of 6 % during the 20 year term. The value of his monthly PMTb must be:
    a. $524.67
    b. $645.78
    c. $430.71

13. Suppose you want to deposit a single payment now that will provide you with an immediate monthly income of $400 each month for a period of 15 years. The monthly payment will start one month after you deposit the present value amount. The issuing insurance company will pay a nominal rate of 7% compounded monthly for this annuity. What present value payment will be required to purchase this annuity?
    a. $45,645
    b. $44,502
    c. $47,437

14. Mary intends to deposit $2,000 to an IRA account at the beginning of each year for 10 years. She wants to know how much her IRA account will be worth if she can get an annual interest of 8% compounded annually. What would you tell her?
    a. $41,650
    b. $30,301
    c. $31,291

15. Joe has always wanted a new auto. He intends to establish a fund to pay for one at the end of eight years. He has $8,000 now in a mutual fund. Starting now, he thinks he can afford to send uniform annual deposits of $2,000 to his fund. He anticipates an after-tax return of 7% effective annual yield. How much money will he need to add to his accumulated sum (FV) if the new auto will cost $45,000 in eight years?
    a. $9,565
    b. $10,450
    c. $9,298

16. Your father has been withdrawing $1,000 at the end of each month from an account that started with a present value of $100,000. He has just received his sixtieth month withdrawal. The account pays a nominal interest rate of 7% compounded monthly. How much money remains in this account?
    a. $65,980
    b. $70,170
    c. $74,180

17. Brian currently has $15,000 in an account that pays an interest rate of 4% compounded monthly. He needs to withdraw $400 per month for 36 months starting immediately. What will be his account's value at the end of 36 months?
    a. $600
    b. $0
    c. $1,586

18. You intend to deposit $100 each month in your savings account. Your bank pays an annual nominal interest rate of 4.5% compounded daily. You would like to determine the future value of those deposits in 6 years. What did you find it to be?
    a. $8,225.89
    b. $8,281.16
    c. $7,590.00

ANSWERS: 1.b, 2.a, 3.a, 4.b, 5.a, 6.b, 7.a, 8.b, 9.a, 10.b, 11.b, 12.c, 13.b, 14.c, 15.c, 16.b, 17c, 18b.

Present Value:
A Different Way Of
Financial Thinking

LEARNING OBJECTIVES:

Present value concepts are a vital part of financial mathematics. After completing this chapter you will be able to:

1. Understand the principle of equivalence
2. Calculate present value transactions
3. Use present value to compare economic alternatives
4. Place value on prospective money receipts
5. Capitalize annual cash flows
6. Understand the meaning and use of discounted cash flow analysis
   - Net Present Value (NPV)
   - Internal Rate of Return (IRR)

Although the present value concept is very useful and relatively easy to apply, present value is mostly familiar only to finance professionals. In this chapter we bring the present value method into your realm of thinking. At first, present value concepts will seem a little strange. Do not slight this chapter on that account, the present value method is an integral part of the "time value" of money theory. In fact, present value demonstrates the time value of money concepts more clearly than does future value.

A present value method called the *internal rate of return* (IRR) is very useful and necessary to determine the *rate of return* of capital investments. Rate of return is a commonly used term that means the same thing as the annual compound interest rate that you have realized or expect to realize on an investment. The IRR is the general method for calculating the rate of return of a random series of payments and receipts. The commercial financial computer software company "Quicken" applies the internal rate of return method to calculate the performance of your accounts.

WHAT IS PRESENT VALUE?

The present value of money is the value today of a future payment, or stream of payments discounted at some compound interest rate (discount rate). Present value is best explained by the power formula introduced in Chapter 4 (see Formula 4.1). The compounding power formula is the same formula for present value, but rearranged as follows:

Formula 6.1: Present Value of a Single Sum

$$PV = \frac{FV}{(1+i)^n}$$

The symbols are the same as those defined in Chapter 4.

To demonstrate the difference between PV and FV, let's construct a table that includes both the future value and the present value of one dollar using an annual interest rate of 10%:

Table 6.1: Future and Present Values of $1 Invested at an Interest Rate of 10%

End of Year	Future Value	Present Value
0	$1.00	$1.00
1	1.10	0.91
2	1.21	0.83
3	1.33	0.75
4	1.46	0.68
5	1.61	0.62
6	1.77	0.56
7	1.95	0.51
8	2.14	0.46
9	2.36	0.42
10	2.59	0.39

From Table 6.1 it is relatively easy to understand the meaning of future value. One dollar invested at the beginning of year 1 grows to $2.59 by the end ten years: $FV = \$1.00 \times (1+0.10)^{10} = \$2.59$. But present value is the reciprocal of the future value. This means that the number in the present value column, corresponding to a given year, is the value of a dollar today (year 0) if you received that dollar at the end of that year.

Inflation is a similar concept. If the annual inflation rate were 10%, for example, the value of a dollar in the first year would only buy 39 cents worth of goods ten years later.

Example 6.1:

Suppose you will receive one dollar in ten years on a present-day invested amount of money, and you normally earn 10% annual interest rate on money you invest. What amount of money (present value) did you invest today to earn that dollar in ten years?

Solution:

$$FV = \$1.00$$
$$i = 10\%$$
$$n = 10 \text{ years}$$
$$PV = \frac{\$1.00}{(1+0.10)^{10}} = \$0.39$$

Now let's state this another way. If you desire a rate of return of 10% per year on your investments, how much of today' money (present value) would you need to invest today to receive one dollar in ten years? The answer is 39 cents. Any more money than that would mean that you would have received a lessor rate of return on your investment. Table 6.2 demonstrates the trend of present values as a function of interest rates.

Table 6.2: The Present Value of $1 at Various Interest Rates

End of Year	4%	6%	8%
0	$1.00	$1.00	$1.00
1	0.96	0.94	0.92
2	0.92	0.89	0.86

The present value decreases as the interest rate increases. This trend takes some getting use to. Also, the present value decreases as the time increases. For very long-term investments, the present value of a relatively large investment can be deceptively small.

What Is Discounting?

In the jargon of the financial community, the present value process is commonly called *discounting*. From Example 6.1 above, the present value of 39 cents is called the discounted value, and the 10% annual interest rate is commonly termed the *discount rate*. This should not be confused with the more frequently encountered use of the word "discounted" to mean the reduction in the price of an item of merchandise that is being sold for less than its full retail price.

How Much Are You Willing to Pay Now for a Return of Money in the Future?

Example 6.1 emphasizes one of the most important uses of present value analysis. How much should you pay now for the future return of an amount of money? In almost any business or investment venture, you must make an initial investment in order to realize a profit at some time in the future. It is common to think that investing a present sum of money pays large dividends if it earns a relatively large amount of money in the distant future, but this may sound a lot better than it actually is. Make sure you do a present value analysis to see whether or not the investment projection meet your goals.

Example 6.2:

Suppose Robert is offered an opportunity to invest $10,000 in a venture that—if everything goes well—is projected by a reliable due diligence study to return $50,000 in 15 years. Robert's goal is to realize an annual rate of return of 15% on his more risky long-term type of investments. Does this venture have the potential to meet his goal?

Solution:

The maximum amount of money that Robert would be willing to paid now to receive $50,000 in 15 years in order to realize an annual rate of return of 15% on his investment is:

$$PV = \frac{\$50,000}{(1+0.15)^{15}} = \$6,145$$

Based on this evaluation, Robert would not be willing to invest $10,000 in this venture.

THE PRINCIPLE OF EQUIVALENCE

Table 6.1 above demonstrates a very important principle. All the dollar values in the table are equivalent. One dollar at the beginning (year 0) is equivalent to $2.69 in ten years. Similarly, a dollar ten years from now is equivalent to 39 cents today (present value). These statements are only true if the interest rate you realize from your investments or borrowed money is 10%. At a different interest rate, the time value of money changes accordingly.

This principle is termed the *principle of equivalence* by Eugene L. Grant and W. Grant Ireson, two Stanford University professors, in their book *Principles Of Engineering Economy,* fourth edition, (The Ronald Press, 1960). This principle is the basis of the time value of money, because it allows you to equate money at any given time period. We emphasize here that the time value of your money depends upon the *interest rate* you are able to earn with the money you invest. Figure 6.1 shows how some interest rates have varied over time.

Figure 6.1

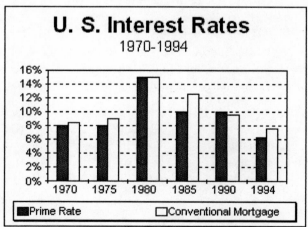

From Figure 6.1, it looks as though the interest rates of 1970—1975 period are about to be duplicated in the mid-1990s. Short-term interest rates, of course, are changed by the Federal Reserve Board in response to the rate of inflation. Although Figure 6.1 presents various interest rates typical of the times, it is incumbent on you to analyze your investments and other available data to determine the realistic discount rates to use for present value calculations. In general, the discount rates selected should be higher for risky as well as long-term ventures. As we saw from Example 6.2, Robert chose a relatively high discount rate because he had both a venture with some uncertainties and a relatively long time duration.

COMPARING THE PRESENT VALUE OF ALTERNATIVES

Present value analysis is useful in comparing the costs of different economic alternatives. A good example is the question of whether to buy a new auto or a used one. The process consists of estimating the expenses and end-of-life-cycle sale value over the period of ownership, and then calculating and comparing the present value of ownership of each option.

In this selection process, the selected discount rates are not necessarily based on the expected rate of return you desire for a future investment opportunity, but rather on the historic rate of return that you have realized on your invested money. The discount rates selected, however, should be greater than the cost of borrowed money.

Example 6.3: Buy a New or Used Auto

Margie needs an auto and has narrowed her selection to two choices: (1) buy a new one for $20,000, or (2) buy a used one for $12,000. She intends to keep her auto six years. She has researched the projected cost of owning each auto and estimates the following:

Cost to own	New Auto	Used Auto
Initial cost	$20,000	$12,000
Annual maintenance	250	700
Gasoline per year	650	800
Insurance per year	1,000	700
Sale value	10,000	2,000

Margie decides to calculate the present value of the cost of ownership. Margie has been an excellent investor: she realizes a rate of return of 12% on her investments. Which alternative is the most economical choice?

Solution:

Table 6.3 shows the present value cost of each option. The costs in parentheses are the annual costs paid by Margie. The annual net cost of both autos in the sixth year is the net of the sale and the value of the six-year cost. For the new auto this is the $10,000 sale price minus $1,900, or a positive return of $8,100.

Table 6.3: Present Value Comparison

Year End	New Auto		Used Auto	
	Annual Net Cost	Present Value Cost	Annual Net Cost	Present Value
0	($20,000)	($20,000)	($12,000)	($12,000
1	(1,900)	(1,696)	(2,200)	(1,964)
2	(1,900)	(1,515)	(2,200)	(1,754)
3	(1,900)	(1,352)	(2,200)	(1,566)
4	(1,900)	(1,207)	(2,200)	(1,398)
5	(1,900)	(1,078)	(2,200)	(1,248)
6	8,100	4,104	(200)	(101)
Totals	($21,4000)	($22,745)	($23,200)	($20,032)

Let's verify the present value of the fifth-year cost ($1,078) of the new auto.

$$PV = \frac{\$1,900}{(1+0.12)^5} = \$1,078$$

Margie will save a present value of $22,745 – $20,032 = $2,713 if she buys the used auto.

If the time value of money had not been considered, the total net absolute cost of the new auto would be only $21,400, compared to $23,200 for the used auto. But remember Margie is successful in investing her money at a 12% interest rate of return. If she buys the used auto she can immediately invest the $8,000 that she saves by not buying the new auto. It is true that she loses the opportunity to invest $300 per year ($2,200 – $1,900) that the used car requires in annual operating expenses over and above those of the new auto, but this does not offset the new auto's absolute cost advantage.

WHAT IS CAPITALIZATION?

You have undoubtedly heard of the term "capitalization." In Example 6.3, we capitalized the annual costs of owning an auto to a single cost, which was the present value. The formal definition of *capitalized cost* used by the financial community is simply the annual costs divided by the interest rate. It is the present value of a perpetual series of annual costs.

Formula 6.2: Capitalization of Costs

$$\text{Captalized Costs} = \frac{\text{Annual cost}}{\text{Interest Rate}}$$

We can best demonstrate this by example.

Example 6.4: Calculating Capitalized Costs

You have determined that, for the remainder of your life, you will need to spend $52 per year on haircuts (neglecting inflation). If you draw the money from an account that pays an interest rate of 6% on your deposited money, what is the capitalized cost of your future haircuts?

Solution:

$$\text{Capitalized Cost} = \frac{\$52}{0.06} = \$867$$

This means that if you deposited $867 in your savings account, you could withdraw enough money annually to pay for your haircuts for the remainder of your life.

This concept may seem trivial, but it has a place in financial thought. It can help you evaluate the relative life-cycle costs of some major expense items relative to your investment rates of return.

Example 6.5:

Bill has retired and would like to get an idea of how much capital he will need if he can realize either 3% or 10% interest on his money. He has estimated some of his expenses.

Solution:

Bill estimated some of his major expenses and capitalized them. The results are shown by the table.

Item	Annual Cost	Capitalized cost @ 3%	Capitalized Cost @ 10%
Food	$5,200	$173,000	$52,000
Auto	6,000	200,000	60,000
Real estate taxes	2,000	67,000	20,000
Home maintenance	1,500	50,000	15,000
Tennis club dues	1,200	40,000	12,000
Cloths	1,500	50,000	15,000
Vacations	3,500	117,000	35,000
Medical	2,500	83,000	25,000
Utilities	2,400	80,000	24,000
Total capitalized cost		860,000	258,000

Bill concludes that he does not have sufficient capital to live on if he only earns an interest rate of 3% on his invested money.

DISCOUNTED CASH FLOW ANALYSIS:
NET PRESENT VALUE

The terms "discounted cash flow analysis" and "net present value" both involve present value operations similar to those we have already presented. As you will see, however, they are unique in analyzing various financial transactions. The terms *present value* and *discounted value* are synonymous. This is a matter of choice. You will probably see it both ways in various publications.

Discounted cash flow analysis is the process of calculating the present value of future cash flows (money paid out and money received). It should be recognized that the cash flows are not necessarily uniform-value cash flows. Also cash flow values can be negative or positive values.

Net present value (NPV) is the discounted cash flow analysis of initial and periodic cash flows calculated with a given discount rate. The discount rate is usually the desired rate of return of a prospective investment. The NPV is used to measure whether the investment will increase or decrease the investor's financial assets as follows:

- If the NPV is positive, the financial assets of the investor increase.
- If the NPV is negative, the financial assets of the investor decrease.
- If the NPV is zero, the investor earns exactly the interest rate used to calculate the NPV.

Understanding the NPV Concept

Net present value can best be understood by starting with a cash flow diagram. For this we will use the same symbols for cash flow that the calculator and computer spreadsheet programs use This will make it easy for you to adapt to calculators.

Cash flow symbols:
CF_0 = Initial cash flow, CF_1 = First period cash flow
CF_2 = Second period cash flow, CF_3 = Third period cash flow, etc.

Cash Flow Diagram

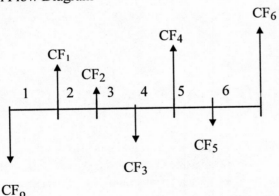

Over the six-year term there are three paid out (negative) cash flows (CF_0, CF_3, and CF_5), and four positive cash flows(CF_1, CF_2, CF_4, and CF_6).

Example 6.6: Calculate Net Present Value (NPV)

Bert opened a mutual fund account with an initial payment of $2,500. He later added $2,000 and $1,500 at the beginning of the years 2, and 3, respectively. At the beginning of year 4 he withdrew $1,000, and at the end of year 4 the mutual fund company reported that his balance was $6,800. Bert would like to realize at least 7% on his investments. Perform a NPV discounted cash flow analysis to see whether or not he did.

Solution:

To visualize the process, we draw the cash flow diagram.

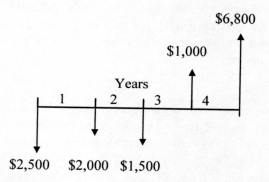

The present value of the cash flows are shown in Table 6.4 where the present value of $1 at 7% is also is calculated. The cash values are multiplied by the present value of $1 and appear in the last column. These are added to get the NPV. Note that for the year column, we designate end of year. Zero is the start of the first year. Thus the present value calculations shown in a given row are for the completion of that year. This is also apparent from the cash flow diagram. At the beginning of year 1 the present value is the same as the initial value $CF_o = (\$2,500)$.

Table 6.4: NPV Discounted Cash Flow Analysis at 7% Interest

Year end	Paid	Received	PV of $1 @ 7%	PV
0	($2,500)		1.000	($2,500)
1	(2,000)		0.935	(1,870)
2	(1,500)		0.873	(1,310)
3		1,000	0.816	816
4		6,800	0.763	5,188
			Net present value	$324

The NPV is positive. This means that Bert realized a rate of return greater than 7%. If the NPV number had been negative, his fund's rate of return would have been less than 7%.

Example 6.7: A Vineyard Investment

George is offered a share in a partnership to develop a vineyard that will start selling grapes in five years. He is offered a share for $15,000. The partnership estimates that each member will pay $2,000 per year for the first four years and then receive $5,000 per year for four years. At the end of eight years they expect to sell the vineyard, and each member should receive $5,000 plus the sales price of $20,000.

Assuming the above values can be realized, George wants to know if this venture has potential to achieve a 14% annual rate of return. He conducts a NPV analysis to evaluate this investment.

Solution:

Table 6.5 shows the results: The NPV is a negative value. George could see that if the partnership kept the vineyard longer it might pay his desired rate, but that the current plan requires too much money early on to realize George's minimum attractive rate of return of 14%.

Table 6.5: NPV of Projected Cash Flows for an Investment Expecting a Rate of Return of 14%

Year End	Cash Flow	NPV $1 @ 14%	NPV of Cash Flow
0	($12,000)	1.000	($12,000)
1	(2,000)	0.877	(1,754)
2	(2,000)	0.769	(1,539)
3	(2,000)	0.675	(1,350)
4	(2,000)	0.592	(1,184)
5	5,000	0.519	2,597
6	5,000	0.456	2,278
7	5,000	0.400	1,998
8	25,000	0.351	8,764
		NPV	($2,190)

DISCOUNTED CASH FLOW ANALYSIS:
INTERNAL RATE OF RETURN

A present value method of discounted cash flow analysis, termed the "Internal Rate of Return" (IRR) is a very useful and necessary method for calculating the rate of return for a series of unequal cash flows. Recall that all formulas in Chapter 5 solve annuities of uniform cash flows. Yet many financial applications in business and investments have cash flows of unequal values. The IRR is a unique method for solving these applications.

Internal Rate-Of-Return (IRR) is the interest rate at which the present value of the net cash flows of an investment equals zero. It is the interest rate (discount rate) at which the net present value (NPV) is zero.

Calculating the IRR, however, requires a trial-and-error method. There are no simple formulas to solve for the internal rate of return. In this process you guess at an interest rate and calculate the net present value. If the NPV is not zero you make another guess and then interpolate to get the correct answer.

We show the IRR calculation method here to get an understanding of the principle. Later in Chapter 8 we show how it is performed by using the financial calculator, and in Chapter 19 where computer spreadsheet programs are very efficient at solving IRR problems.

Calculating the IRR (Trial-and-Error Method)

We demonstrate this process by returning to Example 6.6 which is repeated here for convenience.

Example 6.8:

Although Bert's mutual fund account of Example 6.6 offered a rate of return of greater than 7%, as determined by the NPV analysis, he would now like to know his actual rate of return. Recall that Bert opened the mutual fund account with an initial payment of $2,500, then later added $2,000 and $1,500 at the beginning of the years 2 and 3 respectively. At the beginning of year 4 he withdrew $1,000, and at the end of year 4 his account's value was $6,800. (See the cash flow diagram of Example 6.5.) Let's use the IRR process to find the rate of return Bert realized by this investment.

Solution:

Based on the positive NPV of $324 (Example 6.6) we verified that Bert's fund's return is greater than 7%. Let's select a value of 10% and see whether the NPV is more or less than that value.

Table 6.6 Discounted Cash Flow Analysis at 10% Discount Rate

Year end	Paid	Received	PV of $1 @ 10%	PV
0	($2,500)		1.000	($2,500)
1	(2,000)		0.909	(1,818)
2	(1,500)		0.826	(1,239)
3		1,000	0.751	751
4		$6,800	0.683	4,644
			Net present value	($162)

Because the NPV is a negative $162, we now know that Bert's rate of return is less then 10%. To find the exact rate, we need to perform a linear interpolation as follows:

$$\text{Rate of Return} = 7\% + \frac{\$324}{\$324 + \$162}(10\% - 7\%) = 9.00\%$$

This is a very close result; the precise the rate of return (ROR) is 8.95% by a computer spreadsheet program. (See Example 19.1 of Chapter 19.)

GRAPHICAL REPRESENTATION OF NET PRESENT VALUES

The net present value of the cash flows in Example 6.8 for a range of discount rates are shown on the graph in Figure 6.2. This is a plot of the net present value as a function of the discount rate. Notice that the curve crosses the zero NPV at a discount rate of 9%. Our guess of 7% and 10% gave us a value on both sides of the zero point from which we could interpolate to get the IRR.

Figure 6.2

Net Present Value

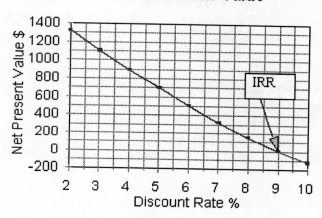

Note that as the discount rate increases, the NPV decreases. This is in keeping with present value characteristics. Also if the discount rate is zero, the NPV is the net value of the actual cash flows. Under a zero discount rate there is no time value of money.

To recap the IRR process, do the following:

1. Guess at an interest rate.
2. Perform a NPV discounted cash flow analysis.
3. Select a second interest rate to get a bracket, that is an interest rate where the NPV is the opposite sign so that you have both a positive and negative NPV result.
4. Interpolate to get the value where the NPV is zero.

The calculations for NPV and IRR are a little cumbersome, but we have gone through them in detail to fully demonstrate the process. It is relatively easy to perform these calculations using hand-held financial calculators or computer spreadsheet programs. Also some financial computer programs, such as Quicken, use the IRR process to calculate the performance of your investments.

Example 6.9: *Internal Rate of Return*

Troy bought 100 shares of stock at a price of $60 per share. One year later he bought another 100 shares at $70 per share. This stock was held by his broker. Four years after his first purchase he sold all 200 shares for a price of $100. There were no dividends declared. What was Troy's annual rate of return on this investment?

Solution:

Initial investment: 100 shares × $60 /share = $6,000
Second-year investment: 100 shares × $70/share = $7,000
Proceeds upon sale: 200 shares × $100/share = $20,000

Cash flow diagram

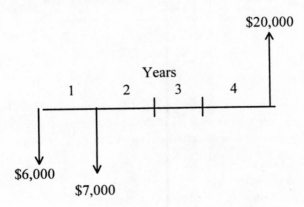

We guessed the rate to be about 13%, so we calculated the present value of 10% and 14%. Good guess, since we have both a positive and negative value. Table 6.7 shows the results.

Table 6.7: NPV of 10% and 14%

Year End	Cash Flow	PV @ 10 %	PV @ 14%
0	($6,000)	($6,000)	($6,000)
1	(7,000)	(6,364)	(6,140)
2	0	0	0
3	0	0	0
4	20,000	13,660	11,842
	NPV =	$1,297	($299)

Interpolation produces:

$$\text{Rate of Return} = 10\% + \frac{\$1,297}{\$1,297 + \$299} (14\% - 10\%) = 13.25\%$$

Can the IRR Process Calculate Annual Rate of Return for Monthly Payments?

The same procedure is used to calculate your ROR on a monthly basis. The periods are monthly if you make some additions to your fund during the year. Then the monthly rate is annualized to an effective interest rate.

Example 6.10:

Jack started a mutual fund account with $1,000 and then sent a payment of $200 at the beginning of each month, starting with the second month. At the end of the year his account reported a final value of $3,395.

Solution:

To demonstrate the process for monthly compounding, we bypassed the trial-and-error process by calculating the IRR with a financial calculator. The table shows that the NPV of the cash flows is zero (thus the IRR) for a monthly discount rate of 0.75%. This is a nominal annual interest rate of 9% and an effective interest rate of 9.38%.

You can keep track of the year-to-date performance of your investments by calculating the IRR any time you receive a financial report of your account value. These reports are usually issued quarterly.

Month	$ CF	$ PV
0	(1,000)	(1,000)
1	(200)	(199)
2	(200)	(197)
3	(200)	(196)
4	(200)	(194)
5	(200)	(193)
6	(200)	(191)
7	(200)	(190)
8	(200)	(188)
9	(200)	(187)
10	(200)	(186)
11	(200)	(184)
12	3395	3,104
NPV		0

Now It's Your turn:

1. Discounting a stream of money or calculating the present worth of a stream of money are the same operations.
    a. True
    b. False

2. A dollar paid to you in six years discounted at a rate of 10% per year has a present value of:
    a. 62 cents
    b. 46 cents
    c. 56 cents

3. What is the present value of $100 paid to you at the end of ten years from now if your rate of return is 8 % per year?
    a. $51.50
    b. $46.32
    c. $42.32

4. What would you be willing to pay today for a venture that will return $1,000 at the end of 4 years, and another $2,000 at the end of 7 years? Since this is a risky venture, you want a rate of return of 20%.
    a. $3,000
    b. $1040
    c. $1620

5. John opened a mutual fund with $2,500. He subsequently sent payments of $1,000 at the beginning of years 2, and 3. At the end of four years his fund was reported to be worth $5,516. John hoped to realize an interest rate of 10% on his investment. Did he get it? (Hint: use NPV)
    a. No
    b. Yes
    c. Probably close enough

6. Can you find the NPV of the new auto's annual net costs shown in Table 6.3? Use an interest rate of 12%.
    a. $21,515
    b. $23,221
    c. $22,745

7. Jack wondered what capitalization would be required to support some miscellaneous expenses that he will have to pay for the remainder of his life. The expenses
   are: (1) $1,500 for real estate taxes, (2) $225 for newspapers, and (3) $105 for
   coffee. Jack earns 9% annually on his capital. What are the capitalized values?
   a. (1) $16,700, (2) $2,500, (3) $1,167
   b. (1) $5,000, (2) $500, (3) $200
   c. (1) $13,500, (2) $1,500, (3) $609

8. Compare the results of capitalizing an annual cost of $1,000 vs. the present value
   of $1,000 annual cost over 30 years, both at an interest rate of 8%.
   a. $16,500 vs. $11,257
   b. $12,500 vs. $12,158
   c. $11,111 vs. $13,200

9. Carl has a house for sale. Its current value is $175,000. Current mortgage rates are
   8.50%. Phil offered Jack a $10,000 down payment and a balloon payment of
   $225,000 in five years. No other payments will be made. What is the present value
   that Phil offering for the house?
   a. $147,635
   b. $159,635
   c. $175,000

10. To receive a future value of $100,000 in 20 years, would you pay $10,000 now if
    you normally earn 15% on your invested capital?
    a. Yes
    b. No

11. Charley issued a note to carry back a loan of $100,000 to the buyer of his house.
    The note is backed by the mortgage on the home. The note is for an interest rate
    of 10% and a term of 10 years. The buyer of the home made 36 payments on the
    note. Charley decided to sell his note to a finance company that earns 12% on its
    money. The monthly payments on the note are $1,321.51, and it has a balance of
    $79,603. How much would Charley receive if he sold this note?
    a. $79,603
    b. $69,875
    c. $74,861

ANSWERS: 1.a, 2.c, 3.b, 4.b, 5.a, 6.c, 7.a, 8.b, 9.b, 10.b, 11.c

Using Compound Interest Tables

LEARNING OBJECTIVES:

In this chapter we present seven basic types of compound interest tables and show you:

1. How tables are configured
2. How tables are identified
3. How to use compound interest rate tables

There are many books of compound interest rate tables sold in bookstores. Such books are of two general types: (1) amortization tables for monthly payments of auto and home loans, and (2) compound interest and annuity tables for more general use. The latter provide individual tables for daily, monthly, quarterly, semiannually, and annual annuities. Many of the books we have examined do not, however, have correct annuity due tables; instead they erroneous use sinking fund formulas for annuity due tables. One book that does offer correct annuity due tables is *Realty Bluebook Financial Tables* by Robert de Heer, (Real Estate Education Company). Mr. de Heer gives credit to Professor Stephen E. Roulac of Stanford University for programming the annuity table values in the book. Professor Roulac does indeed understand the correct use of the annuity due mathematics. Mr. de Heer's book does not apply the out dated sinking fund annuity values.

In this chapter we provide a sampling of compound interest tables. Each of the tables has multiple titles in order to show the different ways they are presented in various published books of tables. We also present a cash flow diagram for each type of transaction. We do not include tables for sinking funds since these do not provide correct annuity results.

It is beyond the scope of this book to provide a complete set of compound interest tables, which would alone fill a book. Also, some compound interest books present tables with eight decimal places. That is a good practice, but to conserve space we will not provide that many significant places for most of our tables since they are intended as example solutions only. The tables provided here were calculated using a personal computer spreadsheet program. This is quite easy to do.

SOME CAVEATS ABOUT COMPOUND INTEREST TABLES

In general, we find that using compound interest tables is a very limited method for solving compound interest problems. Further we recommend that you check the tables you intend to buy by performing some sample calculations using formulas that you know are correctly applied. For example, we have found tables that, in addition to including the erroneous application of sinking fund formulas, use a 360-day year in place of a 365-day year when compounding daily. One book even offers tables for a future value of $1 per period using daily compounding periods. It is illogical that anyone would make payments as frequently as daily for an annuity due type of transaction.

Finally, to be confident using any particular reference of compound interest tables, you should be knowledgeable about the appropriate formulas and their applications. We take umbrage with a statement made in one of the books we reviewed in which the authors stated that "no knowledge of annuity theory is needed," and that " with only simple arithmetic and these tables, anyone can solve the most complex financial problems." In that same book they advertise: "Find out at a glance and to the penny what every dollar you invest will earn." They then use the sinking fund formula in which the example they present is in error by $1,200. In our opinion, the use of such tables without fundamental knowledge of compound interest math is not sound advice.

FUTURE VALUE OF A SINGLE PAYMENT

Table 7.1			
Future Value of $1			
Future Value of a Single Sum			
$FV = PV\,(1+i)^n$			
Period	Interest Rate		
n	4%	6%	8%	10 %
1	1.0 40 0	1.0 60 0	1.0 80 0	1.10 0 0
2	1.0 8 16	1.1236	1.1664	1.210 0
3	1.1249	1.19 10	1.2597	1.3310
4	1.1699	1.2625	1.360 5	1.4641
5	1.2 167	1.3382	1.4693	1.610 5
6	1.2653	1.4185	1.5869	1.7716
7	1.3159	1.50 36	1.7138	1.9487
8	1.3686	1.5938	1.850 9	2.14 36
9	1.4233	1.6895	1.9990	2.3579
10	1.480 2	1.790 8	2.1589	2.5937

Table 7.1 represents this single-payment transaction. All interest rate tables include the period n and the interest rate i. For Table 7.1, the solutions of the expression $(1+i)^n$ are the values in the table according to the period n and the interest rate i. Observe that for a period of $n = 1$ and the interest rate $i = 4\%$, the tabular value is 1.0400. All tabular results have been calculated with the known variable (PV for this transaction) having a value of $1. Referring to Table 7.1, a present value of $1 invested at an interest rate of 4% for a four period term has a future value of $1.1699.

Observe here that the period can be any time period, but the interest rate must correspond to the time period.

The cash flow diagram for the single-payment transaction is:

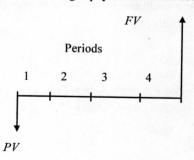

In this transaction, the single present value amount is paid and the future value amount is earned at the end of four periods.

Example 7.1:

Bill invested $1,500 at 8% compounded annually for 4 years. What amount will Bill receive in 4 years?

Solution:

$$PV = \$1,500$$
$$i = 8\%$$
$$n = 4 \text{ years}$$
$$FV = ?$$

From the Table 7.1:
The factor in the table represents $(1+i)^n$ which is $(1+0.08)^4 = 1.3605$.

This is stated as follows:
A present value payment of $1 invested at an interest rate of 8% has a future value of $1.3605 in 4 years.

The future value of $1,500 multiplied the factor 1.3605 provides the sought after result:

$$FV = \$1,500 \times 1.3605 = \$2,040.75$$

Notice that the "n" in the tables is not necessarily the number of years. It is the number of time periods. The interest rates must be chosen as the rate commensurate with the time periods as is done in Example 7.2 below.

Example 7.2:

Paula deposited $1,200 in a credit union account that pays 8% compounded semiannually. What will the future value be in 4 years?

Solution:

We have provided no tables that give explicit solutions for semiannual compounding. Table 7.1 can be used if you modify the interest rate and period—namely the 4 year periods are changed to 8 semiannual periods, and the interest rate of 8% is reduced to a semiannual rate.

$$PV = \$1,200$$
$$i = 8\%/2 = 4\% \text{ per semiannual period}$$
$$n = 4 \text{ years} \times 2 = 8 \text{ semiannual periods}$$
$$FV = ?$$

From Table 7.1 for 4% and 8 periods, the future value of $1 is the factor of $1.3686:

$$FV = \$1,200 \times 1.3686 = \$1,642.32$$

PRESENT VALUE OF A SINGLE PAYMENT

Table 7.2			
Present Value of $1			
Present Value of a Single Sum			
$PV = \dfrac{FV}{(1+i)^n}$			
Period	Discount Rate		
n	4%	6%	8%	10 %
1	0.9615	0.9434	0.9259	0.9091
2	0.9246	0.8900	0.8573	0.8264
3	0.8890	0.8396	0.7938	0.7513
4	0.8548	0.7921	0.7350	0.6830
5	0.8219	0.7473	0.6806	0.6209
6	0.7903	0.7050	0.6302	0.5645
7	0.7599	0.6651	0.5835	0.5132
8	0.7307	0.6274	0.5403	0.4665
9	0.7026	0.5919	0.5002	0.4241
10	0.6756	0.5584	0.4632	0.3855

Example 7.3:

Nine years from now, you will receive a payment of $1,000. What is the present value of this payment now if you realize an annual interest rate of 6% compounded annually?

Solution:

$$FV = \$1,000$$
$$i = 6\%$$
$$n = 9 \text{ years}$$
$$PV = ?$$

From Table 7.2: The present value factor of a $1 payment made in 9 years at an interest rate of 6% is 0.5919:

$$PV = \$1,000 \times 0.5919 = \$591.90$$

FUTURE VALUE OF AN ANNUITY DUE

Table 7.3			
Future Value of $1 per Period			
Future Value of an Annuity Due			
$FV = PMT_b(1+i)\left[\dfrac{(1+i)^n - 1}{i}\right]$			
Period	Interest Rate		
n	4%	6%	8%	10 %
1	1.0 40 0	1.0 60 0	1.0 80 0	1.10 0 0
2	2.12 16	2.18 36	2.2464	2.310 0
3	3.2465	3.3746	3.50 61	3.64 10
4	4.4163	4.6371	4.8666	5.10 51
5	5.6330	5.9753	6.3359	6.7156
6	6.8983	7.3938	7.9228	8.4872
7	8.2142	8.8975	9.6366	10 .4359
8	9.5828	10 .4913	11.4876	12.5795
9	11.0 0 61	12.180 8	13.4866	14.9374
10	12.4864	13.9716	15.6455	17.5312

Cash flow diagram:

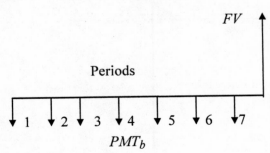

Example 7.4:

A deposit of $1,000 will be made at the beginning of each year for 7 years. The account pays 10% compounded annually. What will be the future value at the end of 7 years?

Solution:

$$PMT_b = \$1,000$$
$$i = 10\%$$
$$n = 7 \text{ years}$$
$$FV = ?$$

From Table 7.3: The future value factor of $1 for 7 periods at 10% per period is 10.4359.

$$FV = \$1,000 \times 10.4359 = \$10,435.90$$

PRESENT VALUE OF AN ANNUITY DUE

Table 7.4			
Present Value of $1 per period			
Present Value of an Annuity Due			
$$PV = PMT_b(1+i)\left(\dfrac{(1+i)^n - 1}{i(1+i)^n}\right)$$			
Period	Discount Rate		
n	4%	6%	8%	10%
1	1.0000	1.0000	1.0000	1.0000
2	1.9615	1.9434	1.9259	1.9091
3	2.8861	2.8334	2.7833	2.7355
4	3.7751	3.6730	3.5771	3.4869
5	4.6299	4.4651	4.3121	4.1699
6	5.4518	5.2124	4.9927	4.7908
7	6.2421	5.9173	5.6229	5.3553
8	7.0021	6.5824	6.2064	5.8684
9	7.7327	7.2098	6.7466	6.3349
10	8.4353	7.8017	7.2469	6.7590

Cash flow diagram

Example 7.5:

You are considering an offer to purchase a note that pays $1,500 at the beginning of each year for a period of 7 years. If you desire to realize a 10% compounded annual rate of return on your investment, how much should you pay for this note?

Solution:

$$PMT_b = \$1,500$$
$$n = 7 \text{ years}$$
$$i = 10\%$$
$$PV = ?$$

From Table 7.4, the present value factor of $1 per period for a period of 7 years at 10% per year is 5.3553.

$$PV = \$1,500 \times 5.3553 = \$8,032.95$$

PRESENT VALUE OF AN ORDINARY ANNUITY

Table 7.5			
Present Value of $1 per period			
Present Value of an Ordinary-Annuity			
$PV=PMT_e \left[\dfrac{(1+i)^n - 1}{i(1+i)^n} \right]$			
Period	Discount rate		
n	4%	6%	8%	10 %
1	0.9615	0.9434	0.9259	0.90 91
2	1.8861	1.8334	1.7833	1.7355
3	2.7751	2.6730	2.5771	2.4869
4	3.6299	3.4651	3.3121	3.1699
5	4.4518	4.2124	3.9927	3.790 8
6	5.2421	4.9173	4.6229	4.3553
7	6.00 21	5.5824	5.20 64	4.8684
8	6.7327	6.20 98	5.7466	5.3349
9	7.4353	6.80 17	6.2469	5.7590
10	8.110 9	7.360 1	6.710 1	6.1446

Cash flow diagram:

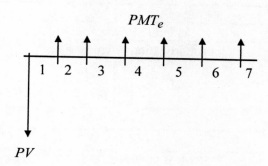

Example 7.6:

What present value amount of money would you need to pay now to buy a note that will pay you $1,500 at the *end* of each year for 7 years if you desire to realize 10% rate of return on you investment?

Solution:

$$PMT_e = \$1,500$$
$$i = 10\%$$
$$n = 7 \text{ years}$$
$$PV = ?$$

From Table 7.5, the present value of $1 per period for 7 years at 10% per year is 4.8684.

$$PV = \$1,500 \times 4.8684 = \$7,302.60$$

Observe that the present value of an annuity depends on the payment mode. Examples 7.5 and 7.6 show this distinction. Failure to recognize this would result in a 10% error in the results. Many of books on compound interest tables do not have the appropriate tables to make this distinction.

UNIFORM PAYMENTS TO AMORTIZE A LOAN

Table 7.6			
Monthly Payment Loans			
Amortization Payment Factors			
$PMT_e = PV\left[\dfrac{i(1+i)^n}{(1+i)^n - 1}\right]$			
Interest Rate			
Months	6.50%	7.00%	7.50%	8.00%
180	0.008711074	0.008988283	0.009270124	0.009556521
240	0.007455731	0.007752989	0.008055932	0.008364401
300	0.006752072	0.007067792	0.007389912	0.007718162
360	0.006320680	0.006653025	0.006992145	0.007337646

Cash flow diagram:

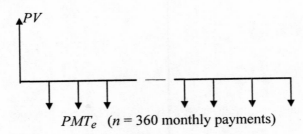

PMT_e ($n = 360$ monthly payments)

Example 7.7:

What monthly payments will amortize a 30-year $250,000 home mortgage offered at an interest rate of 8%?

Solution:

$$PV = \$250,000$$
$$i = 8\%$$
$$n = 30 \text{ years, or } 360 \text{ months}$$
$$PMT_e = ?$$

From Table 7.6, the PMT_e factor to pay off a 360 month 8% annual interest rate loan of $1 is 0.007337646 per month.

$$PMTe = \$250,000 \times 0.007337646 = \$1,834.41 \text{ per month}$$

Notice that the numbers in Table 7.6 have nine decimal places (seven significant digits). This is necessary to get the results accurate to a penny. Calculations of home mortgage monthly payments are usually accurate to the penny.

Table 7.7				
Monthly Payment Loans				
Amortization Payment Factors				
$PMT_e = PV \left[\dfrac{i(1+i)^n}{(1+i)^n - 1} \right]$				
Interest Rate				
Months	6.50%	7.00%	7.50%	8.00%	8.50%
36	.030649	.030877	.031106	.031336	.031568
48	.023715	.023946	.024179	.024413	.024648
60	.019566	.019801	.020038	.020276	.020517

Example 7.8:

What would be your monthly payments if you financed $18,500 of the purchase price of a new car over a term of 60 months at an interest rate of 7.50%?

Solution:

$PV = \$18,500$
$i = 7.50\%$
$n = 60 \text{ months}$
$PMT_e = ?$

From Table 7.7, the monthly payment factor to amortize a $1 loan over a 60-month term at 7.50% is 0.020038.

$$PMTe = \$18,500 \times 0.020038 = \$370.70 \text{ per month.}$$

Now Its Your Turn:

1. Amy deposited $1,350 in a CD account that offered an interest rate of 6% compounded annually. What is the future value of that deposit at the end of 4 years?
   a. $1,704.38
   b. $1,508.39
   c. $1567.56

2. Margaret deposited $500 in a CD account that pays 8% interest compounded semi-annually and that matures in 3 years. What is the future value of the money she will withdraw?
   a. $1050.65
   b. $641.85
   c $632.65

3. How much would John be willing to pay for receipt of $1,500 at the end of 6 years? John normally requires a 10% annual rate of return on his investments.
   a. $946.40
   b. $852.45
   c. $846.75

4. Clarence is the owner of a variety store that will need to be refurbished in 10 years. He estimates that this will cost $10,000 at that time. If he can realize a rate of return of 8% on his investments, what annual payment must he set aside to meet that expense? (Hint: Solve for PMT_b using Table 7.3.)
   a. $758
   b. $639
   c. $864

5. What is the future value of $1,200 paid annually for 7 years if you can get an interest rate of 10% compounded annually?
   a. $11,385
   b. $12,856
   c. $12,523

6. What would you be willing to pay now to receive annuity due payments of $450 for a 5-year term if you desire a nominal annual interest rate of 8% on your investments?
   a. $1,876
   b. $1,940
   c. $1,797

7. The Johnsons have $250,000 in their IRA account. They intend to make uniform monthly withdrawals to deplete this account in 15 years. If they have been earning a rate of return of 8% annually on this mutual fund, how much can they plan on receiving each month?
   a. $2,389
   b. $2,373
   c. $2,568

8. The Jones family has an option the buy a home for $100,000 financed by a 30-year 7.50% mortgage. What will their monthly payments be?
   a. $700.52
   b. $699.21
   c. $756.54

9. The Smiths can afford to make monthly mortgage payments of $650. About how much can they afford to pay for a home if current mortgage rates are 8.00% for 30-year loans?
   a. $105,000
   b. $76,000
   c. $88,584

10. Jack wants to buy a new car but can only afford to pay $150 per month. Interest rates are currently 8.50% for autos. For a four-year term loan, how much can Jack afford to pay for his new car?
    a. $5,300
    b. $6,086
    c. $7,090

11. Your brother has offered to sell you his used BMW and to carry the loan at 6.50% over three years. How much will your monthly payments be if you agree on a price of $8,500?
    a. $280.16
    b. $260.52
    c. $175.82

12. You are offered a GNMA on the secondary market that had an original issue price of $100,000, 30-year term, paying 6.50%. The GNMA has 300 months remaining and the current price is $88,000. Would you buy this issue?
    (Hint: Using Table 7.6, determine the monthly payments you will receive. Then calculate the FV of this loan using Formula 5.6 from Chapter 5. If the remaining principal is larger than the $88,000 you would have to pay for the issue, it is an acceptable investment. This is tough one so give yourself a pat on the back if you get it.)
    a. You would buy it
    b. You would not buy it

ANSWERS: 1.a, 2.c,3 c, 4.b, 5.c, 6.b, 7.a, 8.b, 9.c, 10.b, 11.b, 12.a

Quick-Start the Hewlett Packard HP-12C Financial Calculator

LEARNING OBJECTIVES:

This chapter provides a brief introduction on how to quickly get started using the HP-12C to calculate basic financial functions, including:

1. *FV*: the future value of a compound amount
2. *PV*: the present value of a compound amount
3. *PMT*: the periodic payment amount
4. *n*: the number of compounding periods
5. *i*: the interest rate per compounding period
6. *IRR*: the internal rate of return
7. Calendar date functions

Although the manual that comes with the HP-12C hand-held calculator is excellent, a quick-start introduction to solving compound interest problems is offered here. We show the cash flow diagram for each situation that is being solved by the calculator. The keystrokes are also described and the results shown.

The other financial calculators available operate in a similar manner to the HP-12C. As an alternate, the Hewlett-Packard 10B business calculator also performs the same financial calculations and is more like the general calculators in that it does not use the humorously called "reverse Polish" system.

We assume that you have read this book up to this chapter. If so, you are well grounded in the time value of money concepts. This knowledge is necessary to understand the use of the HP-12C. We also assume that you know some of the basic operations of hand-held calculators.

One of the valuable uses of the financial calculators is their ability to solve explicitly for interest rates and the number of compounding periods. Without a calculator or PC spreadsheet program, solving compound interest formulas for the values of i or n requires some time-consuming applications of rather advanced mathematics.

GENERAL USE OF HEWLETT-PACKARD CALCULATORS

Hewlett-Packard calculators function a little differently from other calculators. They do not have an equal "=" key. The **ENTER** key separates the first number from the second number. To perform an arithmetic operation, you do the following:

1. Key in the first number
2. Press the **ENTER** key to separate the second number from the first,
3. Key in the second number, and
4. Press the +, ×, −, or ÷ key to perform the desired operation.

For the number of decimal places that will be displayed in the calculator window, press the **f** key, then the desired number on the key pad. We shall start with two decimal places. The calculator conveniently rounds the decimal to the number of places you set it. (The keystrokes are set in bold.)

Example 8.1: *Divide 25 by 2*

Keystrokes	Display	Comments
f 2	0.00	Sets two decimal places.
f CLX	0.00	Clears the register.
25	25.	Keys in first number.
ENTER	25.00	Separates the second number from the first.
2	2.	Keys in second number.
÷	12.50	Divides 25 bv 2.

CONFIGURATION OF THE HP-12C FINANCIAL KEYS

The basic financial keys used for solving compound interest problems are at the top and bottom rows of the calculator, as follows:

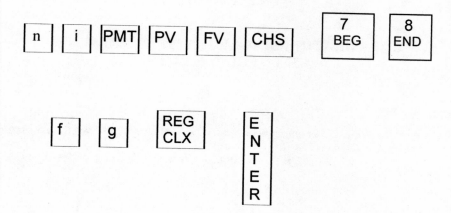

The **f** and **g** keys are called the *prefix keys*. The **f** key is gold color and the **g** key is blue. Pressing the **f** key activates all the keys that have gold writing *above* them. Likewise the **g** key activates the keys with blue letters printer on the bottom of the key. Pressing the **f** key, then the **CLX** key that has **REG** in gold above the key clears the financial and data registers so that you can start a new calculation. If you do not clear the register, the values keyed in stay there, which is all right provided they are the desired values. Pressing the blue **g** key then pressing the **7 BEG** key puts the calculator in the *annuity due* mode, wherein the *PMT* payments entered are made at the beginning of the compounding periods. The word **BEGIN** will appear in the window below the display numbers.

Pressing the blue **g** key, and then the **8 END** key puts the *PMT* payment values in the *ordinary annuity* mode wherein the payments entered are made at the end of the compounding periods. The **END** designation does *not* show in the window.

The **CHS** key changes the input number to a negative number or vice versa when the number displayed is already negative. If you get an "Error 5" indication in the calculator display window, check the sign of the input values of *PV*, *FV*, and *PMT*. Recall that to solve the generalized compound interest Formula 5.6, it is necessary to apply the negative values for cash paid out and positive values for cash received. This applies to the values represented by *PV*, *PMT*, and *FV*. This is also true for the HP-12C because it is programmed to solve the generalized compound interest formula.

Also note that all interest rate values "i" must be keyed in the calculator in percentage form.

CALCULATING SINGLE PAYMENT PRESENT OR FUTURE VALUES

Example 8.2:

If $2,000 is invested at 6% compounded yearly, how much will it be worth in 5 years?

$$PV = -\$2,000, \ i = 6\%, \ n = 5 \text{ years}, \ FV = {}^{'}$$

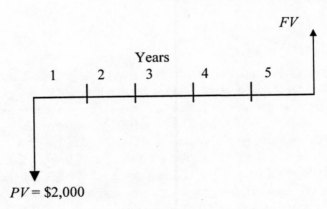

When keying in numbers, only the number itself is keyed in. There are no keys for commas or dollar signs. The negative number is achieved by pressing the **CHS** key prior to keying the number. The calculator will put in the commas and show the minus signs. No dollar or percentage signs are shown in the calculator's window.

Keystrokes	Display	Comments
f CLX	0.00	Clears the registers.
5 n	5.00	Stores the number of years.
6 i	6.00	Stores the interest rate.
2000 CHS PV	− 2,000.00	Stores *PV* (with minus sign for cash paid out).
FV	2.676.45	Calculates *FV* received.

Example 8.3:

Repeat Example 8.2, but do it for daily compounding. If $2,000 is invested at 6% compounded daily, how much will it be worth in 5 years?

$$PV = - \$2,000, \ i = 6\%, \ n = 5 \text{ years}, \ FV = ?$$

Keystrokes	Display	Comments
f CLX	0.00	Clears the registers.
5 ENTER	5.00	Enters the number of years.
365 x	1,825.00	Calculates and stores the number of days in term.
6 ENTER	6.00	Enters the interest rate.
365 ÷	0.02	Calculates and stores the daily interest rate.
2000 CHS PV	− 2,000.00	Stores *PV* (with minus sign for cash paid out).
FV	2,699.65	Calculates *FV* received.

Example 8.4:

What minimum effective interest rate will you need to achieve if you need $5,000 in 7 years and you have $3,500 to invest now?

$$PV = - \$3,500, \ FV = \$5,000, \ n = 7 \text{ years}, \ i = ?$$

Keystrokes	Display	Comments
f CLX	0.00	Clears the registrars.
3500 CHS PV	– 3,500.00	Stores PV (with minus sign for cash paid out).
5000 FV	5,000.00	Stores the FV to be received.
7 n	7.00	Stores the number of years.
i	5.23	Calculates the interest rate.

Example: 8.5:

What is the present value of $10,000 to be received in 10 years, if the interest rate is 6% compounded annually?

$$FV = \$10,000, \ n = 10 \text{ years}, \ i = 6\%, \ PV = ?$$

Keystrokes	Display	Comments
f CLX	0.00	Clears the registers.
10 n	10.00	Stores the number of years.
6 i	6.00	Stores the interest rate.
10000 FV	10,000.00	Stores the FV to be received.
PV	– 5,583.95	Calculates the PV to be paid now.

CALCULATING ANNUITY DUE SERIES OF PAYMENTS

Example 8.6:

Suppose you have $5,000 in an account and, starting now, you will invest $2,000 annually for 5 years. The account pays 8% compounded annually. What will the future value be at the end of 5 years?

$$n = 5, \; i = 8\%, \; PV = -\$5{,}000, \; PMT_b = -\$2{,}000, \; FV = ?$$

$FV = ?$

Years

1   2   3   4   5

$PMT_b = \$2{,}000$

$PV = \$5{,}000$

Keystrokes	Display	Comments
f REG	0.00	Clears the register.
g 7 BEG	0.00 BEGIN	Sets payment mode to Begin.
5 n	5.00.00	Stores the number of years.
8 i	8.00	Stores interest rate.
5000 CHS PV	− 5,000.00	Stores PV (with minus sign for cash paid out).
2000 CHS PMT	− 2,000.00	Stores PMT (with minus sign for cash paid out).
FV	20,018.50	Calculates FV received.

CALCULATING AN ORDINARY ANNUITY SERIES OF PAYMENTS

Example 8.7:

Mike is considering a 30-year home mortgage with an interest rate of 8.5%. He intends to finance $150,000. What will his monthly payments be?

$$PV = \$150{,}000, \ n = 30 \text{ years}, \ i = 8.5\%, \ FV = 0, \ PMT_e = ?$$

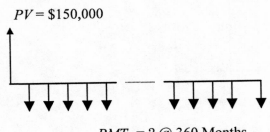

$PV = \$150{,}000$

$PMT_e = ? @ 360 \text{ Months}$

Keystrokes	Display	Comments
f REG	0.00	Clears the register.
g 7 END	0.00	Sets the payment mode to End.
30 ENTER	30.00	Enters the number of years.
12 × n	360.00	Calculates and stores the number of months in the term.
8.5 ENTER	8.50	Enters the nominal interest rate.
12 + i	0.71	Calculates and stores the monthly interest rate.
150000 PV	150,000.00	Stores the loan principal (PV).
PMT	− 1,153.37	Calculated the monthly payment (PMT).

CALCULATING A BALLOON PAYMENT

Example 8.8:

Suppose Mike took the loan of Example 8.7, but intends to pay it off at the end of 20 years. How much would he have to pay?

$PV = \$150,000$, $n = 20$ years, $i = 8.5\%$, $PMT_e = -1,153.37$, $FV = ?$

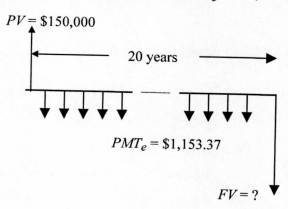

Keystrokes	Display	Comments
f **CLX**	0.00	Clears the registers.
g **8 END**	0.00	Sets the payment mode to End.
20 ENTER 12 × n	240.00	Calculates and stores the number of months.
8.5 ENTER 12 ÷ i	0.71	Calculates and stores the monthly interest rate.
150000 PV	150,000.00	Stores the principal, (PV).
1153.37 CHS PMT	− 1,153.37	Stores the monthly payment (with minus sign for cash paid out).
FV	− 93,024.61	Calculates the balloon payment (FV).

Remember that the negative value means that Mike is making the payments. The positive $150,000 was paid by the lender on Mike's behalf to pay for the home. Because the loan has not been amortized, the remaining principal (balloon payment) must be paid by Mike to discharge the loan.

CALCULATING THE NUMBER OF COMPOUNDING PERIODS

Example 8.9:

If you invested $1,000 at an annual interest rate of 9%, how many years would it take to accumulate $20,000?

$$PV = 0,\ i = 9\%,\ FV = \$20,000,\ PMT_b = -\$1,000,\ n = ?$$

Keystrokes	Display	Comments
f CLX	0.00	Clears the registers.
g 7 BEG	BEGIN	Sets payment mode to Begin.
9 i	9.00	Stores the interest rate.
1000 CHS PMT	− 1,000.00	Stores the payments (with minus sign for cash paid out).
20000 FV	20,000	Stores the *FV* to be received.
n	12	Calculates the number of years to achieve FV.

CALCULATING INTEREST RATES
OF A SERIES OF PAYMENTS

There are two methods for calculating interest rates:

1. Using the compound interest formulas
2. Using the discounted cash flow internal rate of return (IRR) method

Under the first method, the payments *PMT* must meet the definition of *PMT*—namely, equal payments made at regular intervals. The second method can always apply but is mostly used when the payments are not of equal value.

Calculating the Interest Rate of Equal Periodic Payments

Example 8.10:

An $8,000 investment is expected to return a future value of $10,000 at the end of 12-years. It also pays an annual dividend of $600 starting at the end of the first year. What interest rate would the investor realize on this investment?

$$PV = -\$8,000, \ n = 12 \text{ periods}, \ PMT_e = 600, \ FV = \$10,000, \ i = ?$$

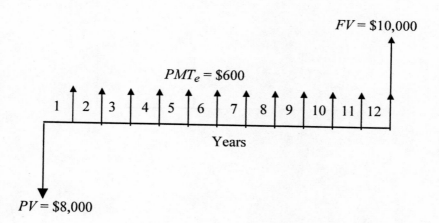

Keystrokes	Display	Comments
f CLX	0.00	Clears the registers.
g 8 END		Sets payment mode to End.
12 n	12.00	Stores the number of years.
8000 PV CHS	$-$8,000.00	Stores the present value payment (minus for cash paid out).
600 PMT	600	Stores dividend payments.
10000 FV	10,000.00	Stores the future value to be received.
i	8.76	Calculates the annual interest rate.

DISCOUNTED CASH FLOW ANALYSIS: NPV AND IRR

In Chapter 6, we presented the net present value analysis (NPV) and the internal rate of return (IRR). Recall that the IRR is simply the discounted interest rate that results when the net present value is zero. We will show how the HP-12C calculates both NPV and IRR. You will get a full explanation of the IRR in Chapter 9 and can read ahead if you wish to clarify its applications.

Recall the cash flow diagram of Chapter 6.

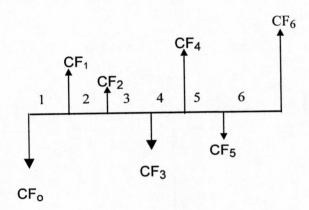

CF_0 is the initial cash flow. On the HP-12C, it is in blue at the bottom the **PV** key. CF_js, at the bottom of the **PMT** key, are the subsequent cash flows. They are keyed in starting with CF_1, and continue to the last value which is CF_6 in this diagram.

The NPV Calculation

Example 8.11:

Bert opened a mutual fund account with an initial payment of $2,500. He later added $1,000, $1,500, and $1,000 at the beginning of the years 2, 3, and 4, respectively. At the end of year 4, he received $7,491. Bert would like to realize at least 7% on his investments. Perform a NPV discounted cash flow analysis to see whether or not he did.

$CF_0 = -\$2,500$, $CF_1 = -\$1,000$, $CF_2 = -\$1,500$, $CF_3 = -\$1,000$, and $CF_4 = \$7,491$. The discount rate is 7%.

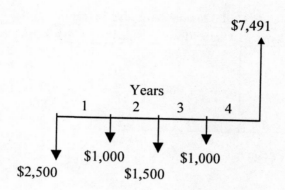

Keystrokes	Display	Comments
f CLX	0.00	Clears the registers.
2500 CHS g Cf₀	− 2,5000.00	Stores Cf_0 (paid out cash flow).
1000 CHS g CFⱼ	− 1,000.00	Stores CF_1 (paid out cash flow).
1500 CHS g CFⱼ	− 1,500.00	Stores CF_2 (paid out cash flow).
1000 CHS g CFⱼ	− 1,000.00	Stores CF_3 (paid out cash flow).
7491 g CFⱼ	7,491.00	Stores CF_4 (received cash flow).
7 i	7.00	Stores discount rate.

Since the *NPV* is positive, Bert did realized a rate of return greater than 7%.

The IRR Calculation

Example 8.12:

Marvin invested in a vineyard that started to pay off in the sixth year. The table shows the cash flow for the life cycle of the project. What was Marvin's rate of return on this investment by the beginning of the tenth year?

Cash Flow for Vineyard Investment

Year	Cash Flow	Year	Cash Flow
0	– $5,000	5	$4,000
1	– 2,000	6	4,000
2	– 1,000	7	4,000
3	0	8	1,000
4	0	9	5,000

The cash flow diagram.

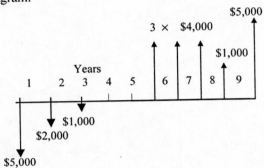

Keystrokes	Display	Comments
f CLX	0.00	Clears registers.
5000 CHS g CFo	– 5,000.00	Stores CF_0 (paid out cash flow).
2000 CHS g CFj	– 2,000.00	Stores CF_1 (paid out cash flow).
1000 CHS g CFj	– 1,000.00	Stores CF_2 (paid out cash flow).
0 g CFj	0.00	Stores CF_3 (zero cash flow).
0 g CFj	0.00	Stores CF_4
4000 g Cfj	4,000.00	Stores CF_5 (received cash flow).
3 g Nj	3.00	Number of times previous cash flow occurs consecutively. (Stores CF_6, CF_7)
1000 g Cfj	1,000	Stores CF_8 (received cash flow).
5000 g Cfj	5,000.00	Stores CF_9 (received cash flow).
f IRR	13.66	Calculates the internal rate of return.

Thus Marvin's IRR is 13.66%.

As a check of the IRR, you could calculate the present value of each value in the table, using an interest rate of 13.66% and then adding them. If the interest rate of 13.66% is accurate, you should get a net present value of zero.

CALENDAR FUNCTIONS

Calendar functions are indispensable for financial math. For example it is frequently necessary to determine the exact term for such investments as long-term bonds, T-bills, etc. The HP-12C can perform these functions very easily.

The process starts with the date format. You must key in the terminal dates to get the number of days between the two dates. We shall use the *day-month-year* format. To do this press, the **g D.MY** keys. You should see "**D.MY**" indicated in the lower right side of the calculator window. To key in the dates, do the following:

1. Key in the one or two digits of the day.
2. Press the decimal point key.
3. Key in the *two* digits of the month.
4. Key in the four digits of the year.

For example, to key in 3 March 1995:

Keystrokes	Display	Comments
3.031995	3.031995	3 is the day of the month. 03 the month and 1995 the year.

Determining the Number of Days Between Dates

Key in the earlier date and press **ENTER**
Key in the later date and press **g   D DYS**

Example 8.13:

You bought a bond with a closing date of July 1, 1995. The bond matured on August 15, 2025. How many days and years are there between these dates. Convert these days to years based on 365 days per year. (Set calculator to display to 6 places)

Keystrokes		Display	Comments
f 6		0.000000	Set six decimal places to show numbers.
g D,MY		D MY	Sets day, month year, format.
1.071995	ENTER	1.071995	Enters 1/07/1995.
15.082025 g Δ DYS		11,003	Enters 15/08/2025 and calculates the number of days between the interval.
365 +		30.145	Converts to the number of years.

Now It's Your Turn

1. Bill invested $2,000 today in an account that earns 12% compounded annually. How much will be in his account at the end of 5 years?
   a. $3,524.68
   b. $4,354.46
   c. $6,589.34

2. How much would Bill have in his account if his money had compounded monthly?
   a. $3,524.68
   b. $3,633.39
   c. $4,354.46

3. How much would Bill have in his account if his money had compounded daily?
   a. $3,563.78
   b. $4,365.68
   c. $3,643.88

4. Don needs $10,000 in 5 years to buy an auto. He can realize an interest rate of 8% compounded daily. How much money must he invest now?
   a. $5,603.49
   b. $6,703.49
   c. $7,603.49

5. If Don could only realize a discount rate of 6% and had $7,600 to invest today, how many months would he need to leave his money in the account if he still needs $10,000? Compounding is monthly.
    a. 56 months
    b. 48 month
    c. 50 months

6. Don still needs $10,000 in the future. He has $7,600 to invest now and can wait 6 years until he needs the money. What minimum annual effective interest rate will he need to realize?
    a. 6.48%
    b. 4.68%
    c. 5.68%

7. Sally currently has an account balance of $1,000. She intends to invest $500 at the beginning of each year for a period of 10 years. She realizes an effective annual interest rate of 7%. What will be the future value of her account at her end of 10 years?
    a. $10,358.95
    b. $8,358.95
    c. $9,358.95

8. Sally and Mike bought a house. They financed $175,000 at a nominal interest rate of 8.75% for a 15 year term loan. What will their monthly payments be?
    a. $1,572.95
    b. $1,749.04
    c. $1,164.28

9. Sally and Mike of question 8 would like to know what the loan balance will be if they were to pay it off in 10 years. What would you tell them?
    a. $84,751.44
    b. $75,683.09
    c. $68,583.05

10. Jenny wants to know what present value amount of money she would need to support her father. She earns an effective interest rate of 8%. Her father needs a cash

flow stream of $2000, $1,000, $500, $600, and $700 over a five year term. The first year payment is to be made immediately.

  a. $5,434
  b. $4,543
  c. $4,345

11. Ben is about to buy a four-flat rental property. He must pay $250,000 now and expects to pay $5,000 the first year, $3,000 the second, and then realize a return of $10,000 over the next 4 years. He expects to sell the building for $400,000 at the end of seventh year. He wants to get a return of 10% on his money. Would he realize that return on this investment?

  a. Yes
  b. No

12. For question 11, what internal rate of return (IRR) would Ben realize on that investment?

  a. 8.29%
  b. 7.64%
  c. 6.38%

13. You opened a mutual fund account with a $5,000 investment. Since then you have deposited $1,000 at the beginning of the second year, and $2,000 each at beginning of the next three years. At the end of five years the mutual fund company reported that your account value was $16,450. You made no withdrawals and left all earned income in the account. What rate of return did you enjoy?

  a. 8.65%
  b. 9.76%
  c. 9.37%

14. Lucky Mort won $3,000,000 in the state lottery. He was disappointed, however, that he does not get the money now but will receive $150,000 a year for 20 years. A financial investment firm offered to buy his stream of payments at a discount rate of 12%. What discounted payment (present value sum of money) would he receive for this annuity? (Don't forget to set the calculator to "BEGIN.")

  a. $3,000,000
  b. $2,361,717
  c. $1,254,866

15. Garth intends to buy a bond on the secondary market. The settlement date is January 14, 1995. The maturity date is July 15, 2005. In how many years will this bond mature?

    a. 10.5 years

    b. 13.6 years

    c. 9.5 years

16. Garth wants to determine his rate of return of his bond. The bond has a coupon interest rate of 7.5% and is discounted so he will pay $850 now for the bond and will receive $1,000 when it matures. His semiannual interest payments are $37.5. What is the rate of return of this bond? (Hint: Assume that the semiannual payment is made to Garth at the end of the first period after he bought the bond.)

    a. 8.52%

    b. 9.82%

    c. 7.50%

ANSWERS: 1.a, 2.b, 3.c, 4.b, 5.a, 6.b, 7.c, 8.b, 9.a, 10.c, 11.b, 12.a, 13.c, 14.c, 15.a, 16.b

Part Two

Applications
of
Financial Math

How to Calculate
Rate of Return
on Investments
(The Bottom Line)

LEARNING OBJECTIVES

After studying this chapter you will be able to:

1. Understand rate of return terminology
2. Calculate rate of return for single payment investments
3. Calculate the rate of return for uniform and nonuniform cash flows
4. Annualize year-to-date performance of investments
5. Convert capital gain to an annual rate of return
6. Understand why the *average rate of return* is not equivalent to the correct *compound rate of return*
7. Understand and use the modified internal rate of return (MIRR)
8. Calculate the rate of return of common stocks under various cash receipt scenarios
9. Understand how mutual fund companies report results and how to calculate your rates of return
10. Understand how you can win big or lose big by leveraging your investments

Your financial well-being can very well depend on the return you realize on your investments. Regardless of the size of your investment portfolio, you undoubtedly have money invested in pension plans, company sponsored 401(k) plans, or the like. Whether you are directing your investments yourself or having someone else doing it for you, you need to monitor what is being reported and understand the results. You should track your investment returns on a continuous basis and make necessary changes as warranted.

THE TERMINOLOGY OF INVESTMENT PERFORMANCE

Perhaps you have heard of such terms as interest rate, yield, current yield, rate of return, discount yield, discount rate, cost of money, and minimum attractive rate of return. These terms all have essentially the same meaning. They are all calculated as the compound rate of interest "i" of the compound interest formulas presented earlier in this book.

In general, the interest rate can be either what you are charged for using someone else's money or how much you charge someone for using your money. Sometimes, however, a profit can be can realized from an investment that pays no interest, such as a the capital gain of a corporate stock, or mutual funds, or a business venture. You need to know how to calculate the rate of return on these types of investments for the purpose of evaluating their performance relative to other alternatives.

Let's define some terms before we discuss their use.

Rate of return (ROR) has the same meaning as the annual compound interest rate realized on an investment or deposit of money. ROR is the term usually applied for the interest rate on an investment as opposed to the interest rate realized on a interest bearing deposit account.

Total rate of return is so termed to assure that the IRR includes all of the financial components making up the earned money. It include any item which contributes to the profit such as interest earned, dividends declared, and capital gains during the time period in question. In general, the rate of return calculation should include all earnings unless stated otherwise.

Yield usually is used when describing the returns of fixed income investments such as bonds. For example *coupon yield* is the stated interest rate based on the par value of a bond. In Chapter 12, bond yields are explained. Dividends declared on common stocks are also referred to as the yield of the stock. In this case the yield does not include capital gains. But yield can also be used for the total returned on an investment, so it requires so examination as to what it is made up of when calculated. In the case of yield to maturity of bonds, it includes capital gains.

Gain is the percent change, or increase, of the initial investment. It is *not* a rate, but often confused with rate of return. The gain is calculated using Formula 2.1 in Chapter 2. The gain is the same as the interest rate only when applied to a one-year period. The gain is mostly quoted as the percentage increase over a number of years. The gain is also sometimes termed the *total cumulative return*.

Average annual return is the gain divided by the number of years over which the gain took place. It is a numerical average, not an accurate representation of the annual compound rate of return. (However, some institutions erroneously mix this terminology with the accurate compound annual rate of return.) One prominent book calls it another view of compounding, which of course, it is not.

Cash-on-Cash is a term used by some to mean the rate of return considering the cash earned on an initial investment. It does not say what happens through out the life cycle of the investment. For example if you invested $1,000 and a year later received $100 your cash-on-cash rate of return would be 10%. The inclusive rate of return can only be determined when the life cycle of the investment is complete.

CALCULATING THE RATE OF RETURN OF A SINGLE-PAYMENT INVESTMENT

One very important use of Formula 4.1 (the power formula) is to find the interest rate (the rate of return) of a single payment investment. To find this rate we simply plug in the numbers and find the unknown, which in this case is the interest rate.

The simplest case for determining interest rates are those where the annual interest earned is known over a one year period. For example if you invested $1,000 for a year and received $100 for its use, the annual interest rate earned would be:

$$\frac{\$100}{\$1,000} \times 100 = 10\%$$

It should be recognized that the original $1,000 must be returned or remain accessible to the investor for this rate of return to be real. Obviously a return of $100 is not a 10% return if the original investment is not intact. This could be considered a cash-on-cash rate of return if the ultimate disposition of the initial investment is not known. For example if you invested $1,000, and received $100 a year for 5 years, but then the investment then worsened and you received no additional payments or the original principal. The rate of return for this venture is − 26%. In this example your cash-on-cash each year was 10%, but you suffered a net loss.

If an investment remains on deposit for a number of years, the solution requires the use of Formula 4.1 to find the annual rate of return. To do this we rearrange the formula to solve explicitly for interest.

Equation 4.1 is:

$$FV = PV\,(1+i)^n$$

$$i = \left(\frac{FV}{PV}\right)^{1/n} - 1$$

Example 9.1: Calculating the Annual Compound Rate of Return

Cass opened a mutual fund account with an initial investment of $4,000. She made no other payments to the fund. She chose to have any money earned reinvested in new shares. At the end of five years the mutual fund company reported her account's value as $6,510. What compound annual rate of return had she realized on this investment?

Solution:

This is a simple single payment situation with 5 year compounding periods. The known values are

$$PV = \$4,000$$
$$FV = \$6,510$$
$$n = 5 \text{ years}$$

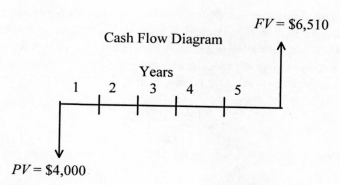

Cash Flow Diagram

$FV = \$6,510$

Years

1   2   3   4   5

$PV = \$4,000$

Using Formula 4.1:

$$i = \left(\frac{\$6,510}{\$4,000} \right)^{1/5} - 1$$

$$= 0.1023, \quad \text{or} \quad 10.23\%$$

Notice that, in this example, Cass does not know how the money was earned. It could have been a combination of interest, capital gains, and dividends on the underlying securities. For this calculation it doesn't make any difference how it was earned, because all earned money was reinvested. The calculation tells Cass that the return on this investment was an effective annual interest rate of 10.23% each year over a five-year period. By virtue of calculating it with a compound interest formula, it is a true compounded annual rate of return. It can be compared to any other investment calculated by the proper compound interest formula.

It should also be noted that the interest rate of return for any given year may not have been 10.23%. For example suppose annual returns were as shown in Table 9.1.

Table 9.1
Rate of return of a $4,000 Initial Investment

Year End	Annual ROR	Year-End Value
1	12.0%	$4,480
2	8.0	4,838
3	15.0	5,564
4	(10.0)	5,008
5	30.0	6,510

The compound rate of return of 10.23% is the annual return rate of return of this mutual fund over five years regardless of what the individual year rates of return were. And it is also not the average annual rate of return. Moreover, you can make this calculation for any number of years. For example, suppose Cass wanted to know what her ROR was after three years. This is calculated as:

$$i = \left(\frac{\$5,564}{\$4,000}\right)^{1/3} - 1$$
$$= 11.63\%$$

The advantage of knowing the annual returns over a period of years is to track the long-term performance of an investment. Some investments make a bonanza in a single year but sacrifice future earnings.

Must Time Periods Be in Whole Numbers of Years?

The answer is "no" provides you use the right fractional period.

Example 9.2: *Calculate Partial-Year Rate of Return.*

George opened a mutual fund account with $4,000. A year and a half later it was worth $4,500. What annual rate of return did George realize?

Solution:

$PV = \$4,000$
$FV = \$4,500$
$n = 18$ months/12 months per year
$\quad = 1.5$ years

Using Formula 4.1

$i = (4500/4000)^{1/1.5} - 1$
$\quad = 8.17\%$

We calculated this result on an annual basis. What results would we get if we performed the calculation using monthly compounding periods? Using Formula 4.1 with monthly periods:

$n = 18$ months
$i = (\$4,500/\$4,000)1/18 - 1$
$i = 0.00656$ per month
$12 \times 0.00656 \times 100 = 7.87\%$ annual nominal rate

Recall that when the time periods are in months, the interest rate is also the rate per month. Multiplying the monthly interest rate by 12 results in the annual nominal annual interest rate.

The effective rate using Formula 4.2, $i_E = \left(1 + \dfrac{i_N}{M}\right)^M - 1$, where M = 12 for monthly compounding, the effective interest rate is:

$$i_E = \left(1 + \frac{0.0787}{12}\right)^{12} - 1$$
$$= 8.17\%$$

By using Formula 4.2, we have converted a nominal monthly interest rate of 0.656% to an annual effective interest rate of 8.17%. It is obvious that the annual nominal interest rate of 7.87% is not, of course, comparable to George's 8.17% effective rate.

How Is A Year-to-Date (YTD) Performance Annualized?

Sometimes it is desirable to extrapolate the current performance of an investment to an annual rate of return. For instance, suppose you had a mutual fund that reported a year-to-date rate of return for a six-month period. You wonder what the annual yield would be if that performance continued for the balance of the year. Example 9.3 demonstrates how this is calculated.

Example 9.3: Annualizing a Year-to-Date (YTD) Rate of Return

You invested $2,000 six months ago in a mutual fund, and the fund currently reports the value is now $2,150. What will the annual yield be if the fund performs as well over the remainder of the year?

Solution:

$PV = \$2,000$
$FV = \$2,150$
$n = 6$ months

The monthly interest rate, using Formula 4.1, is:

$i = (\$2,150/\$2,000)1/6 - 1$
$= (1.0750)0.167 - 1$
$= 1.215\%$ per month

Since the n we used in the formula is in months, the interest rate we solved for is also in months. To convert i to an annual rate we multiply by 12. The annual expected *nominal* yield would be $12 \times 1.215\% = 14.58\%$

The effective yield by Formula 4.2 would be:

$$i_E = \left(1 + \frac{0.1458}{12}\right)^{12} - 1 = 0.1559$$
$$= 15.59\%$$

To project your expected future value at the end of the year, use the power Formula 4.1.

$$FV = \$2,000 \ (1+0.1559)^1 = \$2,312$$

The important lesson here is that the year-end future value is not simply the principal plus a factor of two times the six month earned amount ($2,000 + 2 \times 150=$2,300). Rather it is $12 greater due to the effect of compounding.

CONVERTING A GAIN TO AN ANNUAL RATE OF RETURN

Frequently you will encounter the performance, of such items as mutual funds, reported in terms of gain over a number of years. For example assume a mutual fund, we shall call the *Great Balanced Fund*, reported its performance as follows:

	Cumulative Total Return for the Periods ended 9/30/92	
	5 Year	10 Year
Great Balanced Fund	64.8%	215%

The cumulative total return is simply the gain over the stated duration in years. Gain or percentage change, has a definite place in financial analysis, but it is often confused with the rate of return. One prominent book presents a method of calculating rate of return but does so by using the formula for gain, not compound annual rate of return. This misuse results in a an erroneous value of the annual rate of return.

Calculating the Gain

Recall that gain (percentage difference) as calculated by Formula 2.1 of Chapter 2 is:

$$\frac{\text{Final Value - Base Value}}{\text{Base Value}} \times 100 = \% \text{ Difference}$$

The cumulative total return (gain) of Cass's investment of Example 9.1 is:

$$PV = \$4,000 \text{ (Base value)}$$
$$FV = \$6510 \text{ (Final value)}$$

$$\text{Gain} = \frac{\$6,510 - \$4,000}{\$4,000} \times 100 = 62.75\%$$

This gain took place over five years. The annual compound rate of return over that term was 10.23%. We will next show how gains can be converted to a compound rate of return.

Converting Capital Gain to Annual Rate of Return

To change cumulative total return (gain) to an annual compound rate of return, do the following steps:
(1) Change from percentage to decimal form.
(2) Add 1 to the total return. (this becomes FV/PV)
(3) Raise that number to the $1/n$ power
(4) Subtract 1 from the results and change to percentage form.

Let's do this for the gain of 62.75% over five years:
(1) $62.75\% = 0.6275$
(2) $0.6275 + 1 = 1.6275$
(3) $1.6275)^{1/5} = 1.1023$
(4) $1.1023 - 1 = 0.1023 = 10.23\%$

Let's return to the Great Balanced Fund above and convert the gains to an annual compound rate of return.

Example 9.4: *Convert a Cumulative Return to an Annual Rate of Return*

A mutual fund reported a gain of 64.8% over a five-year period. What is the compound annual rate of return of this investment?

Solution:

(1) 64.8% = 0.648
(2) 0.648 +1 = 1.648 (This value equals FV/PV)
(3) $1.648^{1/5}$ = 1.1051
(4) 1.1051 − 1= 0.1051 or 10.51% per year

Example 9.5:

Convert a cumulative return of 215% over 10 years to an annual rate of return.

Solution:

(1) 215% = 2.15
(2) 2.15 + 1 = 3.15
(3) $3.15^{1/10}$ = 1.1216
(4) 1.216 − 1 = 0.1216 = 12.16% per year

We now know that a 64.8% cumulative gain over 5 years is a 10.51% annual compound rate of return and a cumulative gain of 215% over 10 years is a 12.16% annual return. These values are now comparable to other options where compound rates of return are quoted on an annual basis.

After you repeat these calculations several times, they will become automatic. You will convert much of the mutual fund data you see to make comparisons to other options you might have. This is useful because you might see some big gains over a large number of years that, when analyzed, are not as good as they first appeared.

Are Compound Annual Rate of Return and Average Annual Rate of Return the Same Values?

These two rates of return are not the same. An erroneous method of calculating rate of return used by some authors is to calculate the gain over a number of years, average the gain, and call it the average rate of return. One author calls it: "Another view of compounding." It is not compounding whatsoever. Moreover, we see no valid use for this method because the results are not comparable or useable in time value of money calculations. We will explain the differences here because it is erroneous to mistake the average rate of return for a compound rate of return.

Table 9.2 shows a comparison of the compound and average rates of return. For example a compound rate of return of 10% corresponds to—but is not equivalent to—an average rate of return of 21.18% for a 15-year period. Notice that the value of compound rate of return does not change over time (i.e., is the same for 5, 15, and 20 years), whereas the value of the average rate of return does change.

Table 9.2: Average Rate of Return vs. Compound Annual Rate of Return

Compound Annual Rate of Return	Average Annual Rate of Return On the Original Investment		
	5 Years	15 years	20 Years
5%	5.53%	7.19%	8.27%
10	12.12	21.18	28.64
12	15.25	29.82	43.23
15	20.23	47.58	76.83

The best way to explain the difference is by an example. Suppose you started with an original investment of $1,000 and realized a compound rate of return of 12% over a 15-year period. In 15 years, using Formula 4.1, you would have a future value of:

$$FV=\$1,000\ (1+0.12)^{15} = \$5,473.57$$

Over a 15 year period your total difference (or gain) is:

$$\frac{\$5,474 - \$1,000}{\$1,000} \times 100 = 447.40\%$$

The average gain per year is:

$$\frac{447.40\%}{15\ \text{Years}} = 29.83\%$$

Using the average annual rate of return to find the money earned each year we have: $1,000 × 0.2983 = $298.30 per year. This does not accurately represent the amount of money you received in any of the 15-year periods. For example the actual first year interest earned is: $1,000 × 0.12 = $120.

Perhaps you can ascertain the usefulness of the average annual rate of return method, we cannot. The point is, be sure not to mix them. Moreover, this difference is not well understood by some in the financial community. Many prominent mutual fund companies correctly calculate the compound annual rate of return, but call it the average annual total rate of return.

CALCULATING THE RATE OF RETURN
OF A UNIFORM SERIES OF PAYMENTS

It is necessary to use a financial calculator or a computer spreadsheet program to calculate the rate of return of a uniform series of payments because the formulas we introduced in Chapter 5 are too complex to be solved explicitly for the interest rate. Refer to Chapter 8 of this book where we discuss quick-start instructions for the Hewlett-Packard HP-12C financial calculator. It is quite easy to find the interest rate of most classes of financial problems using an HP-12C or other financial calculators. Interest rates can also easily be solved by the computer spreadsheet programs (see Chapter 19).

THE MODIFIED INTERNAL RATE OF RETURN

The *modified internal rate of return* (MIRR) is an alternative to the conventional IRR technique. The MIRR has been devised to offset some shortcomings of the regular IRR procedure. Recall that the IRR procedure provides a rate of return that implicitly assumes that all cash flows are either reinvested or discounted at the calculated rate. This provides an accurate rate of return when cash flows are paid in only and a single final cash flow is taken. For this situation, every cash flow remains internal until the final withdrawal. We will show later that if there are external cash flows the overall rate of return depends on how these are invested.

Another difficulty of the IRR procedure is due to the fact that where there are several negative and positive cash flows there can be several solutions, all of which provide an accurate zero net present value. In other words the curve in Figure 6.2 could cross the zero value several times.

The MIRR Investment Scenario

It is assumed that an investor has the option to invest in a situation where there will be negative cash flows early on but the prospect of receiving future positive cash flows. The cash to be paid for this investment is currently being held in a low risk holding account that earns a relatively low rate of interest such as money market accounts or short term certificates of deposit. This is a realistic approach since invested money has to originate somewhere. Conversely, positive cash flows received from this investment are reinvested in a more speculative venture, but one that has the potential of higher rates of return. The investor would assume an expected rate of return for the more risky investments, and conduct the MIRR to see if the combination of withdrawn money and reinvested money have the potential to meet his or her desired investment goal.

Calculating the MIRR

The procedure for calculating the MIRR consists of the following steps:

1. Calculate the present value of the negative cash flows at the conservative rate of return.
2. Calculate the future value of the positive cash flows at the speculative rate of return.
3. From the values of the n, PV, and FV, solve for the rate of return using Formula 4.1: (single payment compound interest).

The MIRR is a simple procedure to carry out.

Example 9.6: Calculating the MIRR of a Potential Investment

Ron is considering investing in a planned real estate partnership currently seeking funds. The project will be developed over six years and then be sold. The prospective cash flows over the life of this project are projected as shown in the inserted table. The initial cash investment is $10,000. Annual cash flows are to be paid by Ron at the end of years 1, 2, and 3. Ron expects to receive money at the end of years 4, 5, and 6. Ron calculated an IRR of 12.72% for this investment. A rate of return of 12.72% meets Ron's investment goal, but his past experience indicates that he can only realize a rate of return of 10% on his stock market investments.

Year End	Cash Flow	PV @12.72%
0	($10,000)	($10,000)
1	(2,000)	(1774)
2	(1,000)	(787)
3	(1,000)	(698)
4	3,000	1,858
5	3,000	1,649
6	20,000	9,750
NPV =		0

Ron decides to recalculate this project assuming that he will get 10% on his reinvested money. He will use cash held in his 5% interest bearing financial-management account to make the required payments. Now what is the prospective overall modified rate of return MIRR under this plan?

Solution: Let's show the prospective cash flows for this project. The procedure is to calculate the present value of the paid (negative) cash flows at an interest rate of 5%, the future value of the received (positive) cash flows at 10%, and then calculate the interest rate for these two values. The present and future values are calculated as shown in the table below.

Cash flows of Example 6.9

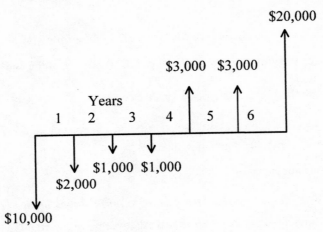

PV of Negative Cash Flows			FV of Positive Cash Flows		
Year End	Cash Flow	PV @ 5%	Year End	Cash Flow	FV @ 10%
0	($10,000)	($10,000)	4	3000	$3,630
1	(2000)	(1,904)	5	3000	3,300
2	(1000)	(907)	6	20000	20,000
3	(1000)	(864)			
	PV	($13,676)		FV	$26,930

Ron has converted his cash flows to a present value and a future value. Now it is possible to calculate the modified internal rate of return by the single payment compound interest power formula. Calculate the modified internal rate of return given that:

$$PV = \$13,676, \ FV = \$26,930, \ n = 6 \text{ years}$$

Formula 4.1

$$i = \left(\frac{FV}{PV}\right)^{1/n} - 1$$

$$= \left(\frac{\$26,930}{\$13,676}\right)^{1/6} - 1$$

$$= 11.98\%$$

Ron's plan of using cash from his 5% account to pay the invested cash, and reinvesting the cash received at 10% results in a modified internal rate of return (MIRR) of 11.98%. Although this is short of the 12.72% IRR results, Ron considers this to be a realistic and acceptable rate of return for his investment opportunities.

Observe why the MIRR of this example was lower than the IRR. Because the present value the sum of the negative cash flows of the MIRR was calculated with a rate (5%) much lower than 12.72%, the *PV* cost of money invested in this venture was greater ($13,767 vs. $13,259). Moreover, the *FV* sum of the MIRR reinvested money was lower (10% vs. 12.72%) due to the lower reinvestment rate.

In the literature it is common to see MIRR scenarios in which the invested money is taken from a relatively low-interest-rate safe liquid account and the positive cash flows are then reinvested at a higher, more speculative rate of return. The procedure can, however, work for any set of cash flows and interest rates.

CALCULATING THE RATE OF RETURN OF COMMON STOCKS

There are two basic ways to receive money from your stock portfolio: (1) take the capital gain by selling the stock, or (2) reinvest or take the dividends. Some companies allow you to reinvest your dividends in more stock shares. This is called the DRIPS program. The DRIP plan is a dividend reinvestment plan where a company in which you own shares reinvests dividends in new shares. Stockbrokers will also do this for you if so requested. The dividends are reinvested at the current price of the shares at the time the dividends are declared.

What you do with the dividends you receive over the period you hold the stock will affect the rate of return you realize on your investment. For example, when you receive your dividends quarterly and reinvest them in another holding account, such as a savings account, you realize a different overall rate of return than if you had reinvested the dividends in more stock shares. Moreover, if you spend your dividends there is no accurate way to determine the compound annual rate of return of your stock holding compared to the Standard and Poor's 500 index. The latter is calculated by assuming that all dividends are reinvested. (This is not, however, to infer that spending dividends is an unacceptable practice.) If no dividends are issued, it is simple, of course, to calculate your annual rate of return on the investment, and the results are comparable to other investments.

Rate of Return of a Stockholding Portfolio Where Dividends Are Reinvested in Additional Shares

Example 9.7: *Reinvesting Dividends in Stock Shares*

On January 1, 1997, Manny bought 100 shares of a stock priced at $45 per share. The stock paid an annual dividend of $2 per share. (The average dividend of 30 Dow Jones stocks on the New York Stock Exchange is about 2.5%.) Dividends were to be reinvested. During the year the price of a share at the end of each quarter was $46, $47, $48 and $49 respectively. Dividends were issued quarterly and the broker's commission was 2%. What annual rate of return did Manny realize during the year of this investment?

Solution:

The present value of this investment consists of the initial price plus the Broker's commission charge, as follows:

Cost of 100 shares at $45 per share..................	$4,500.00	
Commission charge at 2.50% is 0.025 × $4,500...	112.50	
Total cost	$4,612.50	

The dividend of $2 per share totals $200 per year or $50 per quarter. Reinvested dividends will buy shares of stock as shown by the table.

Stock Dividend Reinvestment Data

Date of Issue	Value of Dividends	Value of a Share	No. of Shares
3/31/97	$50	$46	1.087
6/30/97	50	47	1.064
9/30/97	50	48	1.042
12/30/97	50	49	1.020
Total number of shares bought			4.213

At the end of the year, Manny owned 104.21 shares of stock valued at $49 per share. His total end-of-year value is 104.21 × $49 = $5,106.29 (since he did not sell any shares). The compound annual rate-of-return over this year was:

$$\frac{\$5,106.29 - \$4,612.50}{\$4,612.50} \times 100 = 10.71\%$$

This value of 10.71% was Manny's actual rate of return, but it would not be fully comparable to the Standard & Poor's 500 index because the latter does not account for Broker's commissions. Without the commission, Manny's rate of return would have been 13.47%.

For this example, we showed in detail how the dividends would be reinvested, although it is not necessary to know this to calculate the annual rate of return of your stock holdings. When the stocks are held in your account with a brokerage firm, the firm reports the number of shares you hold at the end of the year. This, coupled with the price of the stock at any given time provides the future value for the calculation.

Rate of Return of Stockholdings When Dividends Are Reinvested In a Money Market Account

Example 9.8: Reinvesting Dividends in a Money market Account

Suppose Manny chooses to have his dividends reinvested in money market account that pays an interest rate of 4%. (A brokerage firm will probably do this unless instructed to buy shares with your dividends.) The other conditions of this investment are the same as in Example 9.6. What would Manny's rate of return be on that investment?

Solution:

Figure 9.1 Cash Flow diagram

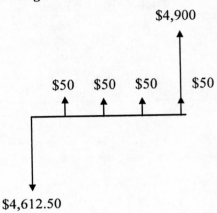

There are four quarterly dividends of $50, and the stock's value at the end of the year is $4,900. The number of shares (100) remains the same. To get the total future value of the investment, we calculate the future value of the dividends compounded quarterly at 4% nominal interest rate:

Date of Issue	Value of Dividend	Future Value of $1 @ 4%	Future Value of Dividends
3/31/97	$50	$1.03	$51.50
6/30/97	50	1.02	51.00
9/30/97	50	1.01	50.50
12/30/97	50	1.00	50.00
Total future value of dividends			$203.00

The combined cash flow diagram for the stock and reinvested dividends is:

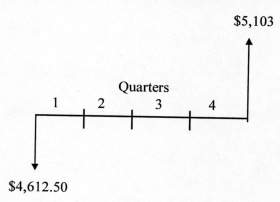

$5,103

Quarters

The annual rate of return is:

$$\text{Total future value} = \$4,900 + \$203 = \$5,103$$

$$\text{ROR} = \frac{\$5,103 - \$4,612.50}{\$4,612.50} \times 100 = 10.63\%$$

Rate of Return of Stockholdings When Dividends Are Spent

Since the dividends are not reinvested it is not possible to accurately determine the annual rate of return of your stockholding comparable to something like the Standard & Poor's 500 index. This is a quandary if you would like to accurately calculate the rate of return of your investment. But, as a bench mark for any given year, you could still calculate the internal rate of return.

If you want to spend your dividends, you would determine the future value of your holdings and/or past performance by calculating the capital gains only. For other types of stocks, such as utility stocks that pay relatively large dividends but enjoy very little growth, the dividends will be your major contributor to income.

Example 9.9: *Calculating Stock Holdings Where Dividends are Spent as Received*

Solution:

There are two methods for doing this: (1) calculate the internal rate of return, and (2) calculate the capital gains only. Using the cash flows of Figure 9.1 and the HP-12C calculator, the IRR is 2.5832% quarterly which becomes an effective interest rate of 10.74%.

To calculate the annual capital gain:

$$\frac{\$4,900 - \$4,612.50}{\$4,612.50} \times 100 = 6.23\%$$

Had it not been for the broker's commission the capital gain for the first year would have been:

$$\frac{\$4,900 - \$4,500}{\$4,500} \times 100 = 8.89\%$$

Summary of Rate of Return Calculational Methods for Stocks

Examples 9.7 through 9.9, results summarized in the table below, compare the rates of return for the circumstances and calculational methods used.

Dividend Disposition	Rate of Return %
Reinvest dividends in stock	10.71
Reinvest dividends in money market at 4%	10.63
Spend dividends, calculate capital gain	6.23
Internal rate of return	10.74

The IRR method results in a higher rate of return because the mathematical process assumes that the dividends earned the same interest rates as the IRR value.

HOW MUTUAL FUNDS REPORT ANNUAL INCOME AND HOW TO CALCULATE YOUR RATE OF RETURN

It is relatively simple to calculate your rate of return of mutual funds. Mutual fund companies do a good job of reporting the results of your mutual fund holdings. To retain their tax-exempt status, mutual funds are required to distribute at least 90% of their earnings each year. They usually make distribution quarterly. Distributed earnings from a mutual fund are identified by three categories: dividends, short-term capital gains, and long-term capital gains. Capital gains are earned when the fund sells some securities at a profit. Dividends are earned as the securities held in the fund issues them. The net asset value (NAV) of each share of a fund is calculated daily to reflect the value of all the securities held, including any cash that may be in the account. This results in a current daily share price.

Let's track the annual report and calculate the annual rate of return of a mutual fund we will call ABC. Assume that all distributions are reinvested and that we make additional cash investments throughout the year. The Table 9.3 shows how the ABC Mutual Fund will typically report the annual transactions.

Table 9.3: ABC Mutual Fund's 1995 Investment Account Statement

Trade Date	Transaction Descriptions	Dollar Amount	Share Price	Share Amount	Shares Owned
	BEGINNING BALANCE @ 12/31/94	3,331	18.07		184.334
01/31	PURCHASE BY CHECK	500.00	17.81	28.074	212.408
02/28	PURCHASE BY CHECK	1,000.00	17.52	57.078	269.486
3/26	INCOME DIV REIN	75.46	17.13	4.405	273.891
3/26	LT CAP GAIN REIN	2.67	17.13	0.157	274.048
6/24	INCOME REIN	76.73	17.70	4.335	278.383
8/31	PURCHASE BY CHECK	1,000.00	18.64	53.648	332.031
8/31	EXCHANGE FROM ANOTHER FUND	4,014.39	18.51	216.877	548.908
9/24	INCOME REIN	153.69	18.39	8.357	557.265
12/16	INCOME REIN	206.19	18.00	11.455	568.720
12/16	LT CAP GAIN	111.45	18.00	6.192	574.912
12/31	ENDING BALANCE		18.16		547.912

PAID THIS CALENDAR YEAR	Income Dividends 512.07	+	Short-Term Gains	+ Long Term 114.14	=	TOTAL DISTRIBUTIONS 626.21

From this account we can calculate the annual beginning balance and ending balance.

Beginning share price × No. of shares held = Beginning balance
$$\$18.07 \times 184.344 = \$3331$$
Ending share price × No. of shares held = Ending balance
$$\$18.16 \times 574.912 = \$10,440$$

Summary of the Annual Cash Flows

Transaction	Date	Amount $
Beginning balance	12/31/94	(3,331)
Purchase shares	1/31	(500)
Purchase shares	2/28	(1,000)
Purchase shares	8/31	(1,000)
Exchange	8/31	(4,014)
Ending balance	12/31/95	10,440

Notice that the distributions are not external cash flows for the purpose of calculating the annual rate of return. Using our money, we purchased shares three times and transferred money from another fund once. The starting balance, the purchased share money, and the transfers are considered to be negative cash flows. The starting balance is actually the amount reported in the account at the end of the previous year. The ending balance is a positive cash flow even though we do not necessarily redeem the shares.

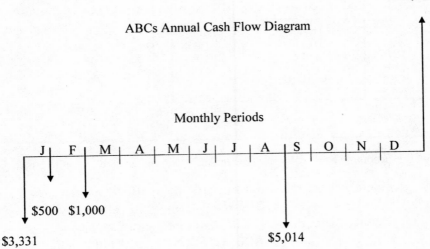

ABCs Annual Cash Flow Diagram

By the internal rate of return method, we calculate (using the HP-12C) that the monthly IRR is 0.762%. This produces an annual nominal rate of 9.15% and an effective rate of return of 9.54%

LEVERAGING: WIN BIG OR LOSE BIG

Perusing the internet reveals that there is considerable interest in *leveraging*. Leveraging your money is a process of investing in which you borrow part of the money you invest. By leveraging, you increase the amount of money invested and you make a profit on the borrowed money as well as your own. If your investment does not make a profit, however, you lose part of your own money as well as part of the borrowed money. You further lose because you must pay interest on the borrowed money. Is said that leveraging is very advantageous in a bull market, but very bad in a bear market.

One way to conveniently leverage is through a brokerage account. Brokerage houses such as Merrill-Lynch and Salomon-Smith-Barney have brokerage margin accounts which allow you to borrow up to 50% of the value of the portfolio you hold in your brokerage account. When you do this, an equal value of the securities in your account are held hostage as collateral for as long as you have your loan. It should be noted here that you can use the borrowed money for what ever you choose, not necessarily for buying securities.

Margin account rules are governed by the Federal Reserve Board's Regulation T, by the National Association of Securities Dealers, and by individual brokerage house rules. Under these rules you can borrow, on the margin, up to 50% of the value of the stocks you buy. Of Course, you could use funds from other sources such as an home equity line of credit where you can usually deduct the interest charged. This would change the performance picture some what.

Most investors involved in leveraging seek a quick profit over a relatively short term, perhaps a few years. Let's see how leveraging works and how the rates of return play out under profitable and unprofitable situations.

Example 9.10: *Leveraging a Profitable Investment*

Charley bought 200 shares of XYZ stock at a price of $100 per share and borrowed half of the cost on the margin. He kept the shares 4 years and then sold them. During this time his shares experienced an increase of 20% per year due to capital gains. No dividends were paid. He was charged an interest rate of 9.50% on the money borrowed from his margin account. Neglecting any commissions, what rate of return did Charley realize on this investment?

Solution:

Initial share price = $100
Shares bought = 200

Charley's equity = $10,000   (*PV*)
Borrowed equity = $10,000

Summery Data of a leveraged Investment

Year End	Finance Charges @ 9.50%	Stock Price	Stock Value
0		$100	$20,000
1	$950	120	24,200
2	1,040	144	28,800
3	1,139	173	34,560
4	1,247	207	41,472
Total	$4,376		

The net money to Charley is: $41,472 − ($10,000 +$4,376) = $27,096 (*FV*)

By Formula 4.1 Charley's rate of return for the 4-year term is:

$$i = \left(\frac{\$27,096}{\$10,000}\right)^{1/4} - 1 = 0.2830 \text{ or } 28.30\%$$

Charley did get a boost by leveraging. Although his stock enjoyed a 20% compound annual rate of return, his overall investment realized a 28.30% compounded annual rate of return.

Example 9.11: *Leveraging an Unprofitable Investment*

Suppose that Charley in the above example did not enjoy an annual increase of 20% on his stock, but instead lost just 5% per share value each year he held it. Every thing else being the same, now what is his annual rate of return?

Solution:

Summery Data of a leveraged Investment

Year End	Finance Charges @ 9.50%	Stock Price	Stock Value
0		$100	$20,000
1	$950	95	19,000
2	1,040	90	18,000
3	1,139	86	17,000
4	1,247	81	16,200
Total	$4,376		

The net money to Charley is: $16,200 - ($10,000 + $4,376) = $1,824$ (FV)

Charley's percentage loss is: $\dfrac{\$1,824 - \$10,000}{\$10,000} \times 100 = -82\%$

Well, it is certainly true. Leveraging in a bear market was a financial disaster. Just a 5% annual loss in the stock price resulted in a 82% loss in Charley's original investment. By leveraging you can lose big even though the annual losses were not too large. It is obvious that the leveraged stock performance needs to exceed the interest rate charges by a significant amount to take advantage of leveraging. During the days before the 1929 market crash, leveraging to 90% was allowed and disaster set in for many. The message is clear, do not get caught leveraging in a bear market.

Now It's Your Turn:

1. The average annual rate of return is a useful method to accurately evaluate and compare your investment returns.
   a. True
   b. False

2. The annual yield of an investment is the same as its annual rate of return
   a. True
   b. False

3. The rate of return, yield, and, total rate of return are all calculated by compound interest formulas.
   a. True
   b. False

4. The gain and the total cumulative return are calculated by the compound interest formulas.
   a. True
   b. False

5. Shirley invested $1,000, and at the end of six years her account's value was reported as $4,250. What was her annual rate of return on this investment? She made no additions to or withdrawals from the account.
   a. 12.73%
   b. 27.27%
   c. 6.25%

6. What was the six-year cumulative total return (gain) of Shirley's account in question 5 above?
   a. 325%
   b. 350%
   c. 27.27%

7. Assume that Shirley's account value (in question 5) was reported as $3,100 at the end of five years. What rate of return had she earned at that time?
   a. 23.12%
   b. 18.45%
   c. 25.39%

8. A mutual fund account started with $5,000, and deposits of $1,000, $500, and $400 were invested at the beginning of years 2, 4, and 5, respectively. All income was reinvested. At the end of 5 years the account value was $9,520. What was the IRR at the end of 5 years? (Hint, draw a cash flow diagram.)
    a. 7.50%
    b. 6.53%
    c. 5.80%

9. An account reported $2,500 on the first of January, and the account value was $3,000 at the end of 19 months hence. What is the nominal annual rate of return of this account?
    a. 12.69%
    b. 10.78%
    c. 11.57%

10. For question 9 above, what is the effective annual rate of return?
    a. 12.20%
    b. 11.57%
    c. 12.79%

11. Bill noticed that the first quarterly report of his mutual fund was $4,193. At the beginning of the year his account had totaled $4,105. With a three-month YTD value of $4,193, what would the annualized rate be if the fund continued to perform at the current rate?
    a. 8.51%
    b. 8.85%
    c. 8.96%

12. The cumulative total gain of a mutual fund is advertised as 320% over a 12-year period. What is the annual compound rate of return of this investment?
    a. 12.70%
    b. 10.98%
    c. 9.87%

13. A mutual fund account started the year with $10,000. All earnings were reinvested. On July 1 the investor deposited $1,000 in the account. At year end, the account's value was $15,000. What was the effective rate of return of this account over that year? Round your answer to nearest 1%. (Hint: Do this problem using quarterly periods.)

   a. 31%

   b. 38%

   c. 33%

15. Steve bought 100 shares of stock for $25 per share. He paid a commission of 2.50%. Each share issues an annual dividend of $1.00, payable quarterly. At the end of two years after receiving his last quarterly dividend, the value of a share was $28. Steve reinvested his dividends in a money market account that paid an interest rate of 4%. What was Steve's annual rate of return on this investment?

   a. 10.52%

   b. 8.33%

   c. 14.64%

16. Roger has an opportunity to invest in shares of a real-estate investment venture. Each share requires $5,000 up front. After that, it is projected that the cash flows for this development will be as shown in the table. What will the modified internal rate-of-return if Roger plans to pay his share from money currently earning 5% in a T-bill fund, and he can invest the positive cash flow in other ventures earning 10%?

Year End	Cash Flow
0	($5,000)
1	(2,000)
2	(2,000)
3	0
4	3,000
5	4,000
6	7,000

   a. 9.50%

   b. 11.21%

   c. 12.50%

ANSWERS: 1.b, 2.a, 3.a, 4.b, 5.b, 6. b, 7.c, 8.a, 9.c, 10.a, 11.b, 12.a, 13.b, 14.b, 15. b, 16.a

Turn Income Taxes to Your Advantage

LEARNING OBJECTIVES:

In this chapter you will learn:

1. The meaning of income tax avoidance
2. How tax deductions save money
3. How to determine your marginal income tax rate
4. How to calculate and apply income tax-equivalent yields
5. How you can use income tax provisions to your advantage
6. Examples of how tax planning can influence your investment decisions

Taxes are, of course, necessary to operate the government. There are opportunities, however, for exercising income tax avoidance, which is perfectly legal and advisable (unlike tax evasion). The U.S. tax laws, as codified in the Internal Revenue Code, provides for tax savings under many circumstances. In this chapter we show how tax deductions save money and present some examples of tax avoidance planning to illustrate some ways you can effectively minimize your taxes.

WHAT IS INCOME TAX AVOIDANCE?

There are many opportunities to legally put into practice income tax avoidance. Tax *avoidance* is simply tax minimization through legal measures whereas tax *evasion* connotes the use of fraud to gain tax advantages. There is a fine line between the two which has tainted the concept of tax avoidance in the minds of some taxpayers. Some taxpayers thus refrain from taking advantage of the perfectly legal and acceptable practice of tax avoidance.

Tax avoidance is accomplished by tax planning. It is necessary to be aware of the savings that can accrue through tax planning. Since tax avoidance is a vast field, we cannot completely address here, we simply show how to calculate tax savings and provide some practical examples of how to plan for tax avoidance

HOW TAX DEDUCTIONS SAVE MONEY

Any time you can take a tax deduction from your gross income, you save money on taxes you would otherwise have had to pay. There are two basic types of deductions available to taxpayers: (1) standard and (2) itemized. These deductions are mutually exclusive. Taxpayers itemize deductions when the amount of these deductions exceeds their standard deduction. Itemizing thus offers a larger potential for tax savings but requires a greater knowledge of the U.S. tax laws to identify allowable deductions.

U.S. tax laws allow taxpayers to deduct from their adjusted gross income (AGI) certain personal specified expenses such as home real estate taxes, medical expenses, and contributions to charitable institutions. Home mortgage interest is deductible. Business expenses incurred in connection with an income-producing activity are deductible. Contributions to a church are deductible. A very important class of deductions consists of IRA and 401(k) plan contributions. Not only do these deductions lower your AGI, but the deducted money grows, tax-deferred, in your qualified accounts.

Calculating the amount of tax savings to be realized by a tax deduction is done as follows:

Formula 10.1: Calculating Tax Savings Due to Deductions

Tax Savings = Value of Tax Deduction × Marginal Tax Rate

Example 10.1: Home Mortgage Interest Tax Deduction

Bill and Kate have a home mortgage on which they paid $10,000 in interest payments last year. They are in the 31% marginal combined federal and state income-tax bracket. How much did they save in income taxes in that year due to the interest they paid? They itemize deductions on the long form.

Solution:

$$\text{Tax Savings} = \$10,000 \times 0.31 = \$3,100$$

HOW TO DETERMINE MARGINAL INCOME TAX RATES

Calculating tax deduction savings and/or equivalent taxable yields involves first sorting out your combined federal/state *marginal* tax rate. If you are fortunate enough to live in a state that levies no income taxes, your task is even easier, since you need only to determine your federal marginal tax bracket.

For a given tax year, you usually need to determine your marginal tax rate just once and store it in your memory. This is true unless you should experience a significant change in your tax situation, such as making a killing in the stock market, which would, of course, jump you to a new tax bracket. Under this circumstance you would be glad to make a new marginal-tax-bracket determination.

What Are Marginal Income Tax Rates?

There are two basic income tax rates: (1) *marginal*, and (2) *average*. The best way to explain these rates is to run through a sample calculation. Average tax rates are included to aid in understanding the overall tax-rate structure.

We start this example by including a 1996 income tax schedule provided by the *1040 Forms and Instructions* pamphlet that the government mails to taxpayers each year. The "married filing jointly" tax table is selected here, but the principle is the same for other categories.

Schedule Y-1—Use if your filing status is **Married filing jointly** or **Qualifying widow(er)**

If the amount on Form 1040, line 37 is: Over —	But not Over —	Enter on Form 1040 line 38	of the amount Over
$0	$40,100	.........15%	$0
40,100	96,900	$6,015.00 + 28%	40,100
96,900	147,700	21,919.00 + 31%	96,900
147,700	263,750	37,667.00 + 36%	140,000
263,750	....	79,445.00 + 39.6%	263,750

In this schedule the *marginal tax rates* are found under the heading, "Enter on Form 1040, line 38." For example, if your taxable income is over $40,100, but not over $96,900, your marginal tax rate would be 28%. No calculations are necessary to determine your marginal rate; all you need to know is your taxable income. *Taxable income* is your income after personal exemptions and standard or itemized deductions have been subtracted from your adjusted gross income. You can readily find your taxable income from your current year's 1040 income tax form. The next example shows how all these tax related items go together.

Example 10.2:

John Q. Taxpayer is married and filing jointly with his wife. Their taxable annual income, on line 37 of tax form 1040, is $125,000.

1. What is their marginal tax rate?
2. How much money is subject to the marginal rate?
3. How much federal income tax must they pay in 1996?
4. What is their average tax rate?

Solution:

1. Their taxable income falls between $96,900 and $147,700, so their marginal tax rate is 31%.
2. The money subject to the marginal rate is $125,000 – $96,900 = $28,100.
3. Income tax payable in 1996 is:
   Base (Pay)............................ $21,919
   Marginal amount ($28,100 × 0.31)...   8,711   (Formula 10.1)
   Total Tax.......... $30,630
4. Their average income tax rate is $30,630/$125,000 × 100 = 24.50%

The first step above was to find that the couple's taxable income lies on the third row of the tax table between $96,900 and $147,700. By inspecting the table, the marginal bracket is found to be 31%. The *average tax rate* is simply the total annual tax bill divided by the taxable income.

Observe that the next dollar of taxable income above $96,900 is an increment that is taxed at 31%. This is the precise meaning of marginal tax rate.

Is The Marginal Tax Rate Appropriate?

A point of confusion often exists on whether to use the average tax rate or the marginal tax rate when considering the tax rate to be applied to the next dollar earned. *The marginal tax rate should always be applied.* The following example verifies this statement.

Example 10.3:

At the beginning of 1996, the Smiths know they will be in the 31% bracket since they will have a taxable income of $100,000 based on their projected 1996 earnings. They have just inherited $60,000 and have the option of investing this money either in tax-free municipal bonds at 5.50 % or in a taxable mutual fund earning 7.97%. As we will show later, for a marginal tax rate of 31%, 7.97% is the exact equivalent taxable yield of a 5.50% tax-free security. In other words, they are break-even values.

The Smiths file jointly and live in a state that does not levy state income taxes. Compare the Smiths' tax-free and taxable net incomes for each of these two scenarios.

Solution:

The Smiths' $60,000 inheritance is not taxable, but any money earned in the future from investing it is, unless the earnings are from tax-free securities.

   Annual return on the tax free Muni (Municipal) bonds:
      $60,000 \times 0.055 = $3,300.
   Annual return on the taxable Mutual Fund:
      $60,000 \times 0.0797 = $4,782.

Results of the Smiths' tax situation are provided in the table below. You can check the values by using the 1996 tax table provided above.

	Tax-Free Munis	Taxable Mutual Fund
Taxable income	$100,000	$100,000
Investment income	3,300	4,782
Total taxable income	100,000	104,782
Taxes to be paid	22,880	24,362
Net income	$80,420	$80,420

Observe that the after-tax income for the tax-free Munis and taxable mutual funds are equal. This demonstrates the validity of using the marginal tax rates for the calculation of equivalent yields of taxable and nontaxable investments

Combined Effective Federal and State Marginal Tax Rate

State income tax rates influence your applicable marginal tax rate. This requires an additional calculation to arrive at a *combined effective federal and state marginal tax rate*. (If you live in a state that has no state income taxes, you can skip this section and proceed to the next.) The formula for calculating the effective state tax rate requires that you know both your state tax rate and your federal marginal tax rates.

Formula 10.2: Effective State Tax Rate

$$\text{Effective State Tax Rate} = \text{State Rate} \times (1 - \text{Federal Rate})$$

Example 10.4:

Tom's taxable income is $41,000 and he files jointly with his wife. Tom is in the 28% federal tax bracket. He lives in California where his state tax rate is 9.3%. What is Tom's effective state tax rate?

Solution:

$$\text{Effective state tax rate} = 9.50\% \times (1 - 0.28)$$
$$= 6.7\%$$

Your *combined effective marginal tax rate* is obtained by adding your federal marginal tax rate to your effective state tax rate.

Formula 10.3: Combined Effective Marginal Tax Rate

Combined Effective Marginal Tax-Rate = Effective State Tax Rate + Federal Marginal Tax-Rate

For Example 10.4 above, Tom's combined effective federal and state marginal tax rate is:

$$28\% + 6.7\% = 34.7\%$$

We are now ready to calculate tax-equivalent yields using these methods to calculate marginal tax rates.

CALCULATING TAX-EQUIVALENT YIELDS

The amount of money that you earn and get to keep from an investment differs depending on whether you must pay income taxes on it or whether it is a tax-free or tax-deferred investment. Most municipal bonds, for instance, earn money that is free of state and federal income taxes so you keep all the interest you earn. In contrast, you must pay income taxes each year on interest earned on securities such as corporate bonds. There is, however, an equivalence between taxable and nontaxable investments. The same equivalence exists between before-tax and after-tax rates of returns. The best buy depends on your marginal income tax bracket, so you must calculate tax-equivalent yields to determine which investment is the most favorable. Here we introduce three tax-equivalent formulas, which are actually the same except for their terminology. The first formula for calculating tax-equivalent yield is:

Formula 10.4a: Converting Tax-Free Yield to Tax-Equivalent Yields

$$\frac{\text{Tax - Free Yield}}{(1 - \text{Marginal Tax Rate})} = \text{Tax - Equivalent Yield}$$

Example 10.5:

You are in the combined state and federal marginal tax bracket of 34%. You notice that the yield of a tax-free municipal bond is 6.50%. What would this be in terms of the tax-equivalent yield of a taxable corporate bond?

Solution:

$$\text{The tax-free yield} = 6.50\%.$$
$$\text{The tax-equivalent yield} = \frac{6.50\%}{1 - 0.34} = 9.85\%$$

In other words a taxable investment of 9.85%, would net the same amount of money as investing in a tax-free security offering 6.50%.

If you are considering an income derived form a tax-free investment compared to that from a taxable investment, Formula 10.4a stated a little differently can provide the answer.

Formula 10.4b: Converting Tax-Free Income to Equivalent Taxable Income

$$\frac{\text{Tax - Free Income}}{(1 \ - \ \text{MarginalTax Rate})} = \text{Equivalent Taxable Income}$$

Example 10.6:

Suppose you were given a gift of $1,000 (gifts are not taxable). How much taxable income would you have had to earn to equal the taxable equivalent amount of this gift? You are in the 28% marginal tax bracket.

Solution: Using Formula 10.4b,

$$\frac{\$1,000}{(1-0.28)} = \$1,389$$

In others words, you need to earn $1,389 in before-tax dollars in order to keep $1,000 after paying the income tax.

Before-Tax and After-Tax Equivalence

Another form of Formula 10.4a also applies to before-tax and after-tax investments. If we substitute after-tax equivalent yield for tax-free yield, and before-tax yield for tax-equivalent yield, we have:

Formula 10.4c: Converting After Tax-Equivalent Yield to Before-Tax Equivalent Yield

$$\frac{\text{After - Tax Equivalent Yield}}{(1 \ - \ \text{Marginal Tax Rate})} = \text{Before - Tax Yield}$$

Example 10.7: *After-Tax vs. Before-Tax Yields*

Ben can realize 10% annually on a taxable investment. He would like to know what his net yield will be after he pays income taxes on this investment. Ben is in the 28% marginal tax bracket.

$$\text{Before-tax yield} = 10\%$$
$$\frac{\text{After - Tax Equivalent Yield}}{(1 - 0.28)} = 10\%$$
$$\text{After-tax equivalent yield} = 10\% \ (0.72)$$
$$= 7.2\%$$

Formula 10.4c is a very useful in planing analysis. For example if you have mutual fund in which you want to compare the after-tax stream of payments against the before-tax stream, you would calculate both using each tax rate. This is demonstrated in the next section.

Observe that, when using Formulas 10.4a, b, or c, the yields can be either in decimal or percentage form, but the marginal tax rates must always be in decimal form. There are several formulas regarding these conversions that have been shown here for clarity of principle. It is not necessary to memorize these, but remember the fact that each involves the quantity (1 – the Marginal Tax-Rate). When changing from a taxable to an after-tax or tax-free value, simply multiply the quantity by the taxable value to get the smaller equivalent tax-free value, and divide the tax-free values by the quantity to get the larger equivalent taxable value.

USING TAX-EQUIVALENT FORMULAS
FOR FINANCIAL PLANNING

The tax-equivalent formulas are useful for financial planning. If you calculated the future sum of money for an annuity due investment using a before-tax interest rate, you would realize a much smaller future value sum *after* you paid annual taxes on the earned income. But if you converted the before-tax interest rate to an equivalent after-tax rate, you would get an accurate after-tax future value. This is demonstrated by the following example:

Example: 10.8:

Suppose Eloise invested $1,500 at the beginning of each year for a 6-year period. The investment pays 10% compounded annually. This is not a tax-free investment. Interest earned is taxable in the year it is earned and Eloise is in the 28% marginal tax bracket. What will the actual after-tax future value of her investment be at the end of 6 years?

Solution:

$$\text{After-tax equivalent yield} = 10\% \,(1 - 0.28) = 7.20\% \quad \text{(Formula 10.4c)}$$
$$PV = 0, \ i = 7.20\%, \ n = 6 \text{ years}, \ PMT_b = -\$1,500$$

Using the annuity due Formula 5.1:

$$FV = \$11,561$$

Let's verify this result by calculating the year-by-year earnings and taxes paid. In the following table, "b" is for the beginning of the year, and "e" is the year end. All other numbers are cash flows. The interest rate we will use to calculate interest in the table is 10%, and the marginal tax rate is 28%.

Table 10.1: Future Value of a Taxable Annuity

Year	Amount Invested	Interest Earned	Income Taxes Paid	Net Interest Earned	Year End Value
1b	$1,500				
1e		$150	$42	$108	$1,608
2b	1,500				
2e		311	87	224	3,332
3b	1,500				
3e		483	135	348	5,180
4b	1,500				
4e		668	187	481	7,161
5b	1,500				
5e		866	242	624	9,284
6b	1,500				
6e		1,078	302	776	11,561

As shown by the shaded value at the end of six years, the calculational results using an after-tax interest rate of 7.20% agrees with the year-by-year analysis with a before-tax interest rate of 10%.

ARE TAX-FREE MUNICIPAL BONDS
APPROPRIATE FOR YOU?

Especially now since the Omnibus Budget Reconciliation Act of 1993 has increased marginal income tax rates retroactively to January 1, 1993, it is more attractive then ever to consider investments in which the earnings are tax-free. In this category are municipal bonds, whose earnings are free of federal income taxes, and usually free of state income taxes too.

Tax-free municipals may be appropriate for you if their tax-equivalent yields are equal to or greater than those of taxable investments. For example, suppose you have been offered a taxable investment that returns 7.00%. You also have the option of buying a municipal bond that is both federal and state tax-free bearing a 5.50% coupon. You are in the 36% marginal tax bracket. The equivalent taxable yield of this Muni is thus 8.59%, which, of course, would be preferred over the taxable 7.00% taxable option.

As part of your financial vigilance, you should continually evaluate tax-free investment options. The more you keep abreast of the tax-equivalent yields, the more you will be able to take advantage of new trends in interest rates and tax rate changes. Once you have assembled your tax-related data and investment options, you can perform tax-equivalent yield calculations. Tax-equivalent yields are different for everyone, depending on his or her marginal tax bracket. Let's try an example with the following situation:

Example 10.9:

John Q. Taxpayer has the following statistics:

- Taxable income $250,000
- Married filing jointly
- Lives in California

Should John buy tax-free muni bonds bearing a 6.00% coupon rate, or buy a taxable stock mutual fund which consistently earns 10%?

Solution:

Inspection of the federal tax table finds John in the 39.6% bracket. For the California tax table, John is in the 11% bracket.

By formula 10.2, John's effective state tax rate is:

$$0.11 \times (1 - 0.396) = 0.066$$

By Formula 10.3 his combined effective state and federal marginal tax rate is:

$$0.396 + 0.066 = 0.462$$

John's taxable equivalent yield for a 6.00% muni bond Formula 10.4a is:

$$\frac{6.00\%}{(1 - 0.462)} = 11.15\%$$

Thus by choosing the 6.00% Muni bond, John would realize an equivalent taxable yield 1.15 percentage points higher than the 10% taxable mutual fund.

Reference Table of Tax-Free Equivalent Yields

The table below provides a quick reference of tax-equivalent yields for a range of federal tax brackets and tax-free yields.

Table 10.2: Equivalent Taxable Yields

Tax Free Yield %	Marginal Tax Brackets					
	15%	28%	31%	36%	39.6%	46.2%
	Tax-Equivalent Yields %					
4.00	4.71	5.56	5.60	6.25	6.62	7.43
4.50	5.29	6.25	6.52	7.03	7.45	8.36
5.00	5.88	6.94	7.25	7.81	8.28	9.29
5.50	6.47	7.64	7.97	8.59	9.11	10.22
6.00	7.06	8.33	8.70	9.37	9.93	11.15
7.00	8.23	9.72	10.14	10.94	11.59	13.01
7.50	8.82	10.41	10.87	11.72	12.42	13.94
8.00	9.41	11.11	11.59	12.50	13.24	14.87

The last column shows the effective combined California marginal tax rates

This table can be used as a guide. Those who live in a state that levies state income taxes should include their state tax rate. The first five columns of the table are tax-equivalent yields that consider *federal marginal* tax brackets only. The last column, under 46.2% (shaded), applies to *California*. It represents the highest possible combined federal and state tax equivalent yields. The California tax bracket is 11%, and the California effective state rate is 6.6%.

TAX AVOIDANCE PLANNING

With some of the income tax formulas in hand, we can embark on some examples of income tax avoidance planing.

The Case of John Wicks, Who Was Tired of Mowing the Grass.

The year was 1985, and John Wicks was tired of mowing the grass and taking care of a big house. The Wicks' children were grown and no longer live at home. John was 55 and his wife Mary was 54. John and Mary decided to sell their home and move into a townhouse, where the grass is mowed and all other outside maintenance is done by the homeowner's association.

The Wicks' home sold for $300,000, but the basis (original price plus additions) in the home was $50,000. The price of the townhouse they elected to buy was $150,000. This resulted in a potential capital gain as follows:

Sale price	$300,000
Less cost basis	(50,000)
Capital gain	$250,000
Less new home cost	(150,000)
Taxable capital gain	$100,000

Mary was upset at the prospect of paying a large capital gains tax. This was not to be, however. John found Section ξ121 of the Internal Revenue Code which allows married couples, at least one of whom is 55 years of age or older, to exclude up to $125,000 ($62,500 for unmarried) of realized capital gain from the sale of their principal residence. This is a one-time allowable exclusion. (This has been changed recently in the U.S. Tax Code to an even more favorable tax situation.) Since the Wicks' capital gain was only $100,000, they did not have to pay any capital gains taxes on the transaction.

Now John did something that confounded everyone. He financed their new townhouse with a down payment of only 10%. He took a mortgage of $135,000 with an interest rate of 9.875% for a term of 30 years. This meant monthly payments of

$1,172.27 ($14,067 annual payments). Mary was again upset at the prospect of rather large mortgage payments so late in life. John's friends thought that he might be getting a little senile, or perhaps just plain crazy.

John was dumb like a fox. He had noticed that high grade municipal tax-free bonds were selling with a coupon interest rate of 10.5%. He took the remaining money from the sale, ($300,000 − $15,000 = $285,000) and bought $285,000 worth of bonds. This meant an annual tax-free income of $285,000 × 0.105 = $29,925.

Interest charged for home mortgage payments is tax deductible. This provided a $13,000 tax deduction for the Wicks. The Wicks were in the 50% income tax bracket in 1985. The deduction provided an annual income tax savings of $13,000 × 0.50 = $6,500. Thus their annual out-of-pocket house payments turned out to be only $14,067 − $6,500 = $7,567. In other words, the government made over 50% of the Wicks' annual mortgage payments.

To sum up, the net annual gain in this move resulted in an annual tax-free income of $29,925 − $7,567 = $22,358. Not too bad, since the Wicks wanted to move to a smaller lower- maintenance newer home. Better yet, how much would John or Mary have had to earn in taxable salary to equal this annual income?

Using Formula 10.4b

$$\frac{\$22,358}{(1-0.50)} = \$44,716$$

Granted, 1985 offered a very rare window of opportunity for the Wicks. The 1986 Tax Reform Act reduced marginal tax brackets. Also, it is no longer possible to buy tax-free bonds offering a coupon interest rate of 10% and at the same time get a home mortgage at a lower interest rate than that of tax-free bonds. The point is, however, there are many opportunities to employ tax savings strategies. To take advantage of these, you must continually analyze your financial options in light of changing financial conditions.

The Case of Bill and Caroline Jones.

The Jones are considering buying rental real estate as an investment. Will this pay a reasonable return? (Watch how income taxes can drive this decision.)

The facts of the case are as follows:
- The Jones are in the 31% marginal income tax bracket.
- The Jones will be an active participant in the property management.
- A four flat rental property is available for $350,000.

- The land value is 20% of the total cost, or $70,000.
- A 25% down payment is required (including closing costs).
- The mortgage interest rate is 8.50% for a 30-year loan.
- The expected rental income is $38,000.

Income tax stipulations are that:
- The owners must be active participants in order to take advantage of the tax provisions.
- Only the building can be depreciated.
- Depreciation is straight line over 27.5 years (After the 1986 Tax Reform Act).
- Deductible expenses are interest on the loan, property taxes, insurance, repairs and maintenance, and depreciation.

The Jones calculated the value of the depreciable items and estimated the taxes, insurance and expected maintenance as follows:
- Mortgage down payment = 0.25 × $350,000 = $87,500
- Mortgage amount = $350,000 − $87,500 = $262,500
- Mortgage payments = $2,018.40 per month, or $24,220 per year
- First year interest to be paid = $22,200
- Depreciation amount = 0.80 × $350,000 = $280,000
- Depreciation is $280,000/27.5 years = $10,181 per year
- Property taxes = $5,000 per year
- Repairs and maintenance = $3,500 per year
- Insurance = $2,000 per year

The financial breakdown for this property consists of the following:

Annual deductible expenses:

Interest	$22,200
Taxes	5,000
Insurance	2,000
Maintenance	3,500
Depreciation	10,200
Total	$42,900

Deductible loss from rental property:

Rental income	$38,000
Less expenses	(42,900)
Net loss	($4,900)

Although the Jones would have a loss for the first year, when the income tax benefits are considered, their position changes as follows:

Income:

Rental income	$38,000
Tax savings	1,519*
Total	$39,519

(* Income tax bracket of 31% of the net loss of $4,900 = $1,519)

Outlay:

Mortgage payments	$24,220
Expenses	$10,500
Total	$34,720

Net cash benefit: $4,799

The expense items under outlay are taxes, insurance, and maintenance. Depreciation is not a cash flow deduction but a tax savings deduction. Although depreciation is not a cash flow expense, it should be recognized that some depreciated money must be recaptured if and when the property is sold at a value higher than the book value. At that time the investor must pay income taxes on the recaptured depreciation.

To sum up, the Jones can realize a first year net income of $4,799 and should do as well in subsequent years. Now, what is the Jones' first-year cash-on-cash rate of return on the investment?

Since the money that the Jones invested is the down payment, their first year annual cash-on- cash rate of return is:

$$\text{ROR} = \frac{\$4,799}{\$87,500} \times 100 = 5.48\%$$

Since this is an after tax return, what would their before-tax equivalent return be?

By Formula 10.4c

$$\frac{5.48\%}{1 - 0.31} = 7.94\%$$

The ROR would in actuality be slightly higher because we did not take into account the principal portion of the loan paid back the first year.

Bill and Caroline would have to weigh this return against other options. In view of the fact that the return on this investment is close to what they could realize through tax-free municipal bonds, it is a close call. The point is, however, they should not embark on such an investment until they have gone through an analysis such as this.

Now It's Your Turn:

1. Tax-equivalent yields refer to:
    a. Yields that result from tax-free investments
    b. A value judgment between tax-fee and taxable-investments
    c. Yields that result from taxable investments

2. Taxpayers in higher income-tax marginal brackets can realize greater taxable-equivalent yields.
    a. True
    b. False

3. The practice of income tax avoidance is wholly acceptable, income tax evasion is not.
    a. True
    b. False

4. To find your federal marginal income tax rate, you must:
    a. Perform a calculation
    b. Inspect a federal tax rate schedule
    c. Both of the above

5. The easiest way to find your taxable income is:
    a. Estimate it for next year
    b. Consult your last year's income tax return
    c. Rough out next year's income tax return

6. Your filing status is "married filing jointly". Your 1996 taxable income was $40,000. What was your 1996 federal marginal tax rate?
    a. 15%
    b. 31%
    c. 28%

7. For question 6 above, what would your tax-equivalent yield be if you are offered a tax-free 5.50% coupon bond? (You live in a state that has no income tax.)
    a. 6.55%
    b. 7.64%
    c. 7.46%

8. If you lived in a state that levies a state income tax and your state tax bracket is 9.0%, what would your effective state tax rate be if your federal marginal tax rate was 31%?
    a. 6.21%
    b. 7.25%
    c. 8.12%

9. A Californian in the highest possible income tax bracket is considering a tax-free bond with a yield of 4.50%. What will her tax- equivalent yield be if she elects to buy this bond? (Hint: See Table 10.2 for the marginal tax rate.)
    a. 7.03%
    b. 7.45%
    c. 8.36%

10. You are in the 15% tax bracket. Which should you choose: a tax-free municipal bond yielding 5.50% or a taxable corporate bond yielding 6.00%?
    a. The municipal bond
    b. The corporate bond

11. You would certainly choose the corporate bond in Question 10 if your tax bracket was 36%.
    a. True
    b. False

12. What recent event has made it more attractive to consider tax-free securities?
    a. Reduced interest rates
    b. The Omnibus Budget Reconciliation Act of 1993
    c. Reduced spread between tax-free and taxable bonds

13. The Adams are going to invest in a mutual fund that offers a fixed effective annual interest rate of 7.00%. The fund's earnings are taxable. The Adams are in the 28% income tax bracket. What will be the net future value of this fund in 20 years if they invest $4,000 at the beginning of each year?
    a. $125,682
    b. $139,519
    c. $132,824

14. Josh and Mary are considering buying a home. Their monthly payments will be $1,250 per month, for a total of $15,000 per year. Of those payments in the first year, $11,472 will be interest. They are in the 34% combined federal and state marginal income-tax bracket. How much would they realize in federal and state income tax savings that year?
    a. $4,100
    b. $3,000
    c. $3.900

15. Stan owns a rental four-flat apartment. His deductible expenses are: interest $25,000, taxes $3,000, insurance $2,500, maintenance $4,500, and depreciation $15,000. Stan and his wife had a taxable income of $95,000 and file jointly. They live in Nevada, which has no state income tax. How much income tax savings did these deductible expenses represent in 1996?
    a. $14,000
    b. $1,240
    c. $11,200

16. Lucy rents an apartment. She would like to buy a home but doesn't want her monthly mortgage payments to be significantly higher than what she now pays for rent. Lucy is in the 31% marginal income tax bracket. Her current monthly rent is $1,050. Considering that her mortgage payments would be mostly taxable interest, approximately what monthly payment can she afford to make if she buys a house?
    a. $2,000
    b. $1,800
    c. $1,520

17. Ben is considering buying a rental two-flat apartment with an investment of $30,000. The annual rent he expects to receive is $16,000. His deductible expenses should be $20,000, of which $7,000 is depreciation and $10,000 is interest.. His annual mortgage payment will be $12,000. Ben is in the 39.6% marginal income tax bracket. What net cash benefit can he expect the first year? What *before-tax* rate of return can he expect?

   a. $1,450 cash benefit, 7.51% ROR
   b. $1,540 cash benefit, 6.25% ROR
   c. $2,584 cash benefit, 14.25% ROR

ANSWERS: 1.b, 2.a, 3.a, 4.b, 5.b, 6.a, 7.b, 8.a, 9.c 10.a, 11.b, 12.b, 13.b, 14.c, 15.a, 16. c, 17.c

What Inflation Does to Your Financial Life

(Are You Keeping Up?)

LEARNING OBJECTIVES:

When you have completed this chapter, you will be able to:

1. Understand inflation terminology and how to deflate a series
2. Determine whether you income is keeping up with inflation
3. Track the progress of your investments in relation to inflation
4. Consider inflation in your financial and retirement planning

Inflation erodes the value of money. Inflation needs to be recognized by everyone because it affects our future financial condition. Inflation has always been present, but it has increased in volatility since 1971 when President Nixon took the United States off the gold standard. In the *Death of Money*, Joel Kurtzman explains that this gave rise to the volatility of money. There was no longer the monetary anchor previously enjoyed. Inflation was built into the new system from its very start. Although inflation is quite low at the present time, we may be in for some inflationary periods in the future, especially if the government needs to monitize the debt in order to keep up with its debt payments.

THE EFFECTS OF INFLATION ON INCOME

Until now we have been talking about the time value of money that increases due to investment earnings. Inflation, however, decreases the value of money. A dollar today will be worth less in the future. We will need more dollars in the future to maintain our living standards.

How can we determine whether we are keeping up with inflation? We can analyze our income relative to inflation. We can also track our investments and make changes to keep ahead of inflation. Of paramount importance, we can take inflation into account when planning for retirement. There are simple procedures for analyzing inflation. But first, some definitions.

Constant dollar is the value of a dollar used as a reference in a base year. A constant dollar has a constant value that is *not* adjusted for the effects of inflation.

Consumer price index (CPI) is the percentage rate of change in the cost of living over a given time period. The CPI is published by the U.S. Department of Labor. It is calculated monthly to measure the changes in consumer prices of such things as housing, food, and electricity. Each year the CPI is annualized to provide the annual rate of change in consumer prices. The CPI is used to adjust items such as Social Security payments.

Real dollar is the value of the constant dollar adjusted for the effects of inflation in the years after the reference or base year. Real dollar is also referred to as *real income*. The value of real dollars over time shows the degradation of the value of money due to inflation.

Real interest rate is the current interest rate minus the current inflation rate.

Real income is income (in real dollars) that is adjusted in purchasing power as a result of inflation.

Suppose you want to know the real dollar value over the last three-year period. We selected the years 1989, 1990, and 1991 to demonstrate this calculation. We found that the CPI for these years was 4.65, 6.11, and 3.06, respectively. This means that the cost of living increased by 4.56%, 6.11%, and 3.06%, over these three years. In tabular form this information, including constant dollars, appears as follows:

Table 11.1: Real Dollar Calculation

Year End	CPI	Price Index 1989 = 100%	Constant Dollars	Real Dollars
1989	Base	100.00	$100	$100.00
1990	6.11	106.11	$100	$94.24
1991	3.06	109.36	$100	$91.44

This calculation starts by selecting a base year. For Table 11.1, we selected the year 1989 as the base year. We assigned the value of 100.00% as the base price index and $100.00 as the constant dollar base amount. We then constructed the price index values based on the changing CPI.

According to the CPI of 1990, the cost of living increased by 6.11% during that year. We increase the base value of the 1989 price index 6.11% by multiplying it by 1.0611 (1.0611 × 100 = 106.11). The year 1991 saw a CPI increase of 3.06%. The 1991 price index value then becomes 109.36 (1.0306 × 106.11 = 109.36). The method of applying the percentage gain of the CPI to calculate the price index is a shortcut using Formula 2.1 from Chapter 2.

To get real dollars, divide the base value of $100.00 by the index value of the year in question. For 1990, $100.00/1.0611 = $94.24, and for 1991, $100.00/1.0936 = $91.44. Notice that we divide the 1989 base amount (constant dollar) by the index number in decimal form. Always divide the index number for any given year into $100.00, the base value for the base year.

The meaning of the real dollar can be appreciated when viewing Table 11.1. In 1991, $100 of 1989 dollars will only buy $91.44 worth of goods and services.

Table 11.2 shows real dollars for the years 1979 through 1992. For practice, you might verify some of these values.

Table 11.2 :Constant Dollar Values

Year	CPI	Price Index 1979 = 100%	Constant Dollars	Real Dollars
1979	Base	100.00	$100	$100.00
1980	12.40	112.40	100	88.97
1981	8.94	122.19	100	81.67
1982	3.87	127.45	100	78.62
1983	8.30	137.74	100	72.60
1984	3.95	143.18	100	69.84
1985	3.77	148.58	100	67.30
1986	1.13	150.26	100	66.55
1987	4.41	156.89	100	63.74
1988	4.42	163.82	100	61.04
1989	4.65	171.44	100	58.33
1990	6.11	181.92	100	54.97
1991	3.06	187.48	100	53.34
1992	2.98	193.07	100	51.79

Notice that, in addition to the real dollar values, the index values turn out to be multiples of the year 1979 ($100). For example, the base value of $100 in 1979 represents a real dollar value of $51.79 in the year 1992, but to offset the effect of inflation you would need to spend $193.07 of 1979 constant dollars in 1992 to get the same goods and services.

Also notice that the real dollar value of $51.79 for 1992 is the present value of the base value of $100 at the uniform annual inflation rate of 5.2% over a 13-year period.

Although the annual rates of inflation (CPI) vary each year, we can determine the uniform equivalent rates of inflation by using the single-payment compound amount Formula 4.1 from Chapter 4. We can apply Formula 4.1 because the rates of inflation are compounded values.

Example 11.1:

Between 1979 and 1992, the cost of living increased 93.07% ($100 to $193.07). What does this represent in terms of a compound uniform annual rate of increase?

Solution:

$$PV = 100$$
$$FV = \$193.07$$
$$n = 13 \text{ years}$$
$$i = ?$$

By rearranged Formula 4.1:

$$i = \left(\frac{\$193.07}{\$100} \right)^{\frac{1}{13}} - 1 = 0.052$$
$$i = 0.052 \text{ or } 5.2\%$$

HOW TO CALCULATE REAL INCOME

Bob would like to track his salary progress. His company has been giving him an annual raise of $1,500 per year. The company asserts that these raises are for the cost of living but that they also include some money for merit raises. In 1988 Bob's salary was

$35,000. How well did his real income keep up with inflation through 1992, and did he get any merit raises during that time?

For this analysis the base salary is $35,000, and because of annual raises it increases $1,500 in constant dollars each year. Using the CPI for the years 1985 to 1992, the results are the following:

Table 11.3: Real Income Analysis of Salary Increases

Year	CPI %	Price Index 1988 = 100%	Salary in Constant $	Real Income
1988	Base	100.00	$35,000	$35,000
1989	4.65	104.65	36,500	34,878
1990	6.11	111.04	38,000	31,221
1991	3.06	114.44	39,500	34,516
1992	2.98	117.85	41,000	34,790

The constant dollar salary of any given year is adjusted for inflation by dividing it by the price index in decimal form. For example, for the year 1989, $36,500/1.046 = $34,878.

Table 11.1 shows that Bob's salary did not keep up with inflation. His real income in 1992 was less than it was in 1988. He would need a 1992 constant dollar of salary of $41,247 just to break even. He did not, of course, get a raise that could be considered a merit raise. If Bob thinks he deserves some additional money to meet the cost of living increase plus a merit raise, he might use this information to plead his case.

The process of converting Bob's constant dollars salary to real dollars is frequently referred to as *deflating a series*.

HOW WELL DOES THE STOCK MARKET
KEEP UP WITH INFLATION?

Some years the stock market results have been good, others not so good. Most stockbrokers like to quote results over the decade of the 1980's. Over that decade some of the good mutual funds realized an annual compound rate of return of 18%. What happened in the decade of the 1970's? Let's see what happened between the years of 1972 through 1978. We will use the Standard & Poor's 500 index of stocks for the stock market performance. The base year is 1972 and the base value starts with an investment of $100. The data are shown in Table 11.4.

Table 11.4
Inflation Adjusted S&P 500 Index Stock Market Values
1972 through 1978.

Year End	CPI %	Price Index 1972 = 100%	S&P 500 Index Change %	S&P 500 Constant Dollar	S&P 500 Real Dollars
1972	Base	100.0	Base	$100.	$100
1973	8.8	108.8	(14.7)	85	78
1974	12.2	122.1	(26.5)	63	51
1975	7.0	130.6	37.2	86	66
1976	4.8	136.9	23.9	107	78
1977	6.8	146.2	(7.2)	99	68
1978	9.0	159.5	6.6	105	66

The S&P 500 constant dollar index, of course, increases or decreases according to the gains or losses in the S&P 500 Index. For example the S&P 500 Index lost 14.7% of its value during 1973. A sample calculation shows the S&P 500 constant dollar (C$) worth for the year 1973, using Formula 2.1 (percentage difference), as:

$$\frac{C\$ - \$100}{\$100} = -0.147$$
$$C\$ = \$85.30$$

The S&P500 real dollars for the year 1973 is $85 ÷ 1.088 = $78.

Now let's calculate the real annual rate of return between the years 1972 to 1978 for the series of real dollars:

$$PV = \$100 \quad (\text{S\&P 500 @ 1972})$$
$$FV = \$66 \quad (\text{S\&P 500 @ 1978})$$
$$n = 6 \text{ years}$$
$$i = \left(\frac{66}{100}\right)^{1/6} - 1 = -0.067 \text{ or } -6.7\% \quad (\text{Formula 4.1})$$

Anyone who invested money in 1972 in an S&P 500 Index fund suffered a compound annual real rate of return loss of 6.7% per year by 1978. This was typical of the stock market in general.

The 1972 to 1978 period was quite volatile. Between 1972 to 1974 alone, investors lost 49% of their investment in real dollars. This might have been caused by the OPEC oil embargo. However, investing is tricky business. If an investor became disgusted at the end of 1974 and pulled her money out of the stock market, she would have missed the returns of 1975 and 1976. During that period the real dollar amount increased a total of 53%.

Let's not leave this subject on a down note. What about some good times in the stock market? Consider the years 1978 to 1986. This span was as about as good as it gets. The results are shown by Table 11.5.

Table 11.5 Inflation Adjusted S&P 500 Index Values, 1978 to 1986

Year End	CPI %	Price Index 1978 = 100%	S&P 500 Index % Change	S&P 500 Constant Dollars	S&P500 Real Dollars
1978	Base	100.0	Base	$100	$100
1979	13.3	113.3	18.4	118	104
1980	12.4	127.4	32.4	156	122
1981	8.9	138.7	(4.9)	148	107
1982	3.9	144.1	21.4	180	125
1983	3.8	149.6	22.5	221	148
1984	4.0	155.6	6.3	235	151
1985	3.8	161.5	24.7	293	181
1986	1.1	163.1	18.5	347	213

What a difference a little time makes. In this time frame, investors more than doubled their portfolio's real dollar value in eight years. Calculate the annualized real rate of return of this period. Did you get 9.91%? The S&P 500 index constant dollar annualized rate of return was 16.8%.

As can be seen from Table 11.5, the largest gains came in the years 1982 through 1986, when the annual rate of inflation dropped below 5%. In that period the S&P 500 index annual gains were considerably higher than the rates of inflation. There was only one year in this series in which money did not grow (1981). In summary, an investment needs to be analyzed in relation to inflation to know just how well it has performed.

How Well Are Those Who Have Their Money in a 2% Passbook Savings Doing?

Consider the Widow Jones, who has $100,000 in a current 2% passbook savings account. She says that she earns $2,000 in interest each year and this is good money. How good is it? She has a marginal income tax rate of 15%. Her after tax rate of return is:

$$2\% \times (1 - 0.15) = 1.70\%$$

In ten years, her $100,000 will grow to an after-tax value of $118,361.

At an annual inflation rate of just 3% this $118,361 will buy only $88,072 worth of goods in ten years. This is calculated as follows:

$$\frac{1}{(1 + 0.03)^{10}} \times \$118,361 = \$88,072$$

THE EFFECT OF INFLATION ON YOUR FINANCIAL PLANNING

In planning for retirement, it is advisable to consider inflation. Your retirement lifetime may even be long enough for inflation to double your living expenses. For example, according to actuarial tables, a man retiring at age 60 has a life expectancy of 18 additional years. His wife of age 60 has a life expectancy addition of 22 years. At an inflation rate of 4%, the cost of living will double in 20 years.

You need to answer several basic questions when planning for retirement:

1. At what age would you like to retire?
2. How much retirement income will you need?
3. How much capital will you need to accumulate to provide your retirement income?
4. What will be the average rate of inflation?

Bob Brinker, the popular host of the radio show "Money Talk," has an interesting term for the amount of money you will need to support your retirement. He calls it your "critical mass." When you have reached the critical mass you can retire.

The critical mass is the sum total of capital holdings that you have or will have to provide the income necessary for retirement. It can consist of such items as pensions, Social Security, 401(k) plans, annuities, portfolio holdings, inheritance, and savings accounts.

Let's take a simple case to demonstrate how inflation is factored into financial and retirement planning. The main point to notice here is that we will conduct this analysis using real dollars rather than constant dollars. Constant dollar planning would leave retirees far short of the long term financial support they need.

Example 11.2: Retirement Planning for Greg and Jean Carson

Greg and Jean decided to develop a retirement plan and analyze the outcome. They developed the follow facts including their retirement goal:

Current age of both	55 years
Current income	$80,000 per year
Current portfolio's value	$200,000
Annual pension at retirement	$50,000 (fixed income)
Social Security at retirement	$18,000 per year
Expected after-tax annual rate of return on investments	7.0%
Money to be invested annually	$10,000
Desired retirement age	62 years (goal)
Desired income at retirement	80% of current (goal)
Expected rate of inflation	4% per year
Retirement duration	25 years

Greg and Jean's home is now paid for, and their children are grown and financially independent. Retirement planning is now foremost in Greg and Jean's minds. Can they meet their retirement goals?

Solution:

Greg and Jean's expected lifetimes are 20 years beyond their desired retirement age of 62. Adding 5 years to this they will plan for living 25 years in retirement. For planning purposes they select 4% as the compound uniform annual rate of inflation.

The first step is to work backward from the 25-year retirement duration to determine the critical mass needed when they retire in seven years. Their desired annual retirement income is $64,000 (80% of $80,000). But, in real inflation-adjusted terms at the start of retirement in seven years, this required income will be:

$$FV = \$64,000\ (1+0.04)^7 = \$84,220\ \text{per year}$$

Because Social Security is adjusted annually according to the cost of living, we can subtract it directly from the Carsons' retirement income. This reduces the balance of their annual retirement income to $66,220 ($84,220 − $18,000).

Now we need to determine the present value of $66,220 escalated at a rate of 4% annually to account for inflation. Table 11.6 shows this calculation year-by-year. It shows that the Carsons will need $578,000 present value dollars at the beginning of retirement, exclusive of their Social Security and constant value pension income.

Table 11.6 is a long table but a simple one. The first column is the number of years in retirement. The second column is the required annual income, exclusive of Social Security and adjusted by an annual increase of 4% to account for inflation. The third column is the fixed pension income. The fourth column is the difference between columns 2 and 3. The fifth column is the present value of one dollar at a 7.0%. The sixth column is the present value of the annual income requirement less the fixed income of $50,000. The total of the annual future values, ($578,000) is the amount needed to support the balance of the Carsons' annual retirement income.

To show how the values in Table 11.6 are calculated, we use the beginning of the 25th year as the example. The following steps are:

1. Calculate the future value of $66,220 at an annual increase of 4%:

$$FV = \$66,220\ (1+0.04)^{24} = \$169,742$$

2. The required net annual income is:

$$\$169,742 - \$50,000 = \$119,742$$

3. Calculate the present value of one dollar out to the end of 24 years at an interest rate of 7%:

$$PV = \frac{1}{(1+0.07)^{24}} = 0.197$$

4. Multiply by the required net annual income by the present value factor to get the present value of the net income:

$$\$119,742 \times 0.197 = \$23,600$$

5. The total required present value to support the Carsons' retirement goal is the sum of $578,000 at the bottom of the sixth column.

To calculate Table 11.6 we used a computer spreadsheet program. Spreadsheets programs are very efficient tools for these kinds of applications. Computer spreadsheet applications are explained in Chapter 19.

Table 11.6
Present Value Calculation of the Carsons' Retirement Income

(1) Year Begin	(2) Required Annual Income @ 4% increase	(3) Fixed Pension Income	(4) Required Net Annual Income	(5) Present Value of 1$ @7.0%	(6) PV of Annual Income @7%
1	$66,220	$50,000	$16,220	1.000	$16,220
2	68,869	50,000	18,869	0.935	17,634
3	71,624	50,000	21,624	0.873	18,887
4	74,488	50,000	24,488	0.816	19,990
5	77,468	50,000	27,468	0.763	20,955
6	80,567	50,000	30,567	0.713	21,794
7	83,789	50,000	33,789	0.666	22,515
8	87,141	50,000	37,141	0.623	23,130
9	90,627	50,000	40,627	0.582	23,645
10	94,252	50,000	44,252	0.544	24,070
11	98,022	50,000	48,022	0.508	24,412
12	101,943	50,000	51,943	0.475	24,678
13	106,020	50,000	56,020	0.444	24,874
14	110,261	50,000	60,261	0.415	25,006
15	114,672	50,000	64,672	0.388	25,081
16	119,258	50,000	69,258	0.362	25,102
17	124,029	50,000	74,029	0.339	25,076
18	128,990	50,000	78,990	0.317	25,006
19	134,150	50,000	84,150	0.296	24,897
20	139,516	50,000	89,516	0.277	24,752
21	145,096	50,000	95,096	0.258	24,575
22	150,900	50,000	100,900	0.242	24,369
23	156,936	50,000	106,936	0.226	24,137
24	163,213	50,000	113,213	0.211	23,882
25	169,742	50,000	119,742	0.197	23,600
Total present value of annual retirement incomes					$578,000

Based on these results, Greg and Jean will need to invest their current portfolio value of $200,000 plus their annual savings of $10,000 at a rate of return sufficient to realize $578,000 in seven years. To determine the future value of this money, two calculations are used.

1. For the single portfolio amount of $200,000, we have:

$$n = 7 \text{ years}, PV = \$200,000, \text{ and } i = 7\%$$
$$FV = \$200,000 \, (1+0.07)^7 = \$321,156$$

2. For the annual investment, we use Formula 5.2 (annuity due).

$$n = 7 \text{ years}, PV = 0, PMT_b = \$10,000, i = 7\%$$
$$FV = \$10,000 \, (1+0.07) \left[\frac{(1+0.07)^7 - 1}{0.07} \right]$$
$$= \$92,600$$

The total amount of money that will be available at the start of the Carsons' retirement years is:

$$\$321,000 + \$92,600 = \$413,600$$

Greg and Jean estimated that in seven years they will need $578,000 to support retirement, but the calculated investment potential is estimated to be $413,600—a shortage of $164,400. Since these calculations depend on some estimates, the Carsons can continue to pursue this goal with the aim of making some changes. Perhaps the inflation rate will be lower than 4%. Moreover, about 40% of the CPI, as calculated by the government, involves the cost of housing and this may not be needed for a retired couple who no longer have a mortgage. Also the Carsons may be able to exceed their expected 7% rate of return on their investments.

This example does strongly indicate that inflation is a major concern that must be considered in retirement planning. It is alarming to notice that in Greg and Jean's case, their annual income needs over their retirement lifetime increased over a factor of more than two.

Present Value Retirement Data

For your convenience, Table 11.7 provides the present value sum of money necessary to support an annual retirement stream for 25 years, starting at $50,000 per year.

This table was calculated using a computer spreadsheet program. The present values of the money have been calculated as a function of various rates of inflation and after-tax rates of return. Referring to Table 11.7, for a uniform annual inflation rate of 3% over that 25 years and an after-tax rate of return of 5% on invested money, a retiree would need $1,002,000 to support his or her retirement's annual stream of money.

Table 11.7
Present Value of Money needed to Support Retirement

	$50,000 Annual Income at Retirement			
	Twenty-Five Years in Retirement			
	After Tax Rates of Return			
Inflation	5%	6%	7%	8%
Rates	Present Value Money			
3%	$1,002,000	$905,000	$823,000	$750,000
4%	1,117,000	1,004,000	907,000	824,000
5%	1,250,000	1,112,000	1,001,000	910,000
6%	1,404,000	1,259,000	1,119,000	1,008,000

The results of Table 11.7 certainly draw attention to the sizable sum of money needed for retirement years. Also, what you realize on your investments has a strong influence. As you can see from the table, you will need about a 40% greater present value sum at the start of retirement if you realize only 5% rather than 8% on your investments. The obvious conclusion is you cannot start too early in planning and saving for retirement. In *The Myth of Retirement*, Craig Karpel states that he does not think that retirement will be possible for a large number of the present-day Baby Boomers.

Now It's Your Turn:

1. If an investor realized a rate of return of 5% on an investment and the CPI that year was 3%, the what was the real rate of return?
   a. 5%
   b. 8%
   c. 2%

2. The rate of inflation is expressed as the CPI and is reported annually by the U.S. government.
   a. True
   b. False

3. The base year is 1987. The year 1988 experienced a CPI of 3.5%. If we select a base value of $100 for the year 1987, what would the real dollar value be in the year 1988?
   a. $92.50
   b. $96.62
   c. $99.65

4. In the year 2000, it is expected that the price index will be 110%, based on a price index of 100% in the year 1995. If the constant dollar was $100 in 1995, what would the real dollar be worth in the year 2000?
   a. $86.96
   b. $89.00
   c. $91.00

5. For question 4 above, how much money in would be needed the year 2000 to buy the equivalent of $100 in 1995 goods?
   a. $86.96
   b. $95.36
   c. $115.00

6. In 1989 the CPI was 4.65%. In 1990 it was 6.11%. How much would an auto manufacturer have to charge at the start of 1992 to keep up with inflation? At the end of 1988 the auto's price was $12,000.
   a. $14,876
   b. $13,325
   c. $12,658

7. Charlie's salary increases and the CPI are shown in the table for the years 19x1 through 19x4.

Year End	CPI %	Price Index 1988 = 100%	Salary in Constant $	Real Income
19x1	Base	100.00	$26,000	$26,000
19x2	4.11		28,000	
19x3	3.19		30,000	
19x4	5.16		33,000	

What is Charlie's real income at the end of 19x4?
   a. $26,894
   b. $29,211
   $27,925

8. For the data shown in the table below, what is the real worth of a dollar at the end of 1984 compared to that of a reference dollar in 1982?

Year End	CPI	Price Index 1989 = 100%	Constant Dollars	Real Dollars
1982	Base	100.00	$1	$1.00
1983	8.30		$1	
1984	3.95		$1	

   a. 92 cents
   b. 97 cents
   c. 89 cents

9. John bought a term life insurance policy on his life that will pay $250,000 to his family upon his death. What amount of money will his family receive in real dollars if he should die 15 years hence? The average annual rate of inflation during that period is estimated to be 6%.
   a. $104,300
   b. $200,500
   c. $128,700

10. Sandy bought $10,000 worth of ABC stock in 19x5. It is now 19x8 and she wants to know the real dollar worth of that stock. The stock market performance of her stock and the annual CPI rates of change are shown in the table. What would you tell her?

Year End	CPI %	Price Index 1972 = 100	ABC Stock Change %	ABC Constant Dollar	ABC Real Dollars
19x5	Base	100.0%	Base	$10,000	$10,000
19x6	14.7		10.2		
19x7	13.4		(6.5)		
19x8	10.6		12.5		

    a. $12,435
    b. $9,874
    c. $8,058

11. The current tuition at a university is about $15,000 per year, give or take a few thousand. If your child is now two years of age, what could you expect the tuition to be at this school when the child is ready to enter college at age 18? Assume that the average annual rate of inflation is 4%. Round the answer to $1,000 dollars.
    a. $18,000
    b. $24,000
    c. $28,000

12. Jake and Ann are going to retire at the end of the year. They think the average rate of inflation will be 3% per year. They need to spend $20,000 per year for the next 5 years to augment their income until they reach age 59 1/2. At that time they can use income from their IRA program. If they are currently making 7% after-tax rate-of-return on the money they have saved to supply the $20,000 per year income, what present sum of real dollar money will they need to support that income stream? The table below is a working form for this analysis.

Year	Living Expenses C$	PV @7% = ? Real Dollars
1	$20,000	$20,000
2		
3		
4		
5		

a. $90,874
b. $92,797
c. $87,056

ANSWERS: 1.c, 2.a, 3.b, 4.a, 5.c, 6.b, 7.b, 8.c, 9.a, 10.c, 11.c, 12.b

Analyzing Corporate Bonds

LEARNING OBJECTIVES:

This chapter shows how financial math can be applied to analyze corporate bonds. You will learn:

1. The cause of bond price volatility
2. How bonds are quoted
3. How prorated bond interest is calculated
4. How to calculate the coupon rate, current yield, and yield to maturity of bonds
5. How bond prices change with interest rates
6. How to construct and interpret yield curves
7. How to analyze price trends of bonds offered on the secondary market

Because bonds constitute a large portion of the investment market, we will apply the mathematical principles learned so far to analyze them. Bonds have a particular jargon and analytical treatment. There are three basic types of bonds: corporate, government, and municipal. Government bonds are discussed in detail in Chapter 13. Municipal bonds are discussed in Chapter 10, where their tax-free characteristics are presented.

Bonds are debt securities that corporations and governments issue to borrow money. A purchaser of corporate bonds becomes a creditor of the corporation. Bonds are issued in two ways. New issues are sold as *initial public offerings* (IPO). There is also a very active secondary market for existing bonds. IPOs are bought from the brokerage groups that underwrite them. Secondary market bonds can be bought from brokerage firms, banks, and mutual fund companies. Bond prices for sale as IPOs or on the secondary market can be quite volatile. Prices are quoted daily in *The Wall Street Journal* and other financial papers.

WHAT CAUSES BOND PRICE VOLATILITY?

Interest rate changes strongly influence bond price swings. Bond prices change inversely to the changes in interest rates. When marketplace interest rates change, bond prices will change to compensate. This is necessary to equalize the bond's yield commensurate with other fixed-income securities. If an existing bond has a coupon rate of 5% and investors now can get a return of 7%, due to marketplace interest-rate changes, the bond's price would have to drop to provide the bond buyer with a yield of 7%.

The volatility of bond prices is a relatively recent phenomenon. In "*A history of Interest Rates*," Sidney Homer and Richard Sylila show that yields on high-quality corporate bonds took 20 years (1900 to 1920) to rise from 3.5% to 5%, and another 20 years (1920 to 1940) to decline from 5% to 2.8%.

The increasing national debt has caused bond prices to rise. U.S. government debt has exploded from $1 trillion in 1980 to more than $5 trillion now. The current value of overall bond debt has reached $8.8 trillion, up 370% since 1980. However, this debt is not the sole cause of bond price volatility.

Interest rates became relatively low in the Federal Reserve Board's attempt to bring the U.S. out the recession of 1991. Interest rates of 30-year government bonds were as low as 5.8%. This caused bond investors to snap up bonds at ever lower rates. Thinking that interest rates would remain low, these investors leveraged their money by buying bonds with funds borrowed at even lower rates. Investors believed that interest rates would remain low because of the recession in both American and foreign economies. The recent Orange County debacle in California is a classic example of what can happen with this kind of thinking: County financial managers failed to recognize that interest rates were again on the rise.

The Fed, fearing inflation, started to raise interest rates on the money it lent to member banks, which drove existing bond prices down and interest rates up. This devaluation of bonds resulted in significant losses, especially to investors who are short-term traders. Giant portfolios of older bonds suffered losses in value and reversal of bond prices caused many bond investors to sell their holdings in an attempt to minimize their losses. A lack of demand then resulted as many took advantage of safer, less volatile CDs and money market yields. A relatively large market developed for discounted bonds that appeared attractive. With long bond yields of 6.5%, the real return after inflation is more that 3%.

In 1995, however, the Fed reduced interest rates due to a perceived slowing of the economy. The 30-year Treasury bond interest rate dropped to 6%. Bond prices again rose, and some bond mutual funds reported annual profits as high as 30%. This was due to capital gains, since the interest rates of high-grade corporate bonds varied from a high of about 8.70% to a low of 7.00% in 1995. It is wholly obvious that large institutional investors play the bond market to take advantage of capital gains caused by price volatility rather than what they can earn from the coupon interest.

We explain this bond scenario to make readers aware of the difficulty surrounding bond purchases. Bonds bought as initial issues or on the secondary market require a particularly extensive analysis to properly evaluate these options. A crystal ball to determine where interest rates are going would also be helpful.

INITIAL PUBLIC OFFERING (IPO) OF BONDS

Corporate bonds are initially offered at *par* and have a *face value* of $1,000 each. Associated with the par or face value is the coupon rate. The *coupon rate* is the nominal interest rate paid on the face value of a bond. Bond interest is usually paid semi-annually, exactly at six-month intervals. Bonds can be issued at various maturity lengths. Long-term bonds are issued for 20 to 35 years. Intermediate maturities range between 10 to 20 years. Debt issues with maturities of less than 10 years are usually called *notes*.

Example 12.1: Calculation of Semiannual Payments to Bond Holders

An IPO bond has a coupon rate of 8.00% and matures in 30 years. How much will the bond holder receive in semiannual and annual interest payments for each bond held? At the end of 30 years what is the total of the final payment?

Solution:

$$INT = PV \times i \times n$$
$$PV = \$1,000$$
$$i = 0.08/2 = 0.04 \text{ per semiannual period}$$
$$n = 1 \text{ semiannual period}$$

The semiannual interest payment is:

$$INT = \$1,000 \times 0.04 \times 1 = \$40$$

The annual interest payment is:

$$INT = 2 \text{ semiannual periods per year} \times \$40 = \$80 \text{ per year}$$

The last payment at the end of 30 years includes the last interest payment and the redeemed face value of the bond.

$$\text{Last payment} = \$40 + \$1,000 = \$1,040$$

Regardless of what happens to the subsequent market price of a bond, two things are constant: (1) the coupon rate remains the same throughout the term, and (2) the face value is paid when the bond's term matures. In the above example the semiannual payment will always be $40 and the face value of $1,000 will be redeemed at the end of the term—provided, of course, that the issuing organization does not declare bankruptcy and/or default on its debt. In this regard, bond obligations are senior to stock. Bond payments must be made before stock dividends in the case of default.

It should be noted that although the semiannual interest is calculated by a simple interest formula, it is not simple interest, but it is a form of compound interest. There are two reasons for this. First, the principal is not paid along with the interest payments. Second, the opportunity exists to reinvested the interest paid semiannually. If this is done, each semiannual reinvested interest again earns interest throughout the term. This is tantamount to compounding.

Proration of Interest

Bond buyers and sellers should be aware of how bond interest is prorated when bonds are bought and sold. Whether buying or selling new or secondary issues, the settlement date is rarely on the specific interest payment date. Where the settlement date is between the *interest payment dates* (IPD), the interest accrued between the last IPD and the settlement date is paid by the buyer to the seller. This is done because the buyer will receive the total interest payment at the next IPD, even though he or she did not hold the bond throughout that semiannual period.

The calculation of accrued interest is done by the simple interest method using *ordinary* interest time periods (i.e., a 360-day year, and 30-day month). The settlement date is not counted in the total days since the IPD. The following example demonstrates this.

Example 12.2: Proration of Bond Interest

A 10% coupon bond settles on November 13. The seller held 20 bonds. The IPD are July 1 and January 1. How much accrued interest must the buyer pay to the seller?

Solution:

Determine the number of days between July 1st and November 13th. Do not count the settlement date.

July	30 days
August	30 days
September	30 days
October	30 days
November	12 days
Total	132 days (There actually are 135 calendar days in this interval.)

$n = 132$ days
$i = 0.10/360 = 0.0002778$ per day
$PV = 20$ bonds $\times$ \$1,000 per bond $= \$20,000$ (based on par value)
$INT = \$20,000 \times 0.0002778$ per day $\times 132$ days $= \$733.39$

For this transaction, the bond buyer must pay the seller \$733.39 of accrued interest upon purchasing these bonds. The next January 1 is the interest payment date. The buyer recoups the accrued interest payment upon receipt of the total semiannual payment of \$1,000.

INTERPRETING BOND QUOTATIONS

Bonds on the secondary market are sold through stock brokerage firms and/or banks. Bonds traded daily are listed by such periodicals as *The Wall Street Journal*. A person interested in following the bond market transactions can follow the published daily bond quotations.

Bond Quotations on the Secondary Market

The following are bond quotations selected at random from *The Wall Street Journal*.

Table 12.1: Bond Quotations

Bonds	Cur Yld	Vol	Close	Net Chg.
ATT 8.10s98	8.2	60	99	+ 1/4
ATT 8⅝ 31	9.0	237	96¼	+ 1/4
AmBrnd 9 ⅛ 16	9.2	25	101	+ 1/2

- **ATT 8.10s98** is an American Telegraph & Telephone 8.10% coupon bond that matures in 1998. The "s" has no meaning, it is a place holder because there is no fraction in the quoted coupon rate quote.
- **8.2 Cur Yld** is the current yield of 8.2%.
- **Vol** means that 60 bonds traded during the period.
- **Close** is the price that the bonds traded at the close of the daily secession.
- **Net Chg** is the difference between the closing price of the previous session and the current session. The change is expressed as the percentage of the par value. A one-half percent positive change (called a one-half point change) is a $5 increase per bond (0.005 × $1000 = $5).

Bond traders refer to a one-point change in the bond price as a $10 change. A two-point change is $20. This terminology is different than that of a basis point. Recall that one basis point is a difference of one-hundredth of a percentage point. If a bond's yield is 8.50% and it changes to 8.75%, this is a change of +0.25 (1/4) percentage points, which is 0.25% × 100 = 25 basis points.

Converting Bond Price Quotes to Dollar Value

This can be a little confusing. The quoted bond prices are expressed as a percentage of par value. A bond price quoted as 82 is 82% of $1,000 = $820. To convert the quote to dollar value, simply multiply it by ten.

Bond Quote	Dollar Value
82	$820
90	$900
95	$950

Bond prices are usually not in round numbers, but in fractional amounts. For example:

Bond Quote	Dollar Value
87 1/4	$872.50
91 3/8	$913.75
96 3/4	$967.50

The simplest way to convert a fractional quote is to change the fraction to a decimal, add it to the whole number, and multiply by ten. For example, 87 1/4 is $87 + 0.25 = 87.25$. The price of the bond is $87.25 \times 10 = \$872.50$.

Bond Ratings

Bond ratings are not included with the quotes, but anyone buying a bond should know its rating. The ratings can be obtained from the bond brokers. The four top ratings by Moody's Investor Service are:

Ratings	Meaning
Aaa	Highest quality
Aa	High quality
A	Upper medium quality
Baa	Medium quality

Bonds rated below Baa levels are considered speculative in increasing degrees. Baa is also called "bank quality" because banks are not permitted by the federal government to buy bonds below this quality.

We emphasize the need to know the quality of a bond prior to buying it. For example, suppose it is possible to buy a bond offering a current yield of 16%. This appears attractive, but the company that issued this bond may be in bankruptcy or close to it. A total loss of invested money is possible.

ANALYZING BOND YIELDS

"Yield" is the term used for the rate of return of bond investments. We have discussed the coupon yield. There are three other yields used in reference to bonds: (1) current yield, (2) yield to call, and (3) yield to maturity (YTM).

The Current Yield

The current yield is the yield produced by the annual fixed interest paid divided by the current market price paid for the bond.

Formula 12.1: Current Yield

$$\text{Current Yield} = \frac{\text{Annual Interest}}{\text{Current Price}}$$

Formula 12.1 shows that the current yield increases as the price decreases. In other words, deeply discounted bonds return greater yields. (This, of course, should be taken with the caveat that the bond rating is acceptable.)

Example 12.3 Calculating Current Yield.

An AT&T bond rated Aaa has a quoted coupon rate of 8 5/8 and a price of 96 1/4. What is the current yield of this bond?

Solution:

First calculate the annual interest:

$$\text{INT} = \$1,000 \times 0.08625 = \$86.25$$
$$\text{Current Yield} = \frac{\$86.25}{\$962.50}$$
$$= 8.96\%$$

This is the second bond listed in Table 12.1. The current yield quotes are rounded to the nearest tenth, or 9.0 for this bond's current yield.

Yield to Call (YTC) and Yield To Maturity (YTM)

These two yields are technically the same thing. Only the term of the investment varies. These yields are the rate of return when the calculation includes the total cash flows throughout the term. Recall that the current yield only involves the annual interest payment and the price paid for the bond.

For a yield to maturity, the length of the term extends between the date of purchase and the maturity date. Some bonds have a call provision in which the issuer can redeem the bond principal at or after a defined date. Calling a bond is particularly advantageous to the issuer if interest rates should drop. In that case the issuer will call the bonds and issue new bonds at the lower coupon rate. The length of the callable term is between the purchase date and the call date.

Calculating YTM

There are two basic methods to accurately calculate the YTM, and one method to esti- mate it. The estimation method provides results that are fairly close to the accurate methods. However, the exact methods are even easier than the estimation method if the HP-12C financial calculator or a computer spreadsheet program is used.

Example 12.4: Calculate the Yield-to-Maturity.

A 30-year bond with a par value of $1,000 can be purchased on the secondary market at the beginning of the year for 70 1/2. Its coupon rate is 10% and it will mature in 6 years from the date of purchase. What will its YTM be to the buyer if it is held to matu- rity?

Solution:

This is a 30-year bond (24 years old) that will mature in 6 years. The bond pays semi- annual interest, so there will be 12 interest payments prior to maturity. Each payment will be 10% of $1,000 divided by 2, or $0.10 \times \$1,000/2 = \$50$. The values are: $PV = -\$705$, $PMT_e = \$50$, $FV = \$1,000$, $n = 12$ periods. Using the HP-12C calculator, the interest rate $i = 9.15\%$. Since this is the semiannual rate, multiply it by 2 to get the annual nominal yield. The annual yield to maturity is thus 18.30%

The cash flow diagram for this transaction is:

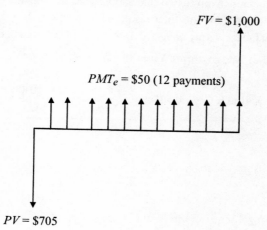

$FV = \$1,000$

$PMT_e = \$50$ (12 payments)

$PV = \$705$

The Internal Rate of Return (IRR) Method

The internal rate of return can also be used to calculate bond YTM. The values in the table below verify the results. Each pay period is six months. The NPV is zero when calculating the present value of the cash flows of Example 12.4 with a semiannual interest rate of 9.15%. Keying in the tabular values using the IRR procedure of the HP-12C (and a computer spreadsheet) also produces a semiannual interest rate 9.15%. These results are verified by the table below which shows the NPV of the year-by-year present value of the annual cash flows at an interest rate of 9.15%.

Pay Period	Cash Flow	PV @ 9.15%	Pay Period	Cash Flow	PV @ 9.15%
0	($705)	($705)	7	50	27.09
1	50	45.81	8	50	24.82
2	50	41.97	9	50	22.74
3	50	38.45	10	50	20.83
4	50	35.23	11	50	19.08
5	50	32.27	12	1,050	367.16
6	50	29.57			
				NPV =	0

YTM by the Approximate Method:

The approximate method involves two calculations. The results from these two calculations are averaged to produce the final result. The approximate method is quite a lengthy procedure, but the results are quite accurate. The first calculation is Formula 12.2.

Formula 12.2: Approximate Yield to Maturity (first calculation).

$$\frac{\text{Par Value} \times \text{Coupon Rate} + \dfrac{\text{Par Value} - \text{Price}}{\text{Years to Maturity}}}{\text{Price}}$$

Let's solve this for the data of Example 12.1.

$$\text{Par value} = \$1,000$$
$$\text{Coupon rate} = 10\%$$
$$\text{Price} = \$705$$
$$\text{Years to maturity} = 6 \text{ years}$$

$$\frac{\$1,000 \times 0.10 + \dfrac{\$1,000 - \$705}{6}}{\$705} = 0.2116$$

The second calculation is Formula 12.3 as follows:

Formula No. 12.3: Approximate Yield to Maturity (second calculation).

$$\frac{\text{Par Value} \times \text{Coupon Rate} + \dfrac{\text{Par Value} - \text{Price}}{\text{Years to Maturity}}}{\text{Par Value} - \dfrac{\text{Par Value} - \text{Price}}{\text{Years to Maturity}}}$$

$$\frac{\$1,000 \times 0.10 + \dfrac{\$1,000 - \$705}{6}}{\$1,000 - \dfrac{\$1,000 - \$705}{6}} = 0.1569$$

Averaging the results of Formulas 12.2 and 12.3:

$$\text{YTM} = \frac{0.2116 + 0.1569}{2} = 0.1842 \text{ or } 18.42\%$$

The approximate method's result of 18.42% is higher by only 0.11% percentage points to the exact yield of 18.30%. Any of the three methods are acceptable for calculating the YTM.

Calculating the Yield To Call (YTC):

The process is exactly the same as those demonstrated for the YTM except that the time duration to the callable date is used in place of the maturity date. Many bonds that have 30-year maturities are callable in 10-years after issue at the option on the issuer of the bond. There is usually a call price premium offered as an inducement for the buyers. It is common to see a price premium of, say, 103, which means that when called the redeemed amount will be $1,030 rather than $1,000 for each bond at maturity.

A bond buyer should always be aware of the call features. It is disconcerting to buy a bond on the secondary market at a premium that is called shortly thereafter. The bond holder then receives the call price, not the premium value paid. This results in a loss of principal. Calculating the yield to call will warn an investor against this type of loss.

Example 12.5: Calculate the Yield to Call

Marge is considering a bond purchase on the secondary market. The bond has a price of 115, a coupon rate of 13%, and is callable in ten years. The bond was issued eight years ago and is callable at a price of 102. The current market coupon yield for bonds is 8%. Is this a good buy considering that the bond can be called in two years.

Solution:

First notice that at a price of 115, the current yield is 11.3%. This looks to be an attractive buy. Let's calculate the yield to call to see if it is. The data for this bond are:

$$PV = -\$1,150$$
$$PMT_e = 0.13 \times \$1,000/2 = \$65$$
$$n = 2 \text{ years} \times 2 \text{ semiannual periods per year} = 4$$
$$FV = \$1020$$

Using the HP-12C we find the YTC is 5.90% This would not be a good buy in a bond market yielding 8%. The current yield's value is deceiving for this bond.

CALCULATING THE CHANGES OF BOND PRICES IN RESPONSE TO MARKETPLACE INTEREST-RATE CHANGES

As we stated earlier, bond prices change inversely to the changes in market interest rates. The price adjustment can be determined by the current yield formula.

Example 12.6: Calculate Bond Price As a Function of Interest Rate Change

Calculate the price of a 5% coupon bond necessary to compensate for a current yield of 7%. This bond has 10 years before it matures.

Solution:

$$\text{Current Yield} = \frac{\text{Annual Interest}}{\text{Current Price}}$$

Rearranging this formula to solve for the price we have:

$$\text{Current Price} = \frac{\text{Annual Interest}}{\text{Current Yield}}$$

Annual interest = $1,000 × 0.05 = $50
Current yield = 7%

$$\text{Current price} = \frac{\$50}{0.07} = \$714.29$$

This, however, will probably not be the market price of the bond. The current price calculated in this manner does not take into account the time value of money. If you were considering selling or buying this bond you would need to find the present value based on holding it to maturity, or the yield to call date if there is one. The calculation to determine the price of the bond of Example 12.6 should consider the yield to maturity of 7% because that is the competitive yield of like-kind securities. The data for this calculation are:

$$FV = \$1,000$$
$$n = 10 \times 2 = 20 \text{ periods}$$
$$PMT_e = \$25 \text{ semiannually}$$
$$i = 7.0\%/2 = 3.5\% \text{ semiannually}$$
$$PV = ?$$

Keying in theses values on a calculator we get $PV = -\$857.88$. A bond buyer or seller would be more realistic by setting this price as the acceptable market price for this bond.

Discounted and Premium Bond Prices

Discounted bonds have market prices lower than par value. This is caused by an increase in market interest rates relative to the bond's coupon interest rate. The price of a discounted bond is always less than the par value of $1,000. Conversely, *premium* priced bonds have market prices greater than par value. Premium prices occur when market interest rates have decreased relative to the coupon rate of the bond. Premium prices are always greater than par value.

Table 12.2 shows the market price values of discounted and premium priced bonds. The table is for a bond with a coupon yield of 7%. Two cases are shown: (1) a bond selling on the secondary market at a discount in a current market yield of 9%, and (2) a bond selling at a premium in a market yield of 5.5%.

Table 12.2
Time Path for the Prices of a 30-Year, 7% Coupon Bond, Par Value $1,000, Selling at a Discount and a Premium as It Approaches Maturity

Years to Maturity	Discount Bond Selling to Yield 9.0% Price	Premium Bonds Selling to Yield 5.5% Price
20.0	$816	$1,114
15.0	837	1,152
10.0	870	1,114
5.0	921	1,065
0.0	1,000	1,000

Let's verify a calculation for a bond that matures in 15 years, in which the buyer desires to realize a yield of 9%. The data are:

$FV = \$1,000$

$n = 15 \times 2 = 30$ periods

$PMT_e = \$35$ semiannually ($\$1,000 \times 0.07 / 2 = \$35$)

$i = 9.0\%/2 = 4.5\%$ semiannually (The coupon rate is 7%, but we want a 9% yield.)

$PV = -\$837$ by using a financial calculator or Formula 5.6

THE YIELD CURVES

Yield curves are important for understanding the characteristics of bonds sold on the secondary market. For a series of bond offerings, yield curves are not presented in financial periodicals. A bond buyer should construct such curves as an aid to their bond selection process.

The yield curve below shows of a series of AT&T bonds with different maturities taken at random from *The Wall Street Journal*. We selected these because they are all Aaa rated and thus are comparable. There are two curves on the graph: (1) the yield to maturity (YTM) and (2) the current yield.

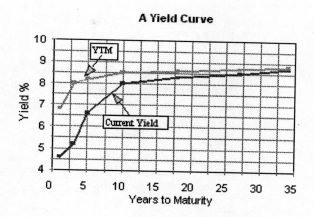

What These Yield Curves Show a Bond Investor

The yield curve shows that yields increase as the maturity dates increase. This is a pronounced characteristic of bonds. It is caused by the fact that bond buyers want higher yields as a hedge against potential interest rate fluctuations. For example, if interest rates should increase, the holder of short-term bonds can afford to wait and recoup their full principal. Holders of long-term bonds, however, would lose some principal if they had to sell in that market. Bond investors want the protection of higher yields in terms of greater annual earnings and/or a smaller loss of principal if they need to sell the bonds.

The curves show that it is not advantageous to buy the AT&T bonds having maturities larger than 10 years. The curves are relatively flat after 10 years. A bond with a 35-year maturity has only a 30-basis-point yield advantage compared to one with a 10-

year maturity. In short, there is no bonus for the interest rate risk of longer maturity bonds.

The yield curve also shows another advantage of plotting both the yield to maturity and current yield. Because financial periodicals quote only current yields, a potential buyer would not see the real advantage of buying some these bonds, whereas the yield curves in show that the desirable maturity range is between five to ten years. In this range the YTM is significantly higher than the current yield. The YTM is the rate of return to the investor. With knowledge of the current yield alone, a bond buyer would probably pass up the profitable 5-year maturity bond.

STRATEGIES FOR BUYING BONDS
ON THE SECONDARY MARKET

Bond buyers should calculate the YTM characteristics of bonds available on the secondary market. Resulting price trends reveal the best strategies for buying bonds on the secondary market. Table 12.3 and Figure 12.2 show the YTM characteristics of a prospective bond offering. Table 12.3 shows the YTM as a function of bond prices and maturities for a bond with an 8% coupon.

Table 12.3: Yield to Maturity for an 8% Coupon Bond

% of	Years to Maturity				
Face	5 Yr	10 Yr	15 Yr	20 Yr	25 Yr
106	6.58%	7.15%	7.34%	7.42%	7.47%
104	7.04%	7.43%	7.55%	7.61%	7.64%
102	7.52%	7.71%	7.78%	7.80%	7.82%
98	8.51%	8.30%	8.24%	8.21%	8.19%
96	9.02%	8.61%	8.48%	8.42%	8.39%
94	9.55%	8.92%	8.73%	8.64%	8.59%
92	10.09%	9.25%	8.99%	8.86%	8.80%

Table 12.3 shows an interesting trend: When bond prices are greater than the par value, the YTM increases as the years to maturity incmrease. For example, a bond bought at a premium price of 106 has a YTM of 6.58% for a 5-year maturity, but increases to 7.47% at a 25-year maturity. Conversely, bonds bought at a discount provide a greater YTM with shorter maturity periods. A 5-year maturity bond bought

at a discount price of 92 offers a YTM of 10.09% compared to 8.80% for a 25-year maturity.

In either case, bond yields become closer to the coupon rate as the maturity durations increase. Figure 12.1 shows these YTM trends for an 8% coupon bond with maturity durations of five and 25-years. The 5-year maturity duration plot is much steeper than the 25-year plot. A person buying a 5-year maturity bond enjoys a greater yield for discounted bond prices but a much larger yield penalty for bonds bought at a premium. The yields do not change as much throughout the bond price range if the premium price bonds are held for the 25-year term.

Figure 12.1

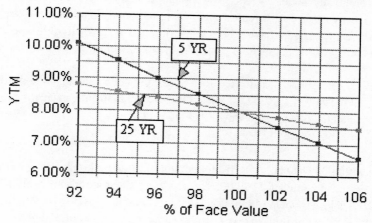

Based on the characteristics discussed above, the following two observations provide a good strategy for buying bonds:

1. The yield to maturity is maximized when buying discounted bonds with relatively short maturity durations.
2. Interest rate risk is minimized when buying premium price bonds with relatively long maturity durations.

IS IT ADVANTAGEOUS TO TAKE CAPITAL GAINS IN A DECREASING INTEREST-RATE BOND MARKET?

The answer here is "not usually." This question comes up when interest rates are dropping and the bond holders can realize a capital gain. In this situation a bond holder has an opportunity to sell his or her bonds, pay a capital gains income tax, and reinvest or spend the profits. Depending upon the options, selling may result in a smaller fixed income.

Example 12.7: *Sell and Take Capital Gains of Bonds?*

Josh—who is 65 years of age—owns 100 tax-free Muni bonds with a coupon rate of 10%. Josh bought the bonds 2 years ago (1985) at par, and they can be called in 10 years from the date of issue. Josh's reason for owning the bonds is to have a fixed annual income. Since interest rates have subsequently dropped to 5.50% for this type of bond, Josh could now sell his bonds for a price of 114. Josh is in the 28% marginal income tax bracket.

Fred, Josh's neighbor, has advised Josh to sell the bonds and take the profit. Fred told Josh that the gain is 14% ($14,000) and that is a great profit. Considering that Josh still needs an annual income, how good is Fred's advice?

Solution:

Josh paid $100,000 (100 bonds × $1,000 per bond) for these bonds. He has enjoyed a tax-free annual income of $10,000. Upon selling these bonds he would receive $114,000. Of this amount, $14,000 is subject to a capital gains tax. He would have to pay $3,920 (0.28 × $14,000) in taxes, leaving a net capital gain of $10,080.

In the current market, Josh can spend his profits and still buy $100,000 worth of bonds at the prevailing coupon rate of 5.50%. His annual income now would be:

$$INT = \$100,000 \times 0.055 = \$5,500$$

Since his previous income was $10,000, he would suffer a reduction of $4,500 per year if he sells, takes the capital gain, and reinvests the balance. The nontaxable present value of the loss of $4,500 for 8 years (the duration to call date) at 5.50% is about $28,000. This certainly doesn't offset the $10,080 after-tax profit Josh made by taking his gain. Fred's advice wasn't very good.

Now It's Your Turn:

1. As current interest rates increase, the price of existing bonds will decrease.
   a. True
   b. False

2. The par value and the face value of a bond is:
   a. $1,200
   b. $1,000
   c. $1,500

3. The semiannual interest payment of a bond is always the same even though the bond is traded at a discount or a premium.
   a. True
   b. False

4. If an 8% coupon bond has a call price of 102, what final payment will the bond holder receive for each bond when they are called?
   a. $1,000 + $80
   b. $1,020 + $80
   c. $1,020 + $40

5. A bond quoted as 89 1/8 actually costs:
   a. $891.25
   b. $890.13
   c. $890.25

6. Banks are not permitted to buy bonds with a Moody rating lower than BAA.
   a. True
   b. False

7. A 8% coupon bond was sold and settled on September 3. The IPDs are July 1 and January 1. How much accrued interest must the buyer pay the seller if 50 bonds were bought?
   a. $825.10
   b. $688.89
   c. $672.35

8. A IPO bond has a coupon of 7.5% and matures in 30 years. How many of these bonds must a person buy to receive a semiannual payment of $562.50?
   a. 18 bonds
   b. 12 bonds
   c. 15 bonds

9. A bond has a price of 77 1/4. How much money has this bond been discounted?
   a.$325.50
   b. $234.45
   c. $227.50

10. A bond quote indicates a net change of +1/4. What is the dollar amount of this change?
    a. $25
    b. $50
    c. $2.50

11. Bond A has a coupon yield of 7.25%, and bond B has a coupon yield of 8.00%. What is the difference in basis points between the yields of these two bonds?
    a. 50 basis points
    b. 70 basis points
    c. 75 basis points

12. What is the current yield of a bond that is priced at $90 with a coupon of 7.5%?
    a. 7.56%
    b. 8.03%
    c. 8.33%

13. A bond has a coupon interest rate of 4.5%, a price of 85, and matures in 3 years. What are the current yield (CY) and the YTM of this bond?
    a. CY 5.29%, YTM 8.24%%
    b. CY 5.29%, YTM 10 45%
    c. CY 4.92%, YTM 10.45%

14. To maximize the yield of a bond purchase, a good strategy would be to buy bonds with the following attributes:
    a. Par value with long maturities
    b. Discounted prices with short maturities
    c. Premium prices with long maturities

15. William owns 10 bonds having a coupon rate of 10%. Interest rates have dropped since William bought these bonds. The current coupon rate of IPO bonds is 8.50%. Based on commensurate *current yields* what would you expect William's bond holding would be worth on the secondary market?
   a. $11,765
   b. $12,351
   c. $10,000

16. Curt is considering buying William's bonds in question 15 above. However, Curt would like to actually realize 8.5% yield on his investment. How much should Curt be willing to pay for William's bonds? William's bonds are callable in 6 years at a price of 103.
   a. $12,542
   b. $10,876
   c. $10,000

17. A series of bonds for sale are shown by the table. These bonds are all Aaa rated and are noncallable.

Bond	Years to Maturity	Price
A 4.00s 98	3	91
B 6.00s 00	5	93
C 7 1/2 05	10	94
D 8.00s 10	15	96

Develop a yield curve and determine which bond you would buy to realize an attractive yield commensurate with interest rate risk. (Give yourself a pat on the back, this one is a lot of work.)
   a. A
   b. B
   c. C
   d. D

ANSWERS: 1.a, 2.b, 3.a, 4.c, 5.a, 6.a, 7.b, 8.c, 9.c, 10.c, 11.c, 12.c, 13.b, 14.b, 15.a, 16.b, 17.c

Analyzing U. S. Government Securities

LEARNING OBJECTIVES:

When you have completed this chapter, you will be able to:

1. Understand the pricing conventions of T-bills
2. Calculate discount, coupon-equivalent, and effective yields of T-bills
3. Calculate the prices and yields of T-bills, notes, and bonds offered on the secondary market
4. Use yield curves to determine how bond yields change with maturity duration
5. Calculate income and pricing conventions of Government National Mortgage Association (GNMA) investments
6. Calculate discount prices of zero-coupon bonds

U.S. Treasury bills, notes, and bonds are considered to be the safest investments in the world. The government uses these securities to finance the national debt. The government debt of approximately $5 trillion represents one of the largest money transactions taking place continuously.

Treasury bills are short-term investments. They provide a competitive return with other short-term options, are highly liquid by virtue of an active secondary market, and are essentially free of default risk. Treasury bills are considered the cornerstone of the money market.

Government National Mortgage Association certificates (GNMAs) are a very popular and safe fixed income investment. An investor can receive monthly amortization payments of principal and interest similar to those that banks receive when they lend mortgage money to homeowners.

Analyses of zero-coupon bonds are included here because they have some advantages to the investment community, but their shortcomings need to be recognized.

U.S. TREASURY BILLS

Treasury bills are government securities sold in minimum denominations of $10,000, and in $5,000 increments thereafter. T-bills are short-term U.S. Treasury IOUs which have maturities of 13, 26, and 52 weeks. They are sold at a discount from face value and are redeemed at full face value at maturity.

How the Original Prices of T-Bills are Determined

The prices of 13 week (91 day) and 26 week (182 day) T-bills are determined by an auction held every Monday throughout the year. Some thirty-six government securities dealers, reporting to the Federal Reserve Bank of New York, buy T-bills through a competitive bidding process. The auctions of the 52-week T-bills take place on the same day, but only once every four weeks.

The dealers of government securities are commercial firms engaged in all forms of securities sales. About ten of these dealers are banks; the remainder are brokerage firms. Some examples are the Bank of America, Citibank, the First National Bank of Chicago, and brokerage firms such as Salomon Brothers, Merrill-Lynch, and Bear Stearns.

T-bills do not pay an intermediate cash flow. The return to the investor is the difference between the face value and the discounted purchase price of the T-bills. Because T-bills are sold to the highest bidder at an auction, there is no stated interest rate that you will receive. You must determine the interest rate by a purchase prospective. A typical report taken from a local newspaper a day after the auction read as follows:

> The Treasury Department sold $12 billion in three-month bills where a $10,000 bill was sold for $9,891.10. A total of $21.1 billion six-month bills were sold where a $10,000 bill sold for $9,76.40. The average discount rate for the three-month bills was 4.31%, and 4.74% for the six-month bills.

Once the sale price is known from the auctions, you can calculate the discount yield, coupon-equivalent yield, and effective yield. The discount yield is calculated by a conventional formula that is flawed because it is not comparable to accurately calculated interest rates. It is, however, necessary to understand the conventions used for calculating the discount yield of T-bills in order to understand market practices, especially the pricing and yields of T-bills on the secondary market.

How T-Bills Yields Are Calculated

There are three ways that T-bill yields are interpreted:

1. Market participants use the *discount yield* (which is not an accurate discount) for buying or selling bills.
2. Market participants use the *coupon-equivalent yield* (bond equivalent) when measuring the rates of return commensurate with bond investments.
3. Financial managers and analysts use the *effective yield* to compare the true annual compound rate-of-return with other compound interest type of investment options.

The third method is, of course, the most realistic method we have advocated throughout this book. In our search for these conventions we found, much to our amazement, that very few books that we examined correctly describe the conventions of applying the three yields described above. Chances are that when you buy a book at your local bookstore the correct methods will not be described.

One book that does correctly describes the conventions used by the financial community is a college textbook entitled *Commercial Bank Financial Management* by Joseph F. Sinkey, Jr., published by Macmillan, 1986. A paragraph from Mr. Sinkey's book aptly describes the situation:

In the banking, finance, economics, and society in general, there are various conventions developed over time that frequently defy logical explanation. When we encounter such conventions we can attempt to change them, but usually we must cope with them. The alternative pricing conventions for Treasury bills represents one of these challenges. See how well you cope with the challenge.

The T-bill Discount Yield

Formula 13.1:T-Bill Discount Yield

$$Discount\ Yield = \frac{F-P}{F} \times \frac{360}{N}$$

Where:

F = face value (future value)of the bill at maturity

P = current market price (present value)

N = number of days to maturity

Reported T-bill yields are calculated by the discount yield Formula 13.1. This formula understates the yield. The flaw in Formula 13.1 is that the percentage gain is obtained by dividing the income received $(F - P)$ by the face value rather than by the initial price. It is also a simple interest formula with a 360-day year, but the value N is based not on a 360-days basis. It uses the actual number of days to maturity. *We reiterate that although Formula 13.1 is not a correct time value of money formula, it is the formula used by dealers when buying and selling T-bills.*

The Effective Yield

Formula 13.2: T-bill Effective Yield.

$$Effective\ Yield = \left(1 + \frac{F - P}{P}\right)^{\frac{365}{N}} - 1$$

Formula 13.2 is a compound interest formula. It is the proper formula to apply in determining the rate of return comparable to other investment opportunities.

The Coupon-Equivalent Yield

Formula 13.3: Coupon-Equivalent Yield

$$Coupon\text{-}Equivalent\ Yield = \frac{F - P}{P} \times \frac{365}{N}$$

The coupon- equivalent yield is a correct discount yield formula because the earned amount $(F - P)$ is divided by the invested amount P. It is an exact simple interest formula. Let's try an example to compare the yields by the three methods.

Example 13.1:

Calculate the discount, coupon-equivalent, and effective yields of a $10,000, 13-week Treasury bill that sold at the auction for $9,891.10.

Solution:

$F = \$10,000$
$P = \$9,891.10$
$N = 91$ days

$$\text{Discount yield} = \frac{10{,}000 - 9{,}891.10}{10{,}000} \times \frac{360}{91} = 4.31\%$$

$$\text{Coupon-equivalent yield} = \frac{10{,}000 - 9{,}891.10}{9{,}891.10} \times \frac{365}{91} = 4.42\%$$

$$\text{Effective yield} = \left(1 + \frac{10{,}000 - 9{,}891.10}{9{,}891.10}\right)^{\frac{365}{91}} - 1 = 4.49\%$$

These results are summarized in Table 13.1. Also included are the 26- and 52-week T-bills offered concurrently on the market with the 13-week T-bills. Observe the difference between the discount yields, coupon-equivalent yields, and effective yields. The discount yields understate both the coupon-equivalent yields and effective yields. You can appreciate the rationale for calculating the effective yields: If you were comparing investment options knowing only the discount yield values you might slight the T-bill option.

Table 13.1: Prices and Yields of a Typical Treasury Bill Auction

Time Period Days	F Face Value $	P Initial Price $	Discount Yield %	Coupon Equivalent Yield %	Effective Yield %
91	10,000	9,891	4.36	4.42	4.49
182	10,000	9,760	4.75	4.93	4.98
365	10,000	9,500	5.00	5.26	5.26

Also observe that all yields are greater as the maturity dates increase. For T-bills, this is a consistent trend. Longer maturity T-bills offer greater yields.

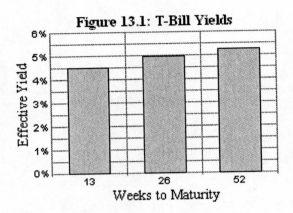

Figure 13.1: T-Bill Yields

T-BILL PRICES AND YIELDS
ON THE SECONDARY MARKET

Government securities dealers provide a very active secondary market. You can buy or sell previously owned T-bills offered by this market. To do so requires a knowledge of how the bills are priced and how this relates to yields.

The price at which dealers are willing to buy T-bills is called the *bid* price. The price at which they are willing to sell is called the *asked* price. The asked price is the price you can expect to pay, plus any commissions that may be charged.

These prices are those at which dealers trade large quantities of T-bills with each other or with other institutions. The difference between the bid and asked prices is the *spread*. The dealer's spread is the profit the dealer makes on the transaction. "Buy low and sell high" is the axiom that dealers live on in the T-bill market. Although the spread is only a few cents per $100 of bills traded, the enormous volume of T-bills, in the millions of dollars, traded amounts to a significant profit.

As already noted, dealers use the flawed discount yield Formula 13.1 to determine the bid and asked prices. Formula 13.1 has been rearranged to provide the price with a known yield. These formulas are necessary because it is the yields that are quoted on the secondary market, not the prices. Table 13.2 is an example of T-bill quotes taken from *The Wall Street Journal*.

Bid price:

$$P_{Bid} = F - y_{Bid} \times F \times \frac{N}{360}$$

Asked price

$$P_{Asked} = F - y_{Asked} \times F \times \frac{N}{360}$$

Table 13.2: Treasury Bills Quoted on the Secondary Market

Maturity	Days to Maturity	Bid	Asked	Chg.	Asked Yield
Dec 29 '94	176	4.65	4.63		4.80
Jan 12 '95	190	4.75	4.73		4.91
Feb 09 '95	218	4.85	4.83		5.02
Mar 09 '95	246	4.93	4.91		5.12
Apr 06 '95	274	5.05	5.03	-0.01	5.26
May 04 '95	302	5.15	5.13	-0.01	5.38
Jun 01 '95	330	5.19	5.17		5.44

The *asked yield* is calculated on the basis of the price using the coupon-equivalent yield formula. The *Chg* column shows the daily change based on the asked yield.

Let's calculate the bid and asked prices of the December 29, 1994 maturity T-bills shown on the first line of Table 13.2.

$$P_{Bid} = 100 - 0.0465 \times 100 \times \frac{176}{360} = 97.73$$

$$P_{Asked} = 100 - 0.0463 \times 100 \times \frac{176}{360} = 97.74$$

Asked yield:

$$\text{Coupon - equivalent yield} = \frac{100 - 97.74}{97.74} \times \frac{365}{176} = 4.80\%$$

Notice that the prices are expressed in percent. The face value is expressed as 100, and 97.74 as a percentage of the face value.

From these results, you can see that the higher bid yield provides a lower bid price to the dealer. The asked price is usually a few cents higher than the bid price. Thus the spread is one cent (97.74 − 97.73 = 0.01 or 1 cent per $100). This spread is the dealer's profit.

We have provided Table 13.3 to show the data listed in Table 13.2 converted to the prices and the effective and tax-free yields. Table 13.3 also shows the equivalent effective taxable yields for an investor who lives in a state that levies a state income tax. T-bills are exempt from state and local income taxes. In other words, a person in a marginal state tax bracket of 9% would have to earn 5.34% on a taxable investment to realize the 4.86% offered by the state-tax-free T-bill shown in row 1 of Table 13.3.

Because bid and asked prices are not published, investors must calculate them. The advantage of being able to calculate the effective yields is that it gives the investor a true comparison to other investment options. Notice in particular that the effective yields and the resulting tax-free yields are higher than the asked yields shown in Table 13.2. The reason that the effective yields are higher is due to the fact that effective yields are calculated by a true compound interest formula whereas the discount yields are not.

Table 13.3: Converted Treasury Bill Data

Maturity Dates	Bid Price	Asked Price	Spread	Effective Yield %	Effective* Yield %
Dec 29 '94	97.73	97.74	0.01	4.86	5.34
Jan 12 '95	97.49	97.50	0.01	4.98	5.47
Feb 09 '95	97.06	97.08	0.01	5.10	6.60
Mar 09'95	96.63	96.64	0.01	5.19	5.70
Apr 06 '95	96.16	96.17	0.02	5.34	5.87
May 04 '95	95.68	95.70	0.02	5.46	6.00
Jun 01 '95	95.24	95.26	0.02	5.52	6.07

* This is the equivalent state tax-free effective yield for an investor that has a marginal state tax rate of 9%. See Formula 10.3a for this calculation.

Testing the Effective Yield Formula

Since we have maintained that the effective interest rate is the true compound rate of return, let's test it with the T-bill data. Recall that the effective interest rate converts the nominal rate to an effective rate that has a compounding period of one year. If that is true, we should be able to accurately calculate the face (future value) of a given T-bill using the price (present value) and the number of days to maturity expressed as a fraction of one year. The formula for this calculation from Chapter 4 is:

Formula 4.1: Future Value of a Present Value Amount

$$FV = PV\,(1+i)^n$$

Example 13.2:

In Table 13.3, the first line has a T-bill that costs 97.74 (asked price) and a face value of 100. This would represent an actual cost of $9,774 and a face value of $10,000. The effective interest rate is 4.86%. The number of days to maturity is 176. Verify the accuracy of the effective interest rate in calculating the face value.

Solution:

$$PV = \$9774$$
$$n = 176 \text{ days or } 176/365 = 0.482 \text{ years}$$
$$i = 4.86\%$$

When we plug in these numbers into Formula 4.1, we should get a present value of $10,000.

$$FV = \$9,774\,(1+0.0486)^{0.482} = \$10,000$$

This illustrates the validity of the effective interest rate being the true annual interest rate equal to a nominal rate using daily compounding.

Buying Treasury Bills

We leave it to you to investigate the many ways of buying T-bills. In general, original issues can be bought by a treasury direct account or through a broker-dealer. On the secondary market it is necessary to buy from a broker-dealer. Remember that you pay the asked price when buying T-bills on the secondary market, whereas if you must sell your T-bills, you get the bid price for them. In addition there is a fee for buying T-bills from a broker-dealer. The fee to buy or sell T-bills is quite nominal. As of this writing, the brokerage firm of Salomon Smith Barney charges $35 per order regardless of the dollar value of the bills bought.

TREASURY NOTES AND BONDS

Treasury notes and bonds are very similar to corporate bonds. However, Treasury bonds are quoted differently in the financial publications. We will show how these differences relate to the analytical process. As is true of corporate bonds, an investor should analyze Treasury note and bond offerings before making a choice.

In addition to original issues, there is a very active secondary market. On the secondary market there are over 150 notes and bonds quoted daily in *The Wall Street Journal*. There is a wide variety of note and bond prices and yields, which depend on the maturity dates and market yield variations. Bond prices change daily. Much analysis is necessary to find the best returns for the duration of time over which you are interested in tying up your money.

Treasury Note and Bond Characteristics

Treasury notes differ from bonds in their lengths of maturity: Notes have maturities in the range of one to ten years, whereas Treasury bonds have maturities of ten to thirty years. The 30-year bonds are referred to as the "long bond" by the financial community. Treasury long bond prices are quoted daily in the media. A price increase means that the yield has decreased, and vice versa.

The payment you receive from owning notes and bonds is interest paid semiannually. Unlike Treasury bills, notes and bonds are not discounted. They sell for the face value (or the market value on the secondary market). They are sold in face value denominations of $1,000. The coupon rate is the nominal annual rate you will receive. For instance, the bond holder of a 7.50% coupon bond will receive a semiannual payment of $37.50. This payment is based on the face value, not on the market price paid for the bond.

Analyzing Notes and Bonds Sold on the Secondary Market

Table 13.4 shows how notes and bonds are quoted in the financial papers. Quotes are as of mid-afternoon. The quotes are slightly different than that of T-bills in that it is the bid and asked prices of bonds that are quoted rather than bid and asked yields, as is done for T-bills.

Treasury note and bond quotes also provide the asked yield, which is the yield to maturity based on the asked price. The bid and asked prices are expressed as the percent of face or par value; the number after the colon is the fraction in thirty-seconds. For example, the asked price of 90:09 is 90 plus 9/32, or 90.281. The actual price of this note is $902.81. The "n" after the date designates a Treasury note. Notice also that the bond price quotes are not expressed in dollars even though they are called the prices.

Table 13.4: Quotes of Government Notes and Bonds in The Wall Street Journal, July 8, 1994

Rate	Maturity (Mo/Yr)	Bid	Asked	Chg	Asked Yield
5 7/8	Feb 04n	90:07	90:09	+5	7.30
12 3/8	May 04	134:30	134:02	+8	7.32
12	May 04	133:29	134:01	+8	7.39
10 3/4	Aug 05	124:30	125:02	+6	7.40
12 1/2	Aug 09-14	143:04	143:08	+7	7.61

The bond in the last row of Table 13.4 shows a maturity date of August 09—14. The 09 date shown means that this bond is callable in August 2009, five years before the maturity date of August 2014. Not many government bonds are callable, but some are. For callable bonds, the asked yield shown by the table is calculated to the yield to call rather then the yield to maturity.

Calculating the Yields of Notes and Bonds

The formulas for calculating the current yield and the yield to maturity were presented in Chapter 12. Let's check the current yields and the yield to maturity of some values in Table 13.4.

Example 13.3:

On the secondary market, Phyllis bought the Treasury bond listed in the last row of Table 13.4. The asked price is 143:08, coupon yield is 12 1/2%, and call date is August 2009. What is the current yield and yield to call?

Solution:

The annual interest earned is: $\$1,000 \times 0.125 = \$125$

The price of the bond is: $10 \times 143 + \dfrac{8}{32} = \$1,432.50$

The current yield is:

$$\frac{\$125}{\$1432.50} = 0.0873 = 8.73\%$$

The yield to call:

$$PV = -\$1,432.50$$
$$FV = \$1,000$$
$$PMT_e = \$125/2 = \$62.50 \text{ per semiannual period}$$
$$n = 15 \text{ years} \times 2 = 30 \text{ semiannual periods}$$

Using a financial calculator to solve Formula 5.4:

$$i = 3.807\% \text{ semiannually, or } 7.61\% \text{ annually}$$

Because of the high coupon rate of 12 1/2%, this bond probably originated about 15 years ago. Phyllis will realize a current yield of 8.73%—well short of the coupon yield—because she paid a premium of $432.50 per bond. Since she will receive $1,000 in 15 years when the bond matures, she will suffer a capital loss equal to the premium value. Phyllis would probably do better to find a shorter-term bond to limit the interest rate risk.

Price Trends of Treasury Notes and Bonds

The price trends of notes and bonds are shown by a yield curve. The yield curve is a characteristic of the yields available across the spectrum of maturities at any given point in time. The increase of bond yields as the maturity dates extend is well known. The data shown in Figure 13.3 are taken from *The Wall Street Journal* of January 12, 1995.

The yield curve of Figure 13.3 is flatter than usual. Rising short- and intermediate-term interest rates and falling long-term interest rates result in a flattened curve. Between the maturities of three and ten years, the yields are fairly constant. The yields out to 30 years are not significantly higher. An investor does not have to buy securities with long maturities to get a good return. This fact offers an investor the opportunity to choose the maturity range with minimum interest rate risk. The only reason to buy long-term bonds is to lock in the prevailing interest rates. This would be the strategy if it is assumed that interest rates have peaked and will fall in the near future.

Figure 13.3: Gov. Bond Yields

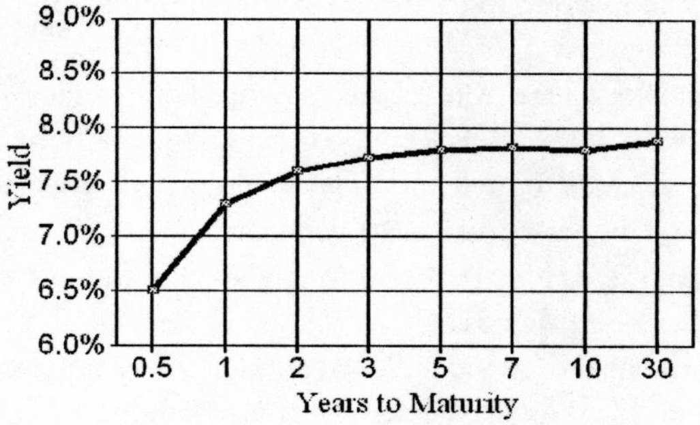

To further demonstrate yield-price trends, Table 13.5 provides a comparison of yields over a one year period for T-bills, notes, and bonds.

Table 13.5: Yield-Price Trends

Treasury	Yields		Percent
Securities	12/29/93	12/28/94	Increase
3-Month T-Bill	3.06%	5.60%	83%
6-Month T-Bill	3.21	6.51	102
2-Year Note	4.19	7.69	84
5-Year Note	5.10	7.80	53
10-Year Note	5.69	7.78	37
30-Year Bond	6.25	7.80	25

These yield changes took place because the comparable interest rate also changes throughout the year. It is obvious that interest rate changes influence the yields of short-term securities much more than those of long-term maturity securities.

GOVERNMENT NATIONAL MORTGAGE ASSOCIATION (GNMA) (GINNIE MAE CERTIFICATES)

The Government National Mortgage association is a corporation of the U.S. government functioning under the Department of Housing and Urban Development (HUD). A GNMA certificate represents a portion of a pool of home mortgages insured by the

FHA. GNMA certificates (called "Ginnie Maes") are guaranteed by the U.S. government. GNMAs are also referred to by the financial community as "Mortgage-Backed Securities."

Home buyers can take a loan from a bank, savings and loan, or stock broker. These financial organizations sell the loans to the government, which then pools this money and sells GNMA certificates to investors. The homeowners who secure the loans pay monthly principal and interest over a 30-year term. After deducting handling and insurance fees, the payments are "passed through" on a monthly basis to the investors who bought the GNMA certificates.

Since GNMAs are backed by the U.S. government, they are considered to be very safe investments. Individual GNMA certificates are bought through brokers in increments of $25,000. They can also be bought in lessor amounts through mutual funds or on the secondary market.

An incentive for buying GNMAs is the fact that they usually offer returns that are about half a percent higher than the returns on Treasury bonds.

How to Determine the Monthly Payment an Investor Will Receive

The monthly payments you would receive as a GNMA investor are determined by calculating the payment (PMT_e) of an ordinary annuity. The results of a $100,000 GNMA principal amount with an interest rate of 7% over a 30-year term is shown in Table 13.6. The method of constructing a mortgage schedule is presented in Chapter 14.

Table 13.6

GNMA Mortgage Payment Schedule			
Principal			$100,000
Interest rate			7.00%
Number of monthly payments			360
Monthly payment			$665
Month	Interest Payment	Principal Payment	Principal Balance
			$100,000
1	$583	$82	$99,918
2	$583	$82	$99,836
3	$582	$83	$99,753
4	$582	$83	$99,669
5	$581	$84	$99,585
6	$581	$84	$99,501
7	$580	$85	$99,416
8	$580	$85	$99,331
9	$579	$86	$99,245
10	$579	$86	$99,158
11	$578	$87	$99,072
12	$578	$87	$98,984
20	$574	$92	$98,267
21	$573	$92	$98,174

The monthly payment include both principal and interest. This has been confusing to some investors who did not realize that the payments are not similar to those of bonds, which pay interest only and the principal at maturity. The GNMA payments completely amortize the loan with monthly payments. There is no final balloon payment of principal.

If you invested $100,000 in the GNMA certificates of Table 13.6, you would receive a monthly payment of $665. However, homeowners with a mortgage in a GNMA pool will on average not keep their mortgages for 30 years. Due to such actions as refinancing, selling their homes, and some paydown of advanced mortgage payments, the average GNMA investment is completely amortized in about 12 years. This means that some monthly payments to the investor will consist of more principal than the schedule shows. The payments received are very well identified by the payment agent as to the amount of interest and principal received. The investor always receives all of his or her money back at the stated interest rate. This is guaranteed by the U.S. government.

Buying GNMAs on the Secondary Market

There is also a very active secondary market for GNMAs. This market is a little more complex than that of T-bills and bonds. A sampling of GNMA quotes on the secondary market taken from *The Wall Street Journal* of January 10,1995 is shown in Table 13.7.

Table 13.7
Mortgage-Backed Securities

Representative issues quoted by Salomon Brothers, Inc.

30-Year	REMAIN TERM (Years)	WTD-AVE LIFE (Years)	PRICE (DEC) (Pts-32nds)	CASH FLOW YIELD*
GNMA 6%	28.8	13.2	82-24	8.51%
GNMA 7%	28.3	12.1	89-06	8.73
GNMA 8%	27.9	10.8	95-06	8.90

*Based on projections from Salomon's prepayment model, assuming rates remain unchanged from current levels.

The information on the first line of this table means:

1. The GNMA was originally issued at a nominal interest rate of 6%.
2. It has 28.8 years remaining of the original 30 year term.
3. It has an expected life of 13.2 years wherein all of the principal and interest will be paid back over that time.
4. It will cost 82 24/32% of the remaining principal to buy this issue.
5. Salomon Brother's computer model predicts a cash flow yield of 8.51%.

Perhaps the best way to analyze the situation of buying a GNMA on the secondary market is to follow an example. We can use the information of Tables 13.6 and 13.7 to facilitate this.

Example 13.4:

Curt wants to buy about $100,000 worth of GNMA certificates on the secondary market. He has selected the offering in the second row of Table 13.7.

1. How much will he have to pay for those issues?
2. How much monthly payment will he receive on average?
3. What will his yield be on this investment?
4. How much money did the original investor who sold this GNMA lose?

Solution:

To determine the remaining principal, Curt is buying a GNMA that has 28.3 years remaining. This means that the GNMA has been in existence $30 - 28.3$ years $= 1.7$ years or about 20 months. If we go down Table 13.6 to 20 months, we find the remaining principal to be $98,267.

1. The price that Curt must pay for these certificates is 89-06/32% of the remaining principal or $0.89188 \times \$98,267 = \$87,642$. This is a discounted price of $10,625. Since interest rates must have increased and are currently higher than 7%, the market price for his GNMA decreased to account for the higher interest rate.
2. Curt will receive scheduled monthly payments of $665. Since Table 13.7 shows that the expected lifetime of this GNMA is 12.1 years in place of the remaining 28 years, additional principal will be received. We can calculate a uniform monthly payment based on the new conditions, as follows:

$$PV = \$98,267, \; n = 12.1 \text{ years} \times 12 = 145 \text{ months}, \; i = 7\% \div 12 = 0.5833\%$$

Using a financial calculator to solve Formula 5.4 for PMTe, we have:

$$PMT_e = \$1,000$$

3. To determine Curt's yield to maturity on this investment, we have:

$$PV = \$87,642, \; n = 145 \text{ months}, \; PMT_e = \$1,000, \; FV = 0, \; i = ?$$

Using a financial calculator:

$$i = 0.7738 \text{ per month or } 9.29\% \text{ per year}$$

The original investor lost $10,625 of the remaining loan principal of $98,267. He lost some money because he sold into a relatively high interest-rate market. If the original owner had not sold these GNMAs he would have continued to receive all of his money at an interest rate of 7%.

Although a lengthy process is involved in analyzing GNMAs offered on the secondary market, the rewards can be gratifying. GNMAs are good fixed income investments for someone who wants to receive a monthly income in which some principal is spent very slowly.

The largest complaint registered against GNMAs is the early payback of principal. Also some investors did not recognize that they were getting some principal back with each monthly payment. They were delighted with the monthly payments until they realized that their principal was being systematically reduced. If recognized, this should not be troublesome. An investor can reinvest this principal. The principal and interest payments received monthly are clearly identified.

ZERO-COUPON BONDS

Zero-coupon bonds are Treasury bonds that pay no interest until the bonds mature. Interest that would be paid semiannually is allowed to compound, and a lump sum is paid at maturity. Zero-coupon securities are always sold or traded at a discount from their face or maturity values because they offer no intermediate cash flows. Zero-coupon bonds got their start in 1985, when the Treasury offered Separate Trading of Registered Interest and Principal of Securities (STRIPS).

The major advantages offered by zeros are:

1. The full effect of compounding exists because the bond holder does need to reinvest the semiannual interest to realize compounding.
2. The rate of return is locked in throughout the maturity duration.
3. Being Treasury bonds, zero-coupon bonds are exempt from state and local income taxes.
4. Zero-coupon bonds are discounted so a bond holder pays a smaller present value amount to buy these bonds.
5. These bonds are not callable. If you buy them at a high coupon rate, they cannot be redeemed by the government in a low interest-rate market.

The major disadvantages are:

1. The interest earned each year is taxed in the year earned, even though this interest accrues but is not received in cash. Unless the bonds are held in a tax-deferred retirement account, bond holders must pay annual taxes out of their own pocket until the bonds mature.
2. Because of the non-interest-payment feature, zeros fluctuate more in price on the secondary market as market interest rates change.

From these advantages and disadvantages, it follows that zeros should be bought with the aim of holding them until maturity. They also should be held in a tax-deferred account. The buyer should be satisfied with the rate of return of the bonds and the maturity duration. These bonds fit very well in IRA or Keogh accounts.

How Zeros Compound

Being a bond, zeros compound semiannually. Bond buyers need to know how much they would have to pay now for the face value of the bond at maturity.

Example 13.5:

You bought $10,000 worth of zero-coupon bonds with a coupon interest rate of 6% and a maturity of 20 years. What is the discounted amount you would pay now to buy these bonds?

Solution:

$$FV = \$10,000$$
$$i = 6\% \text{ annually or } 3\% \text{ semiannually}$$
$$n = 20 \text{ years or } 40 \text{ compounding periods}$$
$$PV = ?$$

$$PV = \frac{FV}{(1+i)^n} \qquad \text{(Formula 4.1)}$$

$$PV = \frac{\$10,000}{(1+0.03)^{40}} = \$3,065.57$$

For a convenient reference, discounted present value prices of zero-coupon bonds are shown in Table 13.8.

Table 13.8: Discount Prices of a $1,000 Zero-Coupon Bond

Years to Maturity	Coupon Rate			
	4%	6%	8%	10%
5	$820	$744	$676	$614
10	673	554	456	377
15	552	412	308	231
20	453	307	208	142
25	372	228	141	87
30	305	170	95	54

These prices are rounded to the nearest dollar. If you were to buy a zero-coupon 30-year maturity bond at a coupon rate of 8%, the price you would pay today is $95 per bond. You would collect $1,000 per bond at the end of 30 years. These discounted prices do not include any broker commissions, which can vary according to the maturity dates.

Calculating the Compounding of Zero-Coupon Bonds Held in a Taxable Account.

This is a complex procedure that needs to be understood, because the return on your investment is compromised by the fact that you must take money out of your own pocket to pay taxes throughout the entire maturity duration. The investor in zero-coupon bonds thus foregoes an opportunity to earn compound interest on the taxes paid. Let's demonstrate this situation by an example.

Example 13.6:
Ralph is considering buying a zero-coupon bond bearing a coupon rate of 8%. The bond matures in 5 years. He would like to compare the after-tax rate of return between having the bonds held in a tax-deferred account versus a taxable account. Ralph can realize an after-tax return of 6% on his invested money. He has a marginal tax rate of 30%.

Solution:
The discounted amount of money for an 8% bond is $676. Table 13.9 shows the semi-annual taxable liability, the taxes paid at a 30 % marginal rate, and the future value of the tax payments over 10 semiannual periods.

Table 13.9: Financial Details of a 5 Year, 8% Zero-Coupon Bond Taxable Investment

5 Year Six-Month Periods	Before Tax Value	Taxable Liability	Taxes Paid @ 30%	FV of Taxes Paid
0	($676)			
1	703	$27	$8.10	$10.57
2	731	28	8.40	10.64
3	760	29	8.70	10.70
4	791	30	9.00	10.75
5	822	32	9.60	11.13
6	855	33	9.90	11.14
7	890	34	10.20	11.15
8	925	36	10.80	11.46
9	962	37	11.10	11.43
10	1000	38	11.40	11.40
Totals	$1000		$97.20	$110

The future net value to the investor of this bond is:

$$\$1,000 - \$110 = \$890$$

The annual rate of return for this investment in which the imputed interest is taxed and paid annually is:

$$FV = \$890$$
$$PV = \$676$$
$$n = 5 \text{ years}$$

$$i = \left(\frac{FV}{PV}\right)^{1/n} - 1 \quad \text{(Formula 4.1)}$$

$$i = \left(\frac{\$890}{\$676}\right)^{1/5} - 1 = 0.0565$$

$$= 5.65\%$$

If the bonds were held in a tax-deferred account, the net after-taxes return on this investment at maturity would be:

Taxable amount at maturity in 5 years = ($1,000 − $676)×0.30 = $97.20
Net to the bond holder = $1,000 − $97.20 = $903

$$\text{After-tax rate of return} \quad i = \left(\frac{\$903}{\$676}\right)^{1/5} - 1 = 0.0596 = 5.96\%$$

Although the taxable and tax-deferred rates of return were not greatly different, this is an example for instructional purposes only. To make a valid comparison, you need to repeat this exercise using conditions specific to your current financial conditions.

Now It's Your Turn:

1. The original price of T-bills is determined by:
   a. An auction
   b. The discount yield formula
   c. The effective yield formula

2. Investors in T-bills receive their profit only when the T-bills mature.
   a. True
   b. False

3. At an auction, the average selling price of 26-week T-bills was $9,685. What is the discount yield, coupon-equivalent yield, and effective yield of these T-bills?
   a. 5.86%, 5.89%, 5.95%
   b. 6.23%, 6.24%, 6.53%
   c. 6.23%, 6.52%, 6.63%

4. If an investor bought five of the T-bills in question 4, how much would she pay initially and how much would she receive at maturity?
   a. $50,000, $45,000
   b. $48,425,$10,000
   c. $48,425, $50,000

5. How much interest did the investor of question 4 receive from the investment?
   a. $1,575
   b. $1,635
   c. $2,575

6. On the secondary market, a T-bill is offered at an asked yield price of 5.25%. This issue will mature in 263 days. What is the selling price and the asked yield of this issue?
   a. 96.86, 5.54%
   b. 96.16, 5.54%
   c. 96.16, 5.63%

7. What price would a dealer have to pay for each T-bill of question 6 if the bid price yield was 5.27%? What would your effective yield be if you bought this issue at the asked price?
   a. 97.15, 5.58%
   b. 96.15, 5.60%
   c. 96.18, 5.60%

8. A Treasury note has an asked price of 90:04. What is the dollar price of each of this note?
   a. $910.25
   b. $9,012.25
   c. $901.25

9. A Treasury bond has a coupon rate of 12 1/2%, an asked price of 125:09, and matures in 15 years. What are the current yield and the yield to maturity of this bond?
   a. 9.98%, 9.33%
   b. 12.5%, 10.5%
   c. 9.33%, 9.23%

10. *The Wall Street Journal* quoted a Treasury bond maturity Mo/Yr as Feb 06-15. At what date can this bond be called?
    a. Feb of the year 2014
    b. Feb of the year 2006
    c. It is not callable

11. GNMA's payments are guaranteed by the federal government.
    a. True
    b. False

12. On the secondary market the U. S. government will guarantee that buyers of an initial issue GNMA will be able to sell the issue before maturity and not lose money.
    a. True
    b. False

13. If you bought a new issue GNMA for $25,000 that has an interest rate of 8.25% and a maturity of 30 years, what monthly payment would you receive? Of the first payment how much is interest? (Neglect the small commission the broker would get for this issue.)
    a. $172.56, $154.78
    b. $187.82, $171.88
    c. $189.98, $175.76

14. If the expected lifetime of the GNMA of question 13 above is 12 years, what might be an average monthly payment you would receive for 12 years?
    a. $274
    b. $325
    c. $256

15. Robert has an opportunity to buy a GNMA on the secondary market. The current principal balance of this issue is $98,984 and the price is quoted as 89-08. Neglecting broker commission, how much would Robert have to pay for this issue?
    a. $98,984
    b. $88,343
    c. $91,343

16. The GNMA of question 15 has a interest rate of 8% and was originally a 30 year GNMA. What regularly scheduled monthly payment will Robert receive?
    a. $833.56
    b. $766.76
    c. $733.76

17. John bought 20 initial-issue zero-coupon Treasury bonds. These bonds have a coupon rate of 7.50% and mature in 25 years. How much did John have to pay for these bonds?
    a. $4,659.97
    b. $3,174.13
    c. $4,578.87

ANSWERS: 1.a, 2.a, 3.c, 4.c, 5.a, 6.b, 7.b, 8.c, 9.a, 10.b, 11.a, 12.b, 13.b, 14.a, 15.b, 16.c, 17.b

Analyze Your Home Mortgage and Save Money

14

LEARNING OBJECTIVES:

This chapter will show how to apply the math to:

1. Calculate annual percentage rates (APRs)
2. Evaluate and select the best available mortgage loan
3. Decide when and how you should refinance your mortgage
4. Develop and use a mortgage loan payment schedule
5. Save money by painlessly prepaying your mortgage
6. Understand and monitor changes to adjustable rate mortgages
7. Calculate balloon payments
8. Understand and avoid negative amortization
9. Understand and calculate reverse annuity mortgages (RAMs)
10. Understand why biweekly payment mortgages are a gimmick

Buying a home is one of the largest and perhaps the best investment you will ever make. As such, the debt secured by a mortgage is probably the largest debt you will have to pay throughout your lifetime. Mortgage loan terms are usually for 15 or 30 years. The debt is an ordinary annuity in which a principal sum is paid by a lending institution and the mortgage is retired by a uniform series of payments made by the owner over the life of the loan term.

The interest paid over the term of the loan is considerably greater than the principal amount of money borrowed. The only way to reduce the amount of interest paid—short of securing a reduction in the interest rate—is to reduce the term of the loan. For an existing loan, this is accomplished by making principal payments in additional to the regularly scheduled mortgage payments.

WHAT IS THE ANNUAL PERCENTAGE RATE (APR)?

The first step in securing a mortgage is, of course, to find the lowest interest rate commensurate with the settlement costs. When you look for a loan, you will have to consider two different interest rates. The first is the *contract rate* and the second is the *annual percentage rate* (APR). The APR is a rather artificial interest rate that is supposed to provide the interest rate charged for the loan by including the total cost of the loan.

The federal Truth-in-Lending Act (Regulation Z) requires the lender to submit to the borrower a truth-in-lending statement within three days after completion of the application. This document must disclose the APR.

Settlement Costs

When you seek a loan, the actual principal required to finance the home is not the only amount of money involved. The settlement costs must also be paid. The settlement costs (more commonly called the closing costs) consist of the origination and discount points, and all the other fees such as title insurance, appraisals, and a host of administration fees, etc. The origination and discount points are expressed as a percentage of the contract amount of the loan.

The total settlement costs are significant when securing a home mortgage. For example suppose the total of the origination and discount points is 2 points for a loan of $100,000. The value of the points would be $2,000 ($100,000 × 0.02 = $2,000). The balance of the settlement costs for a $100,000 loan is on the order of $2,000, which constitutes a total settlement cost of $4,000. Add this to the original loan amount and the total amount you are actually financing for this loan is $104,000.

Calculating the APR

The Truth-in-Lending Act does not define specifically how the APR is to be calculated. Moreover, it is a value that is calculated specifically for each loan. The following example shows you how it should be calculated. It is a method that requires the use of a financial calculator.

Example 14.1: Calculating the APR.

Suppose you are considering a 30-year loan of $100,000 with a stated contract interest rate of 8.00%. There is an origination fee of 2 points and $2,000 in other closing costs for a total of $4,000. The amount you will actually borrow to complete this loan is

$104,000, but the original loan amount necessary to finance your home is $100,000. The procedure is:

1. Calculate the monthly payment you will make for the total amount financed at the stated interest rate and term ($104,000 at 8% for 30 years).
2. Calculate the interest rate (APR) by using the original loan principal ($100,000) and the monthly payment of step 1.

Solution:

1. Calculate the monthly payment:

$$FV = 0, n = 360, PV = \$104,000, i = 8.00\% \div 12 = 0.6667\%$$
$$\text{The calculated monthly payment } PMT_e = \$763.12$$

2. Calculate the APR by keying the following in the financial calculator:

$$FV = 0, n = 360, PMT_b = -763.12, PV = 100,000$$

3. Press the "i" key and read a monthly interest rate of 0.7015. This is a nominal *annual percentage rate* of $12 \times 0.7015 = 8.42\%$.

Effectively, this calculation is for a monthly payment the takes into account the added principal ($104,000) due to the closing costs, but the interest rate APR considers that you borrowed only $100,000. From this example you can see that the additional closing cost of $4,000 added 0.42% to the interest rate of your loan.

What Does the APR Really Mean?

We have found that most lenders do not follow the Truth-in-Lending Act's definition of the APR. Some lenders only include the points, claiming that the balance of the costs are charged by others. In Example 14.1 above, you might be comparing a 8.42% APR of a lender who calculated it correctly versus a lender who only included the points. The latter results in an APR of the 8.21%. Moreover, when lenders advertise an APR they tend to minimize the balance of settlement costs, so you might be in for a surprise when you negotiate the loan.

In our opinion, the best way to compare loans is to ignore the advertised APR. You should critically examine the contract interest rate and all charges in detail and then calculate the APR yourself.

HOW TO COMPARE A NO-POINTS VS. A POINTS LOAN

When financing or refinancing a home mortgage, some lenders offer a no-points loan. The lenders of no-points loans charge a higher contract interest rate to compensate. A no-points loan can be advantageous, especially if you suspect that interest rates are going down in the future and that you might want to refinance soon. Under this circumstance, you can walk away without having incurred the additional cost of points added to your loan balance. The downside to this is that if you keep a no-points loan for a long term you will incur a cost penalty. We will explain this, because it is a trade-off that needs to be analyzed.

Consider the following two loans, Loan 1 charges points, Loan 2 does not.

	Loan 1	Loan 2
Loan amount	$150,000	$150,000
Contract interest rate	7.125%	7.625%
Term (years)	30	30
Points	2.0	None
Additional closing costs	$2,000	$2,000

We can calculate the APR of these loans and compare them as follows:

	Loan 1	Loan 2
Cost of points	$3,000	0
Additional closing costs	$2,000	$2,000
Total amount financed	$155,000	$152,000
Monthly payments (calculated)	$1,044.26	$1,075.85
APR	7.46%	7.76%

The APR of Loan 1 is calculated with the following parameters:

$$PV = \$150,000, \ n = 360 \text{ months}, \ PMT_e = -\$1,044.26, \text{ and the } FV = 0$$

Using the HP-12C financial calculator, we have:

$$i = 0.6213\% \text{ per month or } 7.46\% \text{ per year}$$

In the above example, the lender chose a contract rate of 7.625% for Loan 2 rather then the market rate of 7.125% of Loan 1. The lender did this in order to recover the $3,000 cost of points in about seven years. Since the average homeowner sells his or her home in about seven years, the lender would have not recouped the discounted value of the points if the lender had chosen to recover the cost of the points over the 30-year loan term. Had the lender discounted the point value over a 30-year term, the contract interest rate of Loan 2 would have been 7.420% instead of 7.625%. This would have produced an APR of 7.56%.

Assuming that the borrower took Loan 2 and kept it in place for 30 years, we calculate that the present value of the points due to the larger interest rate would be $6,600. You can see that this is a tricky business. You need to evaluate the real cost of the no-points loan in comparing the two options. It is obvious that you should pay the points of Loan 1 unless you expect to refinance or sell your home in a relatively short time.

WHEN IS IT ADVANTAGEOUS TO REFINANCE?

This is a question that depends on many circumstances surrounding your existing loan situation. When interest rates go down, there is usually a flurry of refinancing. However, refinancing is not always advantageous. Many times homeowners will find that, due to the refinancing costs, their loan principal is even larger after refinancing. Moreover, the homeowners lose money if they sell their homes before the savings in the monthly payments recoup the cost of refinancing.

Because the predominance of loans have significant closing costs, the analytical process leading to a decision will be explored here.

The Simple Payback Analysis

This analysis is easy to perform. The process calculates the time it takes for the monthly savings to pay back the closing costs of the new loan.

Example 14.2: A Decision to Refinance

The Wilsons currently have a $125,000, 30 year mortgage at an interest rate of 9.50%. They intend to live in their home another six years and then retire to Arizona. They have had this loan for five years. Interest rates have dropped and they are offered a new 30-year mortgage with an interest rate of 8.50% and 2.5 points. Their current mortgage payment is $1,051.07 and their current loan balance is $120,301. Should they refinance?

Solution:

The closing cost of 2.5 points is $0.025 \times \$120,301 = \$3,008$, plus $2,000 in other items such as title insurance, and appraisal fees, etc., for a total closing cost of $5,008. Now the new mortgage principal will be:

$$\$120,301 + \$3,008 + \$2,000 = \$125,309$$

The new loan will have monthly payments of $963.52. The new monthly payment is a monthly savings of:

$$\$1,051.07 - \$963.52 = \$87.55 \text{ per month}$$

The time required for the monthly savings to recover the closing costs incurred by the new loan is:

$$\frac{\$5008}{\$87.55 \text{ per month}} = 57.2 \text{ months}$$

Since the Wilsons intend to live in their home for 72 months, this loan looks good.

Although the payback analysis is the most frequently used method it has a serious flaw. It does not consider the time value of money. In some cases it can lead to a wrong decision. A more useful analysis considers the present value of the closing costs savings.

Present Value Analysis for Refinancing

Suppose that the Wilsons in Example 14.2 earn a return of 12%, income tax-deferred, on their money invested in a variable annuity. Does a monthly savings of $87.55 over six years result in a present value larger than the closing costs?

Calculate the present value of the monthly savings.

$$i = 0.12/12 = 0.10, \, n = 72 \text{ months}, \, PMT_e = \$87.55, \, PV = ?$$

Using Formula 5.1 of Chapter 5,

$$PV = \$4,478$$

In view of the fact that the Wilsons will only keep the new mortgage six years, refinancing is not advantageous. The cost of refinancing is $5,008 and the present value of the savings is $4,478.

THE CONVENTIONAL FIXED-RATE MORTGAGE

A fixed-rate mortgage is a loan that has a contract rate of interest that cannot be changed throughout the term of the loan. To understand a fixed-rate mortgage, it is useful to calculate the monthly mortgage payment schedule. This schedule is useful to homeowners who would like to save money on their mortgages.

Calculating the Mortgage Payment Schedule

Table 14.1 shows a mortgage schedule. The first 12 months and the last 5 months of the 360-month payment schedule are shown. We will construct such a schedule and explain what each component means.

Consider the following mortgage data:

Term...............................	30 years
Principal..........................	$100,000
Points.............................	2.0%
Other closing costs..........	$2,000
Contact interest rate.........	7.50%

Step 1. The first step is to determine the monthly mortgage payments. We can use Formula 5.1 of Chapter 5 or Table 7.5 of Chapter 7 to find the monthly payments. Using Table 7.5 we have:

$$PMT_e = \$104{,}000 \times 0.006992145 = \$727.18$$

Make sure you use the *contract interest rate* for this calculation. The APR is for comparison purposes only. We now have the first four values of Table 14.1.

Step 2. The next step is to find the interest and principal payments of each monthly payment. Notice from Figure 14.1 that the sum of any monthly principal and interest payment always equals the monthly payment. For example, for the first payment is the sum of $650.00 + $77.18 = $727.18.

To calculate the interest payment each month, multiply the monthly interest rate times the principal balance of the previous month. The first month's interest payment is:

Monthly interest = 0.075/12 = 0.00625
The previous month's balance = $103,922.82
The number of months $n = 1$
$INT = PV \times i \times n$
$INT = \$103{,}922.82 \times 0.00625 \times 1 = \$649.52$

The principal payment is thus $727.18 − $649.52 = $78.66. This principal is subtracted from the previous month's principal balance to give the next month's principal balance. The second monthly balance is: $103,922.82 − $77.66 = $103,845.16. To complete the schedule, this process continues until all 360 monthly payments have been calculated.

Table 14.1

Home Mortgage Amortization
Payment Schedule

Loan principal			$104,000
Nominal interest rate			7.50%
Total number of monthly payments			360
Monthly payment			$727.18

Month	Interest Payment	Principal Payment	Loan Balance
			$104,000.00
1	$650.00	$77.18	103,922.82
2	649.52	77.66	103,845.16
3	649.03	78.15	103,767.00
4	648.54	78.64	103,688.36
5	648.05	79.13	103,609.23
6	647.56	79.63	103,529.60
7	647.06	80.12	103,449.48
8	646.56	80.62	103,368.86
9	646.06	81.13	103,287.73
10	645.55	81.63	103,206.10
11	645.04	82.14	103,123.95
12	644.52	82.66	103,041.29
356	22.30	704.88	2,863.85
357	17.90	709.28	2,154.56
358	13.47	713.72	1,440.84
359	9.01	718.18	722.67
360	4.52	722.67	0.00

If you desire a mortgage schedule—and we highly recommended it—you can get one from your lender, usually for a fee. With a computer spreadsheet program, a mortgage schedule can be done in about twenty minutes. (See Chapter 19 for spreadsheet applications.) One advantage of the computerized schedule is that once you have a schedule, individual values such as the term, principal, and interest rates can be changed and all the other values change accordingly. This is a valuable tool for comparing various options and also for analyzing "what if" scenarios.

HOW TO SAVE MONEY ON YOUR MORTGAGE

It is apparent that the principal paydown amount of the loan at the beginning of the term is quite small. By the end of the term, the principal payments are larger. Figure 14.1 shows the time-value plot of the amortized loan. The upper curve shows how a home-owner's equity would grow assuming an average appreciation rate of 3% per year. The lower curve shows the amortized loan balance going to zero in 30 years. Observe that the loan balance only drops $25,000 in the first 15-year period but $75,000 during the last 15-year period. It is obvious that making additional principal payments early in the loan is an effective method to reduce the total interest paid to amortize a loan.

Figure 14.1

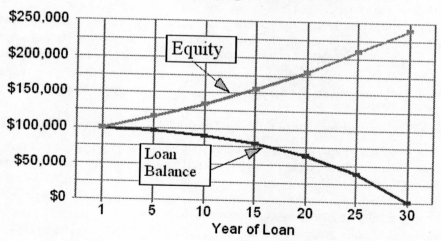

If you were the borrower of the loan in Figure 14.1 and made all 360 payments, you would pay a total of $265,420 ($727.18 × 360 = $265,420) to retire the loan. Of that total, $161,420 is the amount of interest paid. But suppose you systematically made an additional principal payment each month. Most banks and lenders allow this without penalty. Referring to Table 14.1, you could make the first monthly payment of $727.18, and in addition send with it next months' principal payment of $77.66. By doing this you have jumped ahead to the third monthly payment. Now draw a line through the second monthly payment: you will never have to make that interest payment. You have saved an interest payment of $649.52. Then do that each month. Make the payment for that month and send with it the payment of the shaded month. Cross off the shaded month's payments.

Over the first year, you will have saved the interest payments for months 2, 4, 6, 8, 10, and 12. Total interest saved is $3,882.25. To do this, you only had to make additional principal payments of $480 over the first year period. You have thus shortened the mortgage term by six months at this point in the loan process.

Making extra principal payments in the early part of the loan is easy because the principal payments are relatively small. You would not want to do this for the latter months of the loan. In Table 14.4, the last five principal payments are relatively large, so that you would not save much by sending additional principal payments.

One advantage to this method of advanced payments is that you can choose any month to do this. If you are pressed for funds in any given month, you can skip the added principal payment. However, you must always make the regularly scheduled payment of $727.18 every month, even though you have made advanced payments in the past.

If you had selected a 15-year loan term, you would save interest but have to make higher payments every month. The 30-year loan with advanced principal payments gives you flexibility. You can make these payments as long as you like, stopping the practice when the principal payments become too large. Each month that you make a principal payment you are in effect getting a 7.50 % return on your money.

Use the Mortgage Schedule to Keep Track of Annual Interest Payments

For income tax purposes, you can deduct your mortgage interest payments *if you itemize deductions*. Referring to Table 14.1, the total interest payments the first year total is $7,468.74. This is true unless you sent in advanced principal payments. You would, of course, have to calculate the total based on the actual amount paid during the taxable year. If you claim the annual interest paid on your income tax schedule A, it is deducted from your adjusted gross income for a tax saving to you of $2,091.24 (28% of $7,468.74) if you are in the 28% marginal tax bracket. (Marginal tax brackets are explained in Chapter 10.)

Due to this tax deduction, your actual first-year annual cost of the mortgage is reduced to $6,297.33 from the total first year payments of $8,390.57.

SHOULD YOU PAY DOWN YOUR MORTGAGE?

Systematically or wholly paying down your mortgage principal can save you a significant amount of interest. But is it wise to pay down a mortgage even if you should come into some money to do so? Some advisors recommend carrying a large mortgage and never paying it off. This provides a large income-tax deduction. Also they assert that you can certainly can get a larger return on your investments than the rate you are paying for your mortgage.

Suppose, however, that you come into some additional money or a significant raise and can afford to make much larger mortgage payments or even retire your mortgage now. Another option is to invest this new money for income or growth.

Much of this decision is in the eyes of the beholder. To make an informed decision, you at least need to compare the rate of return of your investments versus the economic benefit of paying down your mortgage. Since mortgage interest is deductible, the after-tax rate of your mortgage is the real rate you are paying on your mortgage principal. This is comparable to the after-tax rate of return you expect from your investments or the tax-free rate of return from Munis. Recall from Chapter 10, that the formula to calculate after-tax and before-tax rates is the following:

$$\frac{\text{After - Tax Rate}}{(1 \; - \; \text{Marginal Tax Rate})} = \text{Before - Tax Rate}$$

Let's see how this applies.

Example 14.3: Pay Down the Mortgage or Invest the Money?

John and Mary have a home mortgage bearing an interest rate of 8.00%. Mary has inherited $50,000 and is considering whether to use it to pay down their mortgage or invest it in the equity mutual funds. John and Mary are in the 30% marginal tax bracket. John and Mary feel that they can realize a 12% before-tax overall rate of return in their mutual fund. How does the investment rate of return compare to the rate that of John and Mary pay for their mortgage?

Solution:

The after-tax equivalent rate of John and Mary's mortgage is:

$$\text{Before tax-rate} = 8.00\%$$
$$\text{Marginal tax-rate} = 30\%.$$
$$\frac{\text{After - Tax Rate}}{(1 - 0.30)} = 8.00\%$$
$$\text{After-tax rate} = 5.60\%$$

The after-tax rate of return of John and Mary's taxable mutual fund investment is:

$$12\%(1 - 0.30) = 8.40\%$$

The after-tax rate of return of John and Mary's stock market investments is considerably higher that the cost of money that pays for their mortgage. A wise decision at this time is to invest the money in the mutual fund instead of paying down the mortgage.

THE ADJUSTABLE RATE MORTGAGE (ARM)

This *adjustable rate mortgage* (ARM) is a mortgage in which the interest rate can change periodically according to the changes of the interest rate of some known economic index. Although the process of keeping track of the effects of the interest rate changes of an ARM can be tedious, it is quite important to do so. There have been many reports of mistakes made by lenders which have cost the borrowers considerable sums of money. The following is an excerpt reported in an article by Broderick Perkins in The San Jose Mercury News:

> In recent years, the U.S. General Accounting Office and the Resolution Trust Corporation all found errors, mostly overcharges on ARMs. Depending upon the survey, over charges ranging from $300 to $32,000 were found on 25 percent of the loans. Under the Federal Truth-in-Lending Act, consumers can recover money from erroneous overcharges.

How Does This Process Work?

A current information table in your local newspaper for ARMs might read like this:

Table 14.2: Adjustable Rate Mortgages
(30-year loans of $207,000 or less)

Adjustable Conforming

Lender	Start Rate	Index	Margin	First Adjust. Period	Regular Adjust. Period	Period CAP	Life CAP
Bank A	3.950	11D	2.300	3M	1M	NEG	11.450
Bank B	5.750	6CD	2.625	6M	6M	1.00	11.750

Table 14.2 stipulates the conditions that have the following definitions:

Adjustable conforming means that the maximum amount of the loan is $207,000.

Start rate is the initial interest rate charged, usually artificially low to attract customers. It changes at the first adjustment period.

Index identifies the item that determines how much an ARMs interest rate adjusts. The 11D is the 11th District cost of funds; 6CD is a six-month certificate of deposit.

Margin is a set rate, expressed as a percentage, which is added to the index rate of interest to determine the new adjusted rate. The margin is effective immediately after the first adjustment period.

Adjustment period is how often the interest rate can be changed. The "first adjustment period" means that the start rate will change after that initial period. Thereafter, the interest rate can be adjusted on the stated regular period.

Period CAP is the maximum allowable interest rate change permitted per adjustment period. For Bank B of Table 14.2, the maximum change is 1%. For Bank A the change "NEG" indicates that there is no rate cap and the loan may cause negative amortization. (Negative amortization is explained in the next section.)

Life CAP is the maximum interest rate that can ever be charged over the life of the loan. Let's see how interest rate adjustments are calculated.

Example: 14.4: Calculating Adjustable Rate Mortgage Adjustments

Using the facts of Table 14.2, Bank A, Mary has a loan of $150,000. Her first three monthly payments are calculated at $711.81 for a start interest rate of 3.950% and a 30-

year loan. Let's assume that the interest rate for the 11th District cost of funds (index) is 4.975%. The next step is to calculate the loan balance at the end of the three-month period.

The loan balance after three months using the method to calculate a balloon payment explained in Chapter 5 is:

$PMT_e = -711.81$, $i = 3.950\% \div 12 = 0.32925\%$, $PV = \$150,000$, $n = 3$ months:

FV of the loan balance is found to be $149,343.68

$$\text{After the initial period, the new adjusted rate} = \text{Index} + \text{Margin}$$
$$\text{New adjusted rate} = 4.975 + 2.300 = 7.275\%$$

Now we calculate the new monthly payment to be $1,026.25 based on the balance of $149,343.68 at the beginning of the fourth month and 357 months remaining on the loan. The loan balance at the beginning of the fourth month would be:

$$INT = 0.07275/12 \times \$149,343.68 = \$905.40$$
$$\text{Principal} = \$1,023.72 - \$905.40 = \$118.32$$
$$\text{Loan balance} = \$149,343.68 - \$118.32 = \$149,225.35$$

Now assume the 11D cost of funds went up to 5.000% by the fourth month. The new rate would be:

$$\text{Third month rate} = 5.000 + 2.300 = 7.30\%$$

The new monthly payment would be $1024.53, based on a previous loan balance of $149,225.35 and a remaining loan term of 356 months.

This process goes on each month. If interest rates should decrease, Mary's monthly interest rate will also decrease. This process goes on for as long as she has the loan. The table below summarizes the results for the first five months of Mary's adjustable rate mortgage.

Adjustable Rate Mortgage

Month	Interest Rate	Loan balance	Monthly Payment
0		$150,000.00	
1	3.950	149,781.94	$711.81
2	3.950	149,563.17	711.81
3	3.950	149,343.68	711.81
4	7.275	149,225.35	1,023.72
5	7.300	149,108.61	1,026.25

For those who cannot or do not choose to calculate the progress of their ARM loan, there are organizations that will provide this service for a fee.

What Is the Maximum Payment of This ARM?

Suppose you have had the Table 14.2 Bank A loan and the 11D cost of funds exceeded 9.15%. (This, of course, probably would not happen in such a short of a period of time.) The maximum interest rate that the lender can charge is 11.450%. The calculated maximum monthly payment would now become be $1,473.35 based on a remaining term of 355 months. This payment could not increase regardless of any additional 11D interest rate increases. It could go down if the 11D cost of funds should go below 9.15%.

WHAT IS NEGATIVE AMORTIZATION?

Negative amortization is a variation of the ARM. Negative amortization occurs when the holders of an adjustable rate mortgage experience an interest rate increase but do not want their monthly payments to increase. For the monthly payments to remain constant, the deficiency in interest is paid by being adding to the principal balance. The principal balance thus increases, instead of decreasing as it does under a normal ARM loan.

This type of loan is sometimes preferred by those who know they will sell their home in a short time (say five years or less) and who in do not want higher monthly payments the mean time. In the early part of the loan, the principal increase is not too large and is apparently acceptable to some borrowers.

Consider a loan of $100,000 starting with a rate of 7.50%, as shown by Table 14.3. Suppose the interest rate increased to 9.00% annually after the fifth year. (It probably would not increase that much at a single interval, but we will use it as an example.)

Table 14.3: Negative Amortization

Home Mortgage Amortization
Payment Schedule

Loan principal			$100,000
Nominal interest start rate			7.50%
Total number of monthly payments			360
Monthly payment			$699.21

Month	Interest Payment	Principal Payment	Principal Balance
			$100,000.00
1	$625.00	$74.21	99,925.79
2	624.54	74.68	99,851.11
3	624.07	75.15	99,775.96
4	623.60	75.61	99,700.35
5	623.13	76.09	99,624.26
6	747.18	(47.97)	99,672.23
7	747.54	(48.33)	99,720.55
8	747.90	(48.69)	99,769.24
9	748.27	(49.05)	99,818.30
10	748.64	(49.42)	99,867.72
11	749.01	(49.79)	99,917.52
12	749.38	(50.17)	99,967.68

The new monthly payment at five years becomes $747.18, based on a principal balance of $99,624.26 at 9.00%. For example, $0.09/12 \times \$99,624.26 = \$747.18$. Subtracting that from the fixed monthly payment of $699.21 means that the deficiency of $47.97 must be added to the previous month's principal balance. This is shown in the shaded portion of Table 14.3. This process then continues to add the deficient portion of the interest payment to the loan principal.

Although some may prefer negative amortization, they should be acutely aware that it is happening. It could be quite a surprise to see the principal balance rising if it isn't expected. A negative amortization mortgage can never be paid off. If allowed to continue long enough, the principal balance can exceed the original loan amount.

BALLOON PAYMENTS

We touched on balloon payments in Chapter 5. A balloon payment type of loan usually has a stipulated period during which normal monthly payments are made. At the end of that period, the loan must be terminated by paying the remaining principal balance.

A *balloon payment* at any time in the loan is the same as the balance remaining. There are two methods to find the amount of a balloon payment: (1) look it up from the mortgage schedule, or (2) calculate it using Formula 5.6. (You can also use a financial calculator to do this which is automated use of Formula 5.6.) Example 5.8 of Chapter 5 demonstrates how to determine the amount of a balloon payment.

A 30 in 5 loan is one case in which it is useful to calculate a balloon payment. A 30 in 5 loan means that you have a 30-year loan in which the principal balance must be paid in full at the end of five years.

Example 14.5 A 30 in 5 Home Mortgage Balloon Payment

The Harts have been able to secure a lower mortgage rate loan by agreeing to pay the loan balance in full at the end of five years. The loan principal is $150,000; the interest rate is 7.00% for a term of 30 years. How much money will the Harts need in order to pay off this obligation in sixty months?

Solution:

First find the monthly payment for a 30-year loan. $PV = \$150,000$, $n = 30$ years, $i = 7.00\%$ The monthly payment $PMT_e = \$997.95$. The balloon payment is solved with a financial calculator by using the values of $PV = \$150,000$, $n = 60$, $i = 0.07/12$, and $PMT_e = -\$997.95$. The $FV = -\$141,197$.

THE REVERSE ANNUITY MORTGAGE (RAM)

The *reverse annuity mortgage* (RAM) is a method whereby homeowners can convert some equity in their home to a monthly income. The owners can live in their home while doing this. A RAM loan is particularly applicable to retired people on a fixed income who seek some additional income.

There are many options for RAMs including a government program developed by the Housing and Community Development (HUD) Act of 1987. This program is available to all senior homeowners, regardless of financial status, who meet the following requirements:

- One of the owners are at least 62 years of age,
- They occupy the property as a primary residence,
- The property is free and clear of mortgage debt, or nearly so.

Anyone interested in this type of program should investigate all the options. It should be recognized that the RAM is a negative amortization program. The loan is paid off when the home is sold, when the borrower dies, or when an agreed upon date is reached.

Similarly to the mortgage lending industry, some reverse mortgages are guaranteed by Federal Housing Administration (FHA), and others are not. In our opinion, FHA backed reverse mortgages offer the borrowers greater protection in the overall contracting process and terms.

For those considering a reverse mortgage, there is a Web site that provides comparative information for competing reverse mortgage offerings. The site's Web address is *http://www.reverse.org*. This site is copyrighted by the National Center for Home equity Conversion (NCHEC), an independent not-for-profit organization dedicated to reverse mortgage analysis and consumer information on reverse mortgages.

Financial Characteristics of a Reversal Annuity Mortgage

The best way to see how a reverse mortgage works is to run through an example. Consider a 72 year old couple who have a home valued at $250,000. Assume that the couple chose to take a reverse annuity stream instead of a lump sum payment. The FHA allows monthly annuity payments to be determined based on a predefined percentage value of the home. The lender then calculates the monthly payments based on the resulting value, the couples actuarial expected lifetime, and the prevailing market interest rate.

Suppose the interest rate is 7.50%, the percentage of the homes value is stipulated as 80%, the couples expected lifetime is 15 years, and the closing costs are $6,500.

The monthly annuity payments are calculated using the following data: $FV = 0.80 \times \$250,000 = \$200,000$, $i = 7.50\% \div 12 = 0.625\%$, $n = 15$ years or 180 months, and the closing costs are $6,500, which is the present value of the calculation. The monthly payments to the couple are $PMT_b = \$540.79$. Notice that this is tantamount to the lender buying an annuity in which they pay $540.79 per month to receive $200,000 in fifteen years. According to FHA requirements the lender must make the monthly annuity payments as long as the couple lives. If they live a very long time the lender could lose money on this arrangement. When the couple dies the home is sold and any remaining principal not required to pay the future value of the loan must be returned to the couples' beneficiaries.

Figure 14.2: A Reverse Annuity Mortgage

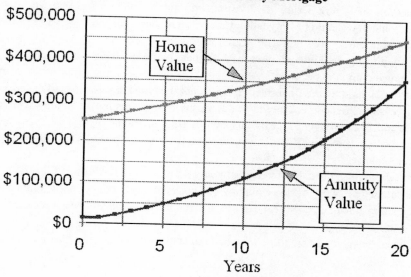

Figure 14.2 shows the values of the annuity and of the home as a function of time. The home's value is assumed to appreciate at 3% per year. This provides some margin for the lender. As the figure shows, when the annuity's value reaches $200,000 in 15 years, the value of the home is $400,000 by that time. Had not the home appreciated, it's value of $250,000 would equal the annuity's future value in about 17 years.

"Creative Financing" of RAM Loans

Upon attending a sales seminar on RAM loans, we learned of a novel approach offered by a local commercial finance company located in Santa Clara County. We term this approach "creative financing." It bears discussion because although it has serious drawbacks, it also has advantages under certain circumstances. It is not an obvious approach, nor can it be understood without a knowledge of financial mathematics.

A commercial finance company offered a RAM loan as follows: A couple 75 years of age have a home valued at $275,000. The finance company offers them a monthly income of $825 as long as both shall live. The company advertise a relatively low discount rate of 4.50%, as opposed to their competitors, who usually charge interest rates as high as 10%. The amount of home equity upon which to base this loan is 33.50% of the home's value, which is $92,000.

How can the finance company afford to do this? Based on these conditions, an interest rate of 10%, a period of 12 years, and a future value of $92,000, the couple's monthly income should be only $480. Can this company make an acceptable return on their investment? A return of 4.5% is not adequate.

They do very well indeed. First they stipulate in the small print of the contract that the finance company becomes sole owner of the home upon the death of the owners. The $92,000 paid by the finance company is not the home equity normally used as the basis to calculate income. The finance company buys an insurance annuity with it. At 4.50% and $92,000 over 12 years this annuity pays the home owners $825 per month as long as they both live. This means that the finance company has no further out of pocket expenses.

So what return does the finance company realize under the terms of this contract? Let's calculate it. The finance company can conservatively count on the home's price appreciating at least 3% per year. Homes in that area historically have appreciated 4.8% per year.

The negative values are those that the finance company pays, the positive those that they receive.

$$PV = -\$92,000$$
$$n = 12 \text{ years}$$
$$PMT_e = 0$$
$$FV = \$275,000 \, (1+0.03)^{12} = \$392,000 \text{ (value in twelve years.)}$$
$$i = ?$$

Using the HP-12C, we get a yield of 12.5%—a much better rate of return than originally stated by the finance company's salesman.

The finance company's salesmen stressed that this arrangement becomes more valuable as the home owners age. Also the salesman pointed out that the couple's descendants should feel good about their folks having this income even though they themselves will never inherit the home or any part of it.

The real downside to this arrangement is the possibility of the elderly couple dying early. If both husband and wife expired in, say, five years, they would have received only $49,500 in absolute cash value for a $275,000 home. Both the finance company and the insurance company then become big winners.

THE BIWEEKLY PAYMENT MORTGAGE: A GIMMICK

This mortgage is a gimmick. It needs to be explained, however, since it is something sold by organizations that take advantage of unsuspecting consumers. Mortgage industry experts report that as many as 12 million homeowners will be solicited to switch this year to biweekly payment plans. The homeowner can be charged a nonrefundable fee as high as $1,000 to have the biweekly payment plans implemented.

Organizations offering this service simply arrange to have your lender repackage your existing 12-month annual payment loan as a biweekly loan. With a biweekly loan you make 26 payments a year instead of 12. Since there are 52 weeks in a year, you can make 26 payments a year by paying biweekly in place of monthly. This repackaged loan is thus retired in about 22 years instead of 30 years.

How the Biweekly Loan Works

Suppose you have a 30-year, 8.00%, conventional $150,000 mortgage. The monthly payments are $1,100.65. Divide this by two and you have biweekly payments of $550.32. So you now pay a total annual payment of $14,308 instead of $13,207 for the 30-year loan schedule. You are simply paying an extra $1,000 annually with the biweekly loan.

The interest rate for 26 annual payments now becomes 8% ÷ 26 weeks = 0.3077%. If you solve for the number of payments for the values of $i = 0.3077\%$, $PMT_e = -\$550.32$, and $PV = \$150,000$, and you will find that 589 biweekly payments will amortize this loan. Your loan term becomes 22.7 years in place of 30 years. The total money you will eventually pay for the biweekly loan is $324,103, of which $174,103 is interest whereas if you paid your original 30-year loan to term, you would have paid $246,234 total interest. The biweekly loan saves money since the loan term has been shortened.

You don't need to pay someone else a fee to do this for you. As explained earlier in this chapter, you can always save interest by making advanced principal payments as desired, and on your own schedule. Also, many of the organizations that package your loan simply take your biweekly payments and make only monthly payments to the lender. They earn some money on the float by doing this.

Now It's Your Turn:

1. For a loan principal amount of $175,000, the lender charges 2.25% points. Because of these points, the home buyer must add how much to the closing costs of this loan?
   a. $2,937.50
   b. $3,937.50
   c. $2,250.00

2. The Smith family needs a home loan principal of $125,000. Their lender charges 2 points, and the balance of closing costs is $3,500. The lender offers a contract interest rate of 8.5% for a 30-year loan. If the Smiths add the total closing costs to the principal, what would their monthly payments be?
   a. $1,700.54
   b. $1,556.78
   c. $1,007.28

3. For question 2 above, what is the APR of this loan?
   a. 8.00%
   b. 9.02%
   c. 8.54%

4. If the lender thinks the $3,500 portion of the closing costs are not included in the APR, what monthly payments and APR would the lender calculate?
   a. $980.36, 8.72%
   b. $1,007.28, 9.02%
   c. $890.36, 8.70%

5. The contract interest rates quoted by lenders of a home loan are:
   a. Nominal interest rates
   b. Effective interest rates

6. If a lender quotes an interest rate of 8.00% for a 360-month loan, what is the effective interest rate realized by the lender?
   a. 8.20%
   b. 8.00%
   c. 8.30%

7. How much interest would the homeowners of Table 14.1 save if they made three monthly payments and sent the next month's principal payment with each regular payment?
   a. $1,945.62
   b. $1,872.20
   c. $1,879.35

8. You have a home loan as follows: term 30 years, principal $150,000, contract rate 8.50%, points 1.5, and other closing costs $2,500. You intend to fold the closing costs into the amount you will borrow. What is the first month's principal payment (PMT_e), interest payment (i), and the principal balance (FV) after the first monthly payment?
   a. $PMTe = 104.75$, $i = \$1,085.14$, $FV = \$154,645.25$
   b. $PMTe = \$95.68$, $i = \$1,094.31$, $FV = \$154,654.32$
   c. $PMTe = \$93.74$, $i = \$1,096.15$, $FV = \$\$154,656.26$

9. For an ARM loan of $200,000 offered by Bank B of Table 14.2, what would the monthly payments of this mortgage be for the first six-month period? The loan term is 30 years.
   a. $1,056.87
   b. $1,043.29
   c. $1,290.67

10. Assuming the one-year treasury bill rate is 5.35%, and the loan balance is $198,475.24 at the end of the first six-month period, what would the monthly payments be for the second six-month period in question 9?
    a. $1,411.02
    b. $1,043.29
    c. $1,493.43

11. If the T-bill rate in question 10 increased 10 basis points during the second six-month period and the loan balance at the end of the second six-month period was $197,663, what would the monthly payments be for the third six-month period?
    a. $1,298.68
    b. $1,507.21
    c. $1,438.05

12. For the loan schedule of Table 14.3, what would be the loan balance after the thirteenth monthly payment?
    a .$100,018.23
    b. $99,992.68
    c. $101,018.23

13. The Carsons have a home mortgage with a current balance of $155,680 and an interest rate of 9.25%. Their original 30-year loan principal was $165,000. They are offered an opportunity to refinance with a 30-year loan at an interest rate of 8.00% and 2.50 points. In addition to the points the balance of the closing costs will be $2,100. Based on a simple payback analysis, how long will it take the Carsons to break even if they refinance? (Round your answer to nearest month.)
    a. 30 months
    b. 35 months
    c. 25 months

14. In Example 14.9, Mr. and Mrs. Johnson felt that the loan buildup was too rapid. They decided to reduce their maximum claim amount to 50%. Under this loan, the total closing costs are $5,000. What monthly income would they receive?
    a. $334.17
    b. $434.17
    c. $343.17

15. Fred wants to compare the total of the annual payments of a 30-year conventional mortgage of $175,000, 7.50% interest rate, with the annual payments of a biweekly mortgage. How do they compare?
    a. $14,684 conventional, $15,907 biweekly
    b. $16,024 conventional, $18,791 biweekly
    c. $17,230 conventional, $19,4870 biweekly

ANSWERS: 1.b, 2.c, 3.b, 4.a, 5.a, 6.c, 7.a, 8.c, 9.b, 10.c, 11.b, 12.a, 13.b, 14.c, 15.a

Tax-Deferred Annuities and Retirement Options

LEARNING OBJECTIVES:

When you have completed this chapter you will be able to:

1. Define the variable tax-deferred annuity and understand its key characteristics
2. Know when it is advisable to buy tax-deferred annuities
3. Calculate the income tax advantages offered by tax-deferred annuities
4. Analyze variable tax-deferred annuity lifetime returns
5. Compare tax-deferred annuities with taxable investments
6. Make informed decisions when selecting annuity payment options
7. Analyze how rates of return influence systematic cash withdrawal programs

As part of your financial planning, you need to consider various tax-deferred annuities and retirement options. An annuity can be a contract with an insurance company or an employer-sponsored retirement plan. Tax-deferred annuities allow you to earn compound interest on your investments without paying income taxes on the earnings or capital gains until the money is withdrawn.

One of the difficult decisions facing owners of annuities or retirement plans is to choose the method of withdrawing the money when it is needed or desired. This is a very important consideration. There are many different withdrawal options offered. You should fully understand and analyze each option to determine the most favorable.

WHAT ARE ANNUITIES?

Generically, an annuity is a series of uniform payments made at equal intervals of time. The payments can be to accumulate a future sum of money (annuity due) or to receive periodic payments of money (ordinary annuity).

Insurance Annuities

An insurance annuity is an investment contract offered by insurance companies. You invest money either in a single sum or periodically. In return, you have the option of either receiving a lump sum, a stream of payments for life, or payments for a defined period. The insurance annuity is a tax-deferred way to accumulate money. The compound interest this money earns grows similarly to a tax-free investment. Once you reach age 59½, you can begin to withdraw your money. Withdrawal prior to age 59½ incurs a 10% penalty unless the annuitant chooses to take a scheduled series of substantially equal periodic payments over his or her lifetime. The interest earned is taxed upon being taken either in a lump sum or as a stream of annuity payments. Unlike IRAs there is no limit to the amount of money that can be invested with an insurance annuity.

The insurance protection feature of an annuity guarantees that your beneficiaries will recoup the money you have invested in the annuity even if it lost money in the underlying investments. But, if the insurance company should undergo bankruptcy, your money could be in jeopardy unless you have invested with a mutual fund.

There are two basic types of annuities. The standard is a *fixed annuity*. You pay a single sum initially; in return, the insurance company pays a *fixed rate* of interest on your money. The fixed annuity can be immediate or deferred. The immediate annuity provides an immediate stream of annuity payments, whereas the deferred stream is taken at a later date.

The other type is a *variable annuity*. A variable annuity is basically an insurance company allied with a mutual fund family. You can choose your investment options offered by a mutual fund family. These investments are called "subaccounts." Insurance companies either have their own mutual funds or work with mutual fund companies that offer some funds set aside specifically for annuities. The rate of return you realize depends on the performance of your subaccount investments.

A fixed annuity contract permits only a single-sum initial payment, whereas a variable annuity allows you to invest over time as often as you like. In this chapter we analyze only variable annuities. Fixed annuity rate of returns are usually too low to be attractive.

Tips on Buying an Insurance Annuity

Annuities are sold by insurance agents, brokers, bankers, financial planners, mutual fund families, etc. As such, there usually are sales commissions and early withdrawal penalties. It is a well-kept secret that some mutual fund families have allied with insurance companies to offer annuities in which there are no sales commissions nor withdrawal penalties. These annuities usually have lower expense ratios and fees. In addition, if the underlying insurance company should become bankrupt, your money is still intact with the mutual fund family. One such fund family that offers tax-deferred annuities is the Vanguard Group of funds.

WHEN SHOULD YOU BUY A TAX-DEFERRED ANNUITY?

Financial planners recommend that tax-deferred annuities be considered only when there are no other tax-deferred options available to you. Insurance annuities usually have higher inherent costs and fees than other tax-deferred options, such as IRAs, 401(k)s, or company-sponsored retirement or savings plans. The insurance-associated annuity has annual costs of a $30 to $50 maintenance fee, a charge of about 0.75% for management, and a 1.00% to 1.50% charge for insurance. The annuity insurance fees are over and above those costs incurred when investing in securities that are not under the annuity umbrella. Thus it is advisable to compare the returns from an annuity with those of taxable investments that have lesser charges.

Also, you would not buy an annuity under an IRA or a 401(k) plan because these plans already offer the tax-deferred investment feature. Moreover, the money committed to an insurance annuity is not deductible from the investor's adjusted gross income as IRA and 401(k) contributions are.

Annuities are recommended as long-term investments. This is particularly true for younger participants because there is a 10% penalty if the lump sum of money is withdrawn prior to age 59 1/2. There also usually are early withdrawal penalties impose by the insurance company.

ANNUITY PAYMENT OPTIONS

When it becomes time to take money from your annuity or a company-sponsored retirement plan, there are some decisions you will be asked to make. There are many options offered by insurance annuities and employer-sponsored plans. It is extremely important to understand these fully and to analyze the payments to be received. A wise choice can enhance your retirement years.

Options for Taking Annuity or Retirement Payments

Typical payout options are:

- Annuitizing
- Nonannuitized systematic withdrawals
- Lump sum
- Payments for a designated period

Annuitizing means that the insurance company or employer's pension plan will contract to pay the annuitant a monthly lifetime payment or a payment for a certain specified period on time. It is important to note that once a policy is annuitized, no withdrawal or surrender of money is allowed. The action is irrevocable. In general, the annuity payment amount depends on your age, the amount of money you have accumulated, and the interest rate the insurance company or employer will pay. The insurance company will amortize your principal over your expected lifetime as determined by actuarial tables. Once you annuitize and begin to take the annuity stream of payments, you must, of course, pay income taxes on the money received (profits) over and above your original invested principal.

Systematic withdrawal is the process of withdrawing money periodically, such as monthly or annually. There is no contractual agreement that the insurance company will pay you an annuity as long as you shall live. You are simply withdrawing your money. For qualified plans and annuities however, there is a 10% penalty for withdrawing money prior to age 59½.

Lump sum is simply taking all your money and investing it somewhere else or spending it. The disadvantage is that you must immediately pay income taxes on the total amount of the profits. If the money has been in an IRA or some other qualified retirement plan, you can roll the money over into another tax-deferred qualified plan.

Some employer pension plans will not pay a lump sum; rather they require that the employee annuitize.

Payment for a designated period is an annuitized agreement for the insurance company to pay you a monthly payment for a defined number of months. This is called "payments certain." The principal and interest are amortized at a fixed interest rate and a defined time period. This is an option under the annuitizing plans.

Income Tax Implications of Annuity and Retirement Payout Options

Income taxes are levied differently for the withdrawn money depending on whether the policyholder annuitizes or takes periodic withdrawals. These cases are explained as follows

The policy is annuitized

The Internal Revenue Code allows the annuitant to exclude from taxable income (as recovery of capital) the proportion of each payment as calculated by the following formula:

Formula 15.1: Tax-Deferred Annuity Exclusion Amount

$$\frac{\text{Investment}}{\text{Expected Return}} \times \text{Annuity Payment} = \text{Exclusion Amount}$$

The annual *exclusion amount* is considered to be return of principal and is not taxable. The *investment* is the sum total of money you have actually paid. The *expected return* is the total amount the annuitant expects to receive over the payout lifetime of the annuitant. IRS publication 939 *General Rule for Pensions and Annuities* provides the information you need to determine the tax treatment or your annuity. It is a requirement to use the IRS published data for the expected life time calculation used to determine the expected return. The annuity payment is the annual payment the annuitant expects to receive. Once the exclusion amount is known, it is subtracted from the monthly annuity payment and the remainder is the taxable amount. To find the taxes to be paid, the taxable amount is multiplied by the annuitant's marginal tax rate.

IRS Publication 939 must be used for a nonqualified plan (for example, a private annuity, a purchased commercial annuity, or a nonqualified employee plan). A sample portion of the life expectancy Table V from IRS Publication 939 is shown by Figure 15.1. It should be noted that this is an IRS unisex table for the sole purpose of determining the taxable part of your annuity payments, it is not actuarial table per se.

Table 15.1
Table V—Ordinary Life Annuities
One Life—Expected Return Multiples

Age	Multiple	Age	Multiple
50	33.1	70	16.0
55	28.6	75	12.5
60	24.2	80	9.5
65	20.0	85	6.9

Example 15.1: *Income Taxes Exclusion Amount*

Paul purchased an immediate annuity for $100,000 and elected to annuitize. The insurance company agrees to pay Paul $628 per month for as long as he lives. IRS Table V (Figure 15.1) shows that Paul, age 65, must use a multiple of 20 years to calculate expected return amount. What will Paul's exclusion amount be? What will his annual tax load be if he is in the 28% marginal bracket?

Solution:

Investment..................................... $100,000
Annual annuity payment...........(12 × $628) = $7,536
Expected return ....(12 × 20 years × $628) = $150,720

Exclusion amount:

$$\frac{\$100,000}{\$150,720} \times \$7,536 = \$5,000$$

The taxable portion of the annuitant's annual income is thus $7,536 – $5,000 = $2,536. The annual taxes Paul must pay annually are 0.28 × $2,536 = $710.

The above example is a simplified approach to this problem to show how the system in general works. As you might expect Publication 939 is about 80 pages and requires much interpretation.

The policy is not annuitized

All the distributions are considered to be taxable profits until the money is spent down to the original principal. This is the First-In First-Out (FIFO) rule. The original investment (principal) is not taxed since it was already post-tax dollars when it was invested in the annuity.

As example of the FIFO rule, suppose the annuitant has an invested principal of $100,000 over 10 years and the final accumulated amount in the fund is $160,000, or a profit of $60,000. The contract holder upon reaching the age 59 ½ years chooses to annuitize. The distributed income is taxed as follows:

Initial investment:	$100,000
Earned profit	$60,000
Total value	$160,000

Systematic withdrawals:		Comments
Year 1	$20,000	Taxed as ordinary income
Year 2	$20,000	Taxed as ordinary income
Year 3	$20,000	Taxed as ordinary income
Year 4	$50,000	Return of principal
Year 5	$50,000	Return of principal

The distribution is not quite as simple as this because the money in the account continues to accumulated profit so the taxable distribution is a moving target.

In comparison to a nonannuitized payment plan, an insurance company's annuitized plan has the advantage of smaller initial income tax payments.

ANALYZING A TAX-DEFERRED VARIABLE INSURANCE ANNUITY

Examples of subaccount options that you might select for your variable annuity investments are shown in the adjacent table. With variable annuities, an investor directs the investment portfolio selection and can also switch investment options as often as desired.

Let's look at how you might analyze a variable annuity investment plan.

Example 15.2: *A Variable Annuity Plan*

Brad and Joan, both 35 years of age, now have an additional $1,500 to invest annually in their future with the aim of retiring and taking monthly payments when they reach age 60. They currently invest the maximum allowed to their IRA and a company sponsored retirement plan. They would like to supplement these plans with an additional tax-deferred savings plan. They are in the 30% marginal income tax bracket now, but expect to be in the 20% bracket when they retire at age 60. They have bought a variable insurance annuity and would like to know what monthly income they can plan on when they reach 60 years of age.

Subaccount performance by category	
Subaccount Category	Annual 5-yr. total returns, %
Stock Funds	
Aggressive growth	18.00
Growth & income	15.00
Hybrid accounts	
Balanced Fund	12.00
Fixed income funds	
Corp. Bond	7.60
Gov. Bond	6.20
Money Market	4.70
Standard & Poor's 500 stock index	20.70

Solution:

Brad and Joan contracted for a variable tax-deferred annuity and were offered the slate of investments shown in the subaccount listing. Since this is a relatively long-term investment, they selected an aggressive growth stock mutual fund. Although this type of fund has returned 18.00%, they believe this growth rate may be a little high for planning purposes, so they reduced it to 15%. The calculation is done in two phases. The *accumulation* phase and the *withdrawal* phase.

The Accumulation Phase

Brad and Joan will deposit $1,500 per year for 25 years at an estimated rate of return of 15%. Calculate the Future Value of the Tax-Deferred Annuity at the End of the Accumulation Phase:

$$PV = 0$$
$$PMT_b = -(\$1,500 - \$50) = -\$1,450 \text{ (due to the annual fee)}$$
$$n = 25 \text{ Years}$$
$$i = 15.00\% - (1.50\% + 0.75\%) = 12.75\%$$

Here we subtract 1.50% required for the insurance cost of the annuity and 0.75% for the management fees. Solving for the future value, we have:

$$FV = \$244,743$$

Observe that this sum of money is accumulated with an investment of only $1,500 \times 25\text{years} = \$37,500$.

The Withdrawal Phase

The second part of this analysis involves receiving the money. When they become 60 years of age Brad and Joan plan to take uniform monthly payments over a 23-year term. They elected *not* to annuitize this plan with the insurance company. At age 60 the couple expect to be in a reduced marginal tax bracket because of reduced earnings upon retirement. They estimate that their marginal rate will then be 20%. They will no longer make monthly payments but will continue with the same mutual funds, including leaving the money with the annuity until it is spent. The reason for this is to avoid paying income taxes immediately as they would have to do were they to take the full amount in a lump sum payout. The money that remains in the annuity still compounds without being taxed.

Calculate the Annual Payments of the Tax-Deferred Annuity During the Withdrawal Phase

$$FV = 0$$
$$PV = \$244,743$$
$$n = 23 \text{ Years, 276 months}$$
$$i = 12.75 \% \text{ per year, } 1.0625\% \text{ per month}$$
$$PMT_e = \$2,749 \text{ per month (By Formula 5.3)}$$

Since Brad and Joan chose *not* to annuitize, the income tax code requires that taxes are paid on the entire monthly payment until only the sum of money they paid remains in the account. The annual income taxes are $12 \times \$2,749 \times 0.20 = \$6,597$. This tax payment continues until only the paid in sum ($37,500) remains in the account. Most of the annuity payments are derived from earnings of the investment rather than the actual paid in principal. This is true of most relatively long-term investment plans such as retirement pensions.

On a spreadsheet we ran the schedule of principal and interest payments for 23 years and found that the principal amount of $37,500 remains after 22 years. The total taxes paid over the 22-year period is $145,000. The total after-tax money that Brad and Joan netted throughout the life of this investment is about $620,000. This demonstrates how profitable a plan such as this can be since the original investment was only $37,500.

TAX-DEFERRED VARIABLE ANNUITIES VS. TAXABLE MUTUAL FUNDS

Does the tax-deferred annuity offer a significant economic advantage over a taxable mutual fund? This is a question that investors should pursue. Tying up money for a long time, plus the additional annuity insurance charge, are distinct disadvantages of the annuity. We will perform an analysis here of a taxable investment for Brad and Joan. This exercise should not be taken as an absolute answer but as a demonstration of the method. A valid comparison can only be made when the marginal tax rates and expected investment rates of return are known to the investors.

Example 15.3:

Brad and Joan decided to consider a plan that involves investing in a no load mutual fund in which the profits are not tax-differed. Other than that they intend to retain the same conditions as in Example 15.2. What monthly income can they expect upon reaching age 60? Recall that the accumulation period is 25 years and the withdrawal period is 23 years.

Solution:

The Accumulation Phase: Calculate the future value (*FV*) of the taxable mutual fund. First we calculate the after-tax equivalent yield of a taxable investment.

The before-tax interest rate is:

$$i = 15\% - 0.75\% = 14.25\%$$

Here we subtract the management fee of the mutual fund. Since Brad and Joan expect to be in a marginal income tax bracket of 30% during their next 23 years, their after-tax interest rate will be determined. Recall Formula 10.4c:

$$\frac{\text{After - Tax Equivalent Yield}}{(1 - \text{Marginal Tax Rate})} = \text{Before - Tax Yield}$$

After-Tax equivalent yield = 14.25% (1 − 0.30) = 9.98%

The data used to calculate the future value of this annuity is:

$$PV = 0,\ PMT_b = -\$1,500 \text{ per year},\ n = 25 \text{ years},\ i = 9.98\%$$

Using the HP-12C, the $FV = \$161,756$

The Withdrawal Phase

The data to calculate the annual after-tax payments to Brad and Joan over the next 23 years are:

$FV = 0,\ PV = \$161,756,\ n = 23$ years, or 276 months,
$i = 14.25\%\ (1 - 0.20^*) = 11.40\%$, or 0.95% per month
*(Marginal income tax bracket is now 20%.)

The calculated after-tax $PMT_e = \$1,643$ per month

The expected total after-tax return over 23 years is:

12 months per year × 23 years × $1,643 per month = $453,743

The comparison of Brad and Joan's tax-deferred annuity with the taxable investment is shown in Table 15.2.

**Table 15.2: After-Tax Payout Comparison of a
Tax-Deferred Annuity vs. a Taxable Mutual Fund**

	Variable Annuity	Mutual Fund
Total invested money	$37,500	$37,500
FV of 25 year investment	244,743	161,756
Total after-tax income	620,00	453,000
Total advantage	$167,000	

For the parameters selected, the tax-deferred annuity is the clear winner. Even though the tax-deferred annuity has higher burden costs, these costs are offset by the tax-deferred feature.

ANALYZING TYPICAL ANNUITIZED PAYMENT PLANS

When and if you decide to annuitize, the insurance company will offer several options. Some employer-sponsored retirement annuity plans offer only an annuitizing option. A typical insurance company annuity or employer plan will provide annuity tables that stipulate the actual payout amounts for the annuitizing options. To explain and analyze the options, we present some of these tables. These are actual tables taken from a variable annuity contract offered by an insurance company. Each table presents the amount of monthly payment for each $1,000 applied. These tables representative a fixed annuity in which the payments are guaranteed by the company. Income payments will not vary in dollar amount.

To more accurately determine the life expectancy of males and females, we will need an actuarial table. The IRS publication 939 offers such a table and a sample portion of that table is reproduced in Figure 15.3. The multiples are the additional years the person is expected to live upon reaching the corresponding age. For example a 65 year old male should live another 15 years. Throughout this book we will use the values in this table for choosing the expected lifetimes for calculating the rates of return of life insurance policies and annuity payments.

Figure 15.3: Actuarial Table

Age		Multiples
Male	Female	
50	55	25.5
55	60	21.7
60	65	18.2
65	70	15.0

The Single Life Annuity Payment Option

Table 15.4: Single Life Annuities—Male

Age of Payee	Monthly Payments Certain			
	None	120	180	240
60	5.57	5.45	5.31	5.10
62	5.82	5.67	5.48	5.23
65	6.28	6.05	5.77	5.41

There are two basic options here. The first, under the "None" column, shows that for each $1,000 of accumulated value in the annuitant's account, the company will pay a lifetime monthly income of $5.57 to a male who annuitizes at age 60 years. When the annuitant dies, the payments stop even if the annuitant should die soon after he annuitizes.

The "monthly payment certain," option, if selected, means that the insurance company will pay the annuitant's beneficiaries a certain number of months even though the annuitant dies before the elapsed time. For example, if the insured male should die 120 months after the date he annuitized, his beneficiaries would receive monthly payments for 120 additional months in the case where the annuitant had selected the 240 month payments certain option.

Let's perform some calculations to see what rates of return the annuitant actually realizes when he or she annuitizes.

Example 15.4:

Joe has $100,000 accumulated in his annuity and at age 65 decides to annuitize. His spouse is his beneficiary and he elects a 240-month certain option. Joe dies 10 years after he annuitizes. His spouse continues to receive payments for 10 years. What before-tax rate of return did Joe and his spouse realize on his annuity investment?

Solution:

Joe's monthly payments will be:

$$5.41 \times \$100,000/\$1000 = \$541 \text{ per month (Table 15.4)}$$

Find the annual interest rate given:

$$FV = 0, PV = -\$100,000, n = 240 \text{ months}, PMT_e = \$541$$

Using a financial calculator we find:

$$i = 0.227\% \text{ monthly or } 2.73\% \text{ nominal annual rate}$$

Example 15.5:

Suppose Joe, age 65, had selected the noncertain option and lives to his life expectancy multiple of 15 years (Table 15.3).

Solution:

Joe's guaranteed monthly payment will be:

$$PMT_e = 6.28 \times \$100,000/1000 = \$628 \text{ per month (Table 15.4)}$$

Find the annual rate of return given:

$$FV = 0. PV = -\$100,000, PMT_e = \$628 \text{ per month. } n = 15 \text{ years} \times 12 = 180 \text{ months}$$

The calculated annual rate of return is:

$$i = 0.138\% \text{ per month, or } 1.66\% \text{ nominal annual rate}$$

The Designated Period Option

This option provides a monthly payment for a designated period selected by the annuitant. It does not provide income past that period.

Table 15.5: Designated Period Annuity

Payment for a Designated Period	
Year of Payments	Amount of Monthly Payment
10	10.06
15	7.34
20	6.00

Let's check the interest rate of return of this option for a 15 year payment period and $100,000 accumulated funds.

$$PMT_e = 7.34 \times \$100,000/\$1,000 = \$734 \text{ per month}$$
$$FV = 0,\ PV = -\$100,000,\ n = 15 \times 12 = 180 \text{ months}$$

The calculated annual rate of return is:

$$i = 0.323\% \text{ monthly or } 3.88\% \text{ nominal annual rate of return}$$

The Joint and Last Survivor Option

This option guarantees a payment to the male annuitant and to his spouse as long as either of them shall live.

Table 15.6: Joint and Last Survivor Annuity

Age of Male Payee	Age of Female Payee		
	55	60	65
60	4.41	4.62	4.83
62	4.44	4.67	4.91
65	4.48	4.74	5.03

Example 15.6:

Joe decided to consider this option. His spouse is also 65 years of age with an annuity accumulation of $100,000. What rate of return does this option provide Joe and his spouse? Base this on the life expectancy multiple of Joe's spouse.

Solution:

The monthly payments for Joe and his spouse, both 65 of age, are:

$$PMT_e = 5.03 \times \$100,000/\$1,000 = \$503 \text{ per month}$$

The life expectancy multiple for a female 65 years of age is 18.2 years (Table 15.3)

$$FV = 0, PV = -\$100,000, PMT_e = \$503, n = 18.2 \text{ years, or } 218 \text{ months}$$

The calculated annual rate of return is:

$$i = 0.0855\% \text{ monthly or } 1.03\% \text{ nominal annual rate.}$$

Although we used the expected life multiples of Table 15.2 to calculate the rate of return of the annuitants, it is obvious that the annuitant will, expect for the designated periods option, realize a greater rate of return on their money by living longer. If Joe of Example 15.5 lived to age 90 in place of 80, he would realize a rate of return of 5.78% from his annuity investment.

SHOULD YOU ANNUITIZE OR TAKE SYSTEMATIC PAYMENTS?

Most financial advisors say "Do not annuitize if you can avoid it." You can appreciate this answer. Upon annuitizing, you no longer have control over your investment, the action is irrevocable, and the rates of return offered by insurance companies are relatively low. In our examples, which have typical rates of return values, we saw that the highest return offered by the example insurance company is less than 4.00%. For some other options, the rates are below 2.0%. After-tax rates of return would even be smaller.

Let's compare the nonannuitized payment option that Brad and Joan selected in Example 15.2 with an annuitized option.

Example 15.7:

Assume that Brad and Joan, at age 60, decided to annuitize their variable annuity plan of Example 15.2. The insurance company contracts to pay them a lifetime income. Assume that they selected the Joint and Last Survivor option shown in Table 15.6. To be consistent we will select a lifetime of 23 years similar to Example 15.2, but the tax treatment requires an age of 24.2 (Table 15.1) to calculate the exclusion amount. What total income will they receive? Compare this to that of Example 15.2.

Solution:

Recall that Brad and Joan had accumulated a principal sum of $244,743 at the start of the annuity payout time. From Table 15.5 the monthly payments to Brad and Joan, both age 60, will be $4.62 per each $1,000 applied.

Their monthly payment will be: $4.62 × $244,743/$1,000 = $1,131
The annual payment will be: $1,131 × 12 months = $13,572
The expected return will be: $13,572 × 24.2 years = $328,442
The original investment was $37,500

Since Brad and Joan have decided to annuitize, Formula 15.1 is allowed by the IRS Code.

Formula 15.1: Tax-Deferred Annuity Exclusion Amount

$$\frac{\text{Investment}}{\text{Expected Return}} \times \text{Annuity Payment} = \text{Exclusion Amount}$$

The exclusion amount is:

$$\frac{\$37,500}{\$328,442} \times \$13,572 = \$1,550$$

The annual taxable amount is:............... $13,572 − $1,550 = $12,022
Annual income taxes are: .... $12,022 × 0.20 = $2,404
Annual after-tax income is: .... $13,572 − $2,404 = $11,168
The total after-tax income over 23 years is: $11,168 × 23 years = $256,900

Comparison of not annuitizing vs. annuitizing:
Nonannuitized total income......... $620,000
Annuitized total income.............. $256,900
Advantage for not annuitizing....... $363100

The advantage gained here was, of course, due to the greater rate of return on the investment of the variable annuity. In general, the equity stock market out performs the fixed-income market. Upon annuitization, insurance companies usually invest the money in fixed-income government securities. Since annuitized returns offered by insurance companies are not very attractive, you will almost certainly do better by leaving your money invested in the subaccounts of the variable annuity and taking systematic withdrawals. However, many people are more comfortable with a guaranteed lifetime insurance annuity rather than the nonannuitized systematic withdrawal plan. You should analyze your situation and make the choice that suits you best.

HOW RATES OF RETURN INFLUENCE SYSTEMATIC CASH-WITHDRAWAL PROGRAMS

When you retire at age 65 or so, you will need an, income that lasts for the rest of your lifetime. You could live 20 or 30 years in retirement and you do not want your money to run out. Systematically withdrawing your money needs to be planned. Suppose you have an annuity or mutual fund from which you want to take uniform withdrawals over your lifetime. You expect to live 25 years and you own a mutual fund presently valued at $250,000. The annual compound rate of return you can expect to realize on this invested money will greatly influence how much you withdraw and how much you may have as a cushion. It is amazing to see what a little difference in the rate of return can mean to your future sum of money.

For example, if you think you can get a rate of return of 8% annually, you could withdraw an annual sum of (PMT_b) $21,685. At the end of 25 years, the money would be depleted (amortized). But if you actually could realize 10% on this money, you would be able to draw $21,685 per year for 25 years and still have $362,800 left in your account. This is, of course, more then you started with. What a difference 2% more a year makes. Try this calculation with other numbers and see what you get. If your annual rate of return turned out to be 12%, you would have more than a million dollars in 25 years. The method to make this calculation is the same that for a balloon payment, as shown in Chapter 5, Example 5.8. You might plan your withdrawal amounts using a conservative rate of return value and then monitor your progress. If in the future you find that the rates are higher, you could replan and take a larger income.

Now It's Your Turn:

1. A tax-deferred annuity offered by an insurance company offers the same income-tax provisions as a tax-free municipal bond.
   a. True
   b. False

2. A tax-deferred annuity should be considered for a long term investment?
   a. True
   b. False

3. One advantage of an annuity bought through a mutual fund-insurance company is that even if the insurance company declares bankruptcy your investment is still intact.
   a. True
   b. False

4. Garvey is in the 15% marginal tax bracket and expects to earn a 10% return on his investments. Would it be advantageous for him to buy a tax-deferred insurance annuity if it had a 2% insurance charge?
   a. Yes
   b. No

5. You have contracted with an insurance company for a tax-deferred variable annuity. You selected a balance fund as the underlying security. The fund has a history of earning a return of 9.5% annually. You plan to leave the money in the fund during an accumulation period of 20 years. Assuming you invested $1,500 at the beginning of each year, how much would you estimate your future value to be if the fund has a 1.5% cost of insurance and a management fee of 0.75%? There is no maintenance fee.
   a. $109,673
   b. $67,780
   c. $93,839

6. At the end of the accumulation period in question 5 above, you have decided to take monthly payments over a 15-year period. What amount would you expect these payments to be in before-taxed dollars? Assume monthly compounding. For the payout phase, you switch to a corporate bond fund that enjoys a historic annual return of 8.50%.

   a. $581
   b. $1,092
   c. $563

7. What was your total investment in the annuity in question 5 above?

   a. $35,000
   b. $45,000
   c. $30,000

8. Judd is considering a tax-deferred annuity that has an insurance cost of 1.5%. He is currently in the 30% marginal tax bracket. Judd also has an opportunity to enter into a long-term taxable venture that he thinks will return an annual rate of 13%. What interest rate would Judd need to realize in his tax-deferred annuity to equal the taxable venture throughout the accumulation phase?

   a. 10.60%
   b. 13.00%
   c. 9.60%

9. For his retirement plan, John (age 62) has the option to elect a retirement income typical of that shown in Table 15.3. He has a principal sum of $250,000 in his retirement plan. If he elects to take the plan with no certain period, what would his before tax monthly income be?

   a. $1,622
   b. $1,455
   c. $1,458

10. For question 9 above, if John's expected lifetime is 17 years, what rate of return is John realizing on this principal?

   a. 2.07%
   b. 1.56%
   c. 3.56%

11. For the rate of return in question 10, how much of John's principal would he forfeit if he died 10 years after he started his annuity payments? (Same calculation as a balloon payment of a mortgage.)
   a. $114,000
   b. None
   c. $52,000

12. If John lives 25 years during the period he receives a monthly payment of $1,455, what annual rate of return would he enjoy? His principal sum was $250,000.
   a. 3.25%
   b. 6.28%
   c. 4.96%

ANSWERS: 1.b, 2.a, 3.a, 4.b, 5.b, 6.a, 7.c, 8.a, 9.b, 10.a, 11.a, 12.c

How to Analyze Life Insurance Policies

LEARNING OBJECTIVES:

In choosing life insurance policies, you need to compare what you are getting for your money. When you have finished this chapter you, will understand the difference between term and whole life policies and be able to compare competing policies by applying the rate of return method to calculate:

1. Death benefit rates of return
2. Cash surrender value rates of return
3. Rates of return of annuitized insurance policy benefits
4. After-tax rates of return
5. Inflation effects on life insurance death benefits

The primary purpose of life insurance is to replace lost income and/or lost capital due to the death of the provider. A secondary use of life insurance is to gain capital to supplement retirement income. Two basic types of life insurance policies are analyzed in this chapter: (1) *Term* insurance which provides death benefits but builds no cash value, and (2) *Whole life* insurance which provides cash accumulation but costs more for the combination of accumulated cash value and death benefits.

Anyone who has tried to or has purchased cash value life insurance is undoubtedly aware of the complexity of the task. A conclusion drawn in a book entitled *The Investments Reader* (Dow Jones—Irwin, Homewood, Illinois, 1989), edited by Jay Wilbanks, highlights the difficulty of choosing cash value life insurance:

> No financial product is more difficult to buy with confidence than cash-value insurance. The financial planning community is becoming increasingly aware of

this, and consumers are likely to benefit as more questions are asked. In the meantime, keep in mind that you have an alternative to cash-value products: You can buy convertible, guaranteed-renewable term insurance and wait.

METHODS FOR ANALYZING LIFE INSURANCE POLICIES

There are three basic methods for comparing life insurance policies. In his comprehensive book, *The Life Insurance Buyer's Guide*, (McGraw-Hill 1989), William D. Brownlie explains these methods. They are: (1) cash-flow analysis, referred to by the life insurance industry as the "traditional method," (2) the interest-adjusted index method, and (3) compound interest rate of return method. Mr. Brownlie recommends the rate of return method, even though it is not used by the insurance industry per se. He points out that the first two methods have the serious flaw of not recognizing the time value of money, and we agree with that assessment.

The Rate of Return (ROR) Method

The rate of return method is simply the rate of return of a series of cash payments and receipts over the life of the policy. For insurance policies, the rate of return can be calculated for three situations, (1) the premiums (money) paid in relation to the death benefit, (2) the premiums paid in relation to the cash surrender value, and (3) the net cash flows after a policy has been annuitized.

First, let's calculate the ROR for a term policy. There are no dividends declared by term life insurance policies, no cash buildup, only a death benefit. Term life insurance provides only protection.

Example 16.1: Rate of Return Of Death Benefits of a Term Life Insurance Policy

The Policy

- Type: Term life insurance policy
- Insured: A 35-year-old male
- Face value: $250,000
- Annual level premiums for 10 years = $310 per year, paid at the beginning of each year

Let's assume that insured dies at the end of 10 years after taking the policy and the face value is paid to his beneficiary. What is the death benefit rate of return to the beneficiaries?

Solution:

$$PMT_b = - \$310 \text{ per year}$$
$$n = 10 \text{ years}$$
$$FV = \$250,000 \text{ (death benefit) paid at the end of 10 years}$$
$$PV = \$0$$

Calculated result: $\quad i = 80\%$

We used the HP-12C to calculate the interest rate. Remember that the PMT_b is negative since the insured pays this over the lifetime of the policy.

Comparing Two Term Life-Insurance Policies

The ROR can be used to compare how much you will get for your money. Let's do this for two term life insurance policies we received in the mail as solicitations. We shall call them A and B.

Example 16.2: Compare the ROR of Two term Policies

Table 16.1: Annual Rates for Two Ten Year Guaranteed Level Term Life-Insurance Policies.

	Policy A			Policy B	
Issue Age	$250,000		Issue Age	$250,000	
	Male	Female		Male	Female
20	$267	$222	20	$225	$223

It is quite obvious that policy A is more expensive than policy B. However, we will go through the exercise to determine the ROR for a 20-year-old male. It is also useful to determine the present value of the stream of payments. Table 16.2 shows the death-benefit ROR for death of the insured occurring in one, five, or ten years after initiation of the policy. Table 16.3 shows the present value of the stream of premium payments. For practice, you can check some of the results.

**Table 16.2: ROR of Term Life Insurance Policies
for a 20-Year-Old Male**

Years	Death Benefit	ROR A	ROR B
1	$250,000	94,000%	111,000%
5	250,000	269	283
10	250,000	83	87

**Table 16.3 Present Value of the Cost of Premiums
at a Discount Rate of 7%.**

Years	PV of Policy A Cost	PV of Policy B Cost
1	$267	$225
5	1,171	987
10	2,007	1,691

The present value indicates how much current money would be necessary to provide the stream of premium payments if you could realize an after-tax return of 7% on your money.

For term policies, the comparative analysis is relatively straightforward. The ROR method will become more significant for whole life policy comparisons.

ANALYZING A GUARANTEED LIFE INSURANCE POLICY

Let's analyze an actual whole life type of insurance policy. One of the most advertised policies on TV is a $10,000 face-value whole life policy where the insurance company uses a popular old time TV personality to explain that the policy builds cash value while providing financial security for the beneficiaries. The insurance company offers this life insurance policy to people 45 to 75 years of age. We called the company and were sent an application and a sheet that provides the policy premium costs for a $10,000 policy. We subsequently asked for a ledger statement but they would not send one unless we filed an application for the policy and paid the first premium. We did, however, manage to get a sampling of the cash surrender value buildup over time for a few selected years.

The Policy

- Type: Whole life
- Insured: A 65-year-old male
- Face value: $10,000
- The annual premium cost = $792 (guaranteed not to change).

Details of the policy and the results of our calculations are shown in Table 16.4. The first column is the year of the policy since the year of initiation. All values shown by the table are beginning of the year values. The second column is the age of the insured. The third column shows the accumulation of the premiums paid by the insured. The fourth column shows the cash-surrender value as stated by the insurance company. The fifth column shows the cash value rates of return. The sixth column contains the calculated the death benefits rates of return rounded to the nearest percent.

The life expectancy multiple for a 65-year-old male is 15 years, as seen from Table 15.3 of Chapter 15 and repeated here for convenience. So we calculated the policy data through the 80th year of the insured.

Figure 15.3: Actuarial Table

Age		Multiples
Male	Female	
50	55	25.5
55	60	21.7
60	65	18.2
65	70	15.0

Table 16.4: A Guaranteed $10,000 Face Value Whole Life Insurance Policy

1	2	3	4	5	6
Beginning of Policy Year	Age of Insured	Cumulative Premiums Paid	Policy Cash Surrender Value*	Cash Surrender Value Rate of Return	Death Benefit Rate of Return
1	65	$792	$0		25%
2	66	1,584	0		16
3	67	2,376	580	−55%	209
4	68	3,168	890	−45	92
5	69	3,960	1,000	−43	52
6	70	4,752			33
7	71	5,544			22
8	72	6,336			15
9	73	7,128			10
10	74	7,920			7
11	75	8,712	3,010	−19	4
12	76	9,504			2
13	77	10,296			1
14	78	11,088			0
15	79	11,880			-1
16	80	12,672	4,380	−15	-2

* End of year value

Rate of Return Death Benefit Calculations

The ROR for the first two years is relatively low for this policy because the policy does not pay the face value of its $10,000 death benefit the first two years. This is to deter someone who is initially terminally ill from taking this policy and immediately collecting the death benefit. The first-year death benefit is 125% of the first year premium, or $1.25 \times \$792 = \$990$. The second-year death benefit is 250% of the annual premium, or $2.50 \times \$792 = \$1,980$. Calculation of the first year ROR is the following:

$$\text{ROR} = \frac{\$990 - \$792}{\$792} = 0.25 \text{ or } 25\%$$

As a further example let's show the ROR calculation at the end of the eleventh year. Note that the payments are made at the beginning of each year so PMT_b is negative when using the HP-12C calculator.

$$PV = 0$$
$$FV = \$10,000$$
$$PMT_b = -\$792$$
$$n = 9 \text{ years}$$

The calculated death benefit ROR is: $i = 6.7\%$ or 7% rounded

Let's show a cash flow diagram for this policy. Assume the insured paid $792 per year at the beginning of each year and died the end of the ninth year. The insured's beneficiaries receive $10,000.

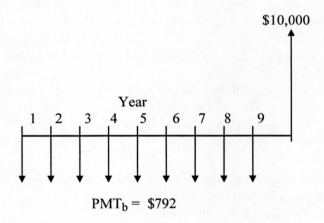

Rate of Return Cash Surrender Calculation

Let's calculate the cash surrender value rate of return for the eleventh year. The parameters are:

$$FV = \$3,010 \text{ received at the end of 11 years.}$$
$$PMT_b = -\$792$$
$$n = 11 \text{ years}$$

Calculated surrender value ROR $i = -19\%$

As seen from Table 16.4, since the cash surrender value rate of return of this policy never does reach positive values, the insured might question the wisdom of the advertised value of this policy. Moreover, if instead of taking the policy, the insured had invested the annual premiums in something like a tax-free Muni fund at an annual rate of 5%, his beneficiaries would get about twice the face value of the death benefit if the insured gentleman expired at his statistical expected age of 80 years.

AN INTEREST-SENSITIVE WHOLE LIFE POLICY WITH VANISHING PREMIUMS

We asked an insurance company to structure a policy for a 35-year-old male that would provide a death benefit of $250,000 for his family. The intent is to provide insurance protection until the insured retires at age 60. To supplement his income upon retirement, the insured would then annuitize the cash-surrender value of the policy over his expected lifetime. The insurance agent recommended a permanent whole life type of life insurance policy that offers a death benefit and in addition builds cash value. After a number of years the premiums are expected to vanish because the insurance company predicts that the premiums paid early on would earn sufficient money to continue paying the insurance death benefits and also provide some cash build-up. The particulars of this policy follow:

The Policy

- Type: Interest sensitive whole life policy with vanishing premiums
- The insured: 35-Year-old male
- Face value: $250,000 death benefit
- Nonsmoker

Table 16.5 shows a ledger statement of financial projections offered by the insurance company. These are projections developed by the computer service of the insurance company to illustrate the expected performance of the policy. The ledger statements are not guarantees of performance but are the expected results based on current practices and financial conditions. Anyone considering a policy should obtain a ledger statement and analyze the results.

The data in Table 16.5 show that the insured pays an annual premium of $2,385 for 14 years. At that time the insurance company projects that the cash value will earn enough to defray the expenses of the policy. The death benefit remains in force, and the excess earnings over insurance cost build cash-surrender value.

In the twenty-sixth year of the policy, the insured becomes 60 years of age, the cash surrender value is $73,395, and elects to receive a lifetime annuity payment estimated by the insurance company to be $460.55 per month. At that time the death benefit no longer exists.

Table 16.5: Financial Illustration of an Interest Sensitive Whole Life Policy

Beginning of Policy Year	Age of Insured	Premiums Paid	Cumulative Value of Premiums	Cash Surrender Value	Death Benefit
1	35	$2,385	$2,385	$0	$250,000
2	36	2,385	4,770	2,023	250,000
3	37	2,385	7,155	4,303	250,000
4	38	2,385	9,540	6,717	250,000
5	39	2,385	11,925	9,291	250,000
6	40	2,385	14,310	12,140	250,000
7	41	2,385	16,695	15,200	250,000
8	42	2,385	19,080	18,457	250,000
9	43	2,385	21,465	21,883	250,000
10	44	2,385	23,850	25,485	250,000
11	45	2,385	26,235	29,390	250,000
12	46	2,385	28,620	33,492	250,000
13	47	2,385	31,005	37,802	250,000
14	48	2,385	33,390	42,333	250,000
15	49	0	33,390	44,561	250,000
26	60	0	33,390	73,395	250,000

Table 16.6 shows the death-benefits rate of return for the policy. At policy year 26, the insured switches to the annuity plan.

Table 16.6: Death Benefits Rates of Return

Year of Policy	Death Benefit	Death Benefit Rate of Return
1	$250,000	10,400%
5	250,000	126
10	250,000	41
14	250,000	24
26	250,000	9

The calculated rate of return of the cash-surrender values are shown in Table 16.7. In the early years of the policy, the cash value builds very slowly.

Table 16.7: Rate of Return of Cash-Surrender Values

Year of Policy	Cash Surrender Value	Rate of Return
5	$9,291	−12.50%
10	25,485	1.46
15	44,561	3.06
26	73,395	4.27

Table 16.8 shows the results of the policy after the insured annuitizes. He receives a monthly payment of $460.55, which is a ten-year certain payout. This means that the insured will receive the payments for the remainder of his life, but if he dies early his beneficiaries will receive these payments for ten years from the start of the annuity.

Table 16.8: Rate of Return of Income from an Annuitized Interest-Sensitive Whole Life Policy

Current Age	Expected Life Multiple	Monthly Income @ Age 60	Cash Surrender Value	Rate of Return
60	18.2 years	$460.55	$73,395	3.67%
60	10 years	460.55	73,395	− 5.46

We calculated the rate of return for two cases: (1) the annuitant will live another 18.2 years, and (2) the 10-year certain period elected by the insured. The life-expected return multiple of a 60 year old male is 18.2 years per Table V (Table 15.3 of this book) of IRS Publication 939. The data for the first calculation are:

$PV = -\$73,395$, $FV = 0$, $PMT_b = \$460.55$, $n = 18.2$ years $\times$ 12 months/year $= 218$ months.

The calculated annual rate of return = 3.67%

The second calculation uses the same values except 120 months in place of 218. The resultant rate of return is: −5.46%,

CONSIDER INFLATION EFFECTS
WHEN PLANNING YOUR INSURANCE NEEDS

Life insurance benefits are paid in constant dollars, so the purchasing power of the money your beneficiaries receive will be considerably less by the time it gets to them. When calculating the amount of insurance you need, you must therefore take inflation into account To show how this is done, we will explain the present value approach. Recall that in Chapter 11 we determined the present value of money required to provide a stream of payments that take into account the effects of inflation. The process is the same when considering insurance. Let's determine the amount of death-benefit money that would provide 15 years of income for an insured person's family at an inflation rate of 4%. For simplicity, we assume that the death-benefit money, upon receipt, is invested by the beneficiaries in a tax-free bond fund.

Example 16.3: Inflation-Adjusted Death Benefit of an Insurance Policy

> Assumptions:
>> Income stream needed..................... 15 years
>> Real annual income needed............ 75% of current income
>> Current after-tax annual income..... $50,000
>> After-tax ROR achievable............. 5.50%
>> Average rate of inflation............... 4.0%

What face value insurance policy should the insured take to provide his family sufficient money to meet the needed income stream?

Solution:

The first-year after-tax income required by the beneficiaries is:

$$0.75 \times \$50,000 = \$37,500$$

Each year, the annual required income increases by 4%. For example, year 2 requires:

$$1.4 \times \$37,500 = \$39,000$$

The amount of each year's income adjusted for an inflation rate of 4% is shown in Table 16.9.

Table 16.9: Annual Incomes Inflated at a Rate of 4.0%

Year	Income	Year	Income
1	$37,500	9	$51,321
2	39,000	10	53,374
3	40,560	11	55,509
4	42,182	12	57,729
5	43,870	13	60,039
6	45,624	14	62,440
7	47,449	15	64,938
8	49,347		

Now we need to determine the present value of the annual income requirements for a discount rate of 5.50%. Recall that a discount rate of 5.50% is that expected by investing the death benefit money in a municipal tax free fund. The present value thus determined will be the real dollar values that account for inflation. The results are shown by Table 16.10.

Table 16.10: Present Values of Annual Incomes at a Discount Rate of 5.50%

Year	PV	Year	PV
1	$37,500	9	33,441
2	36,967	10	32,965
3	36,441	11	32,497
4	35,923	12	32,035
5	35,412	13	31,579
6	34,908	14	31,130
7	34,412	15	30,688
8	33,923		
Grand total = $509,821			

The annual income payments start at the beginning of the year. Let's check the present value for the tenth year. For this we use $n = 9$ years because the present value is calculated for payments made at the beginning of the year. The PV of $53,374 at the beginning of year 10 is from Table 16.9.

$$PV = \frac{1}{(1+0.055)^9} \times \$53,374 = \$32,965$$

Although the inflation-adjusted present value amount is $509,821, if the insured did not consider the effect of inflation for the insured's death benefit, he or she would have selected only $397,112, calculated as follows:

$$FV = 0, PMT_b = \$37,500, n = 15 \text{ years}, i = 5.5\%,$$

The calculated present value $PV = \$397,112$.

Now It's Your Turn:

1. For the same annual premiums, a term type of life insurance policy offers a greater amount of death benefit than a whole life policy.
    a. True
    b. False

2. A term policy builds cash value throughout the policy's lifetime.
    a. True
    b. False

3. The death-benefit rate of return of a $250,000 face-value term policy in which the insured pays $300 at the beginning of each year for 15 years is (round to the nearest whole number):
    a. 53%
    b. 65%
    c. 45%

4. If the policy in question 3 above has a 10-year level annual payment of $250, the 10 year death benefit ROR is:
    a. 87%
    b. 85%
    c. 115%

5. John bought a whole life policy with a face value of $500,000. If he should die in 20 years, how much money in real dollar terms would that policy provide his beneficiaries, if the average rate of inflation over that period was 4%?

   a. $228,193

   b. $500,000

   c. $150,678

6. Ben bought a $10,000 whole life insurance policy. The monthly premiums are $105. Ben's remaining life expectancy is 10 years. What would his death-benefit rate of return be if he lived to his actuarial age?

   a. 7%

   b. 5%

   c. - 5.%

7. Ben decided not to take the policy in question 6, but invested the $105 monthly cost of premiums of in a tax-free mutual fund that returned 5.5%. How much money would his fund be worth in 10 years?

   a. $16,825

   b. $10,000

   c. $12,680

8. An insurance company offers a $12,000 policy for a child at a cost of $3.50 per month for boys. The cost is firm until the child reaches the age of 25. What would the rate of return of the death benefits be when a boy reaches 25?

   a. 18%

   b. 15%

   c. 25%

9. A male 35 years of age bought a whole life policy that will be paid up at age 98. The annual premium payable, for 63 years, is $3,000. At the end of age 65, the expected cash-surrender value is $230,000 and the death benefit is $360,000. When the insured reaches age 65, what are the rates of return of the cash value and death benefit?

   a. 6.53% and 9.34%

   b. 5.52% and 10.23%

   c. 5.52% and 7.90%

10. Bill has a whole life policy. He paid premiums of $150 per month for 18 years. He then annuitized the policy and will receive annuity payments of $260 per month for the remainder of his life. If Bill's remaining life expectancy is 15 years, what amount of his annual payments are excluded from income taxes?

   a. $2,160
   b. $3,126
   c. $1,890

11. For question 10, what will Bill's after-tax rate of return be if he lives for 15 years after annuitizing? His policy's cash value was $34,800 when he started to annuitize, and his marginal tax bracket is 20%.

   a. 3.22%
   b. 4.35%
   c. 2.15%

12. What amount of present value insurance would you need to provide a real dollar after-tax annual income of $30,000 for 5 years if the average rate of inflation will be 3% and you can realize an after tax rate of return of 5%?.

Year Begin	Income Required	Present Value
1	$30,000	$30,000
2	30,900	
3		
4		
5		
Present value total		?

   a. $150,000
   b. $144,00
   c. $11700

ANSWERS: 1. a, 2. b, 3c. 4.b, 5.a, 6.c, 7.a, 8.b, 9.b, 10. a, 11.a, 12.b

How to Make Financial Trade-Off Decisions

LEARNING OBJECTIVES:

In this chapter you will gain information on how to make economically driven decisions, for example, should you:

1. Buy or lease that new auto?
2. Buy a new or used auto?
3. Keep that old appliance or replace it with a new more efficient one?
4. Select a discounted initial payment plan or make time payments?

There are many occasions when you need to choose between economic alternatives such as those listed just above. In the jargon of economics, these deliberations are called "trade-off studies." Trade-offs involve weighing and comparing the cost of each alternative, such as the initial cost of buying a new appliance verses keeping an old appliance that costs more to repair and operate. For example, trading the initial cost of buying a new appliance in favor of keeping the old one that costs more to repair and operate. In business, engineering, and other fields, these decisions are made continuously and must factor in the benefit-cost comparison.

Trade-off decisions are influenced by the interest rates paid or the rate of return from investments realized by those making the decisions. Interest exists as an economic fact: if you borrow money it is necessary to pay interest; if you have money, you have potential to earn a return by investing it. Where a choice is to be made between alternatives that involve different money receipts and disbursements at different times, it is essential to consider interest paid or the rate of return achievable. For example the trade-off involves either paying the money up front to buy a new item but losing the opportunity to invest that money, or not paying the money up front but repairing and keeping the old item because you do so well with your investments that you have an opportunity for more productive use of that capital.

The procedure for conducting these studies is to:

1. Identify and gather the financial data involved for each alternative, such as the capital and operating costs of each in terms of cash flow. These data are gathered over the life cycle of each alternative.
2. Compare the costs of each alternative, either as the present value or the equivalent uniform annual cost of operation.

The Present Value Method

The *present value* method compares the expenditures and incomes at the same point in time. Future expenditures and receipts are discounted with a constant discount rate to reflect the time value of money. All initial cash flows are added to the present value of all future cash flows to obtain a total present value of the life-cycle cash flows of each alternative bring compared. The lowest present value of the alternatives is usually the most favorable choice.

The Equivalent Uniform Annual Cost Method

Equivalent uniform annual costs are obtained by calculating the life-cycle costs of each alternative to an equivalent uniform annual cost using a common interest rate. The *equivalent uniform annual cost* is used because we are comparing nonuniform series of disbursements and receipts in which money has time value. The present value of each alternative is spread out to form a uniform annual cash flow. By this method the nonuniform disbursements of receipts become comparable cash flows.

BUY OR LEASE THAT NEW AUTO?

There are many options available when leasing a new auto. It is important to read and study the contract terms and conditions, especially the fine print. The presentation here is aimed at the economic decision process rather then the multitude of leasing agreements. As such, the lease examined here is a closed end lease: the lessee can return the auto at the end of the lease term, and either turn it in without additional cost, or buy it for the bring-back price agreed upon at the beginning of the lease.

As you will notice, the decision depends on the rate you earn on your invested money, or the interest rate you pay to borrow funds.

Example 17.1: Buy or Lease that New Auto?

Charley needs a new auto and is faced with the question of whether to lease one, pay cash and buy it outright, or finance it over a three year period. Charley would like to also know how the present value of the leased and financed options vary as a function of the interest rate he might earn on his invested money. He selected an interest rate range of 0% to 15%. The facts of the three options are:

1. *Lease the auto*	2. *Buy the auto and pay cash*
Security deposit................$300	Price.........................$17,135
Initial payment $2,000	License and fees...............$350
Payments for 36 months $235	State tax rate.....…..........7.75%
Option to purchase price	
at end of lease period...$10,134	3. *Buy the auto but finance it*
License and fees.................$350	Same prices as option 2
State tax rate....................7.75%	Finance interest rate..... 9%
	Term................. 36 months

If Charley leases the auto, he intends to buy it at the end of the lease period. He thinks that the end-of-lease price appears to be reasonable.

> *Option 1: Lease*
>
> | | |
> |---|---|
> | Initial payment...................................... | $2,000 |
> | State taxes..............(0.0775 × $2,000) | $155 |
> | Security payment.................................... | $300 |
> | License and fees.................................... | $ 350 |
> | Total Initial Payment....................….. | $2,805 |
> | Purchase price at lease end (1.0775 × $10,134) | $10,919 |
> | Monthly payments are (1.0775 × $235)........... | $253 |

Option 2: Pay Cash
The present value purchase price of the new auto is:

Price..	$17,135
State taxes $(0.0775 \times \$17,134)$	$1,328
License and fees........................	$350
Total Cost.......	$18,813

Option 3: Finance
The down payment is 5% of $18,813, or $940.
The monthly payments @ 9.00% are $568.36 to pay the balance of $17,873 financed for 36 months.

Solution:

The present value method of comparison will be used. Table 17.1 and Figure 17.1 show the calculated results. Before we discuss them, let's show an example of how the results are calculated. Consider the case of leasing where Charley's investment rate of return is 8%. The calculated present values are:

Initial payment..	$2,805
PV of 36 payments of $253 @ 8%	$8,128
PV of $10,919 purchase amount in 3 years....	$8,668
Less present value of $300 security deposit.....	($238)
Total present value	$19,363

It should be noted that for a lease payment, the present value of the periodic payments is PMT_b because the first payment is made at the beginning of the month. Also, for simplicity, the present value of all lump sum payments at the end of 36 months was calculated with $n = 3$ years and an 8% nominal interest rate. (We did not calculate the present value of the state license fees for the years 2 and 3, since these would be equal for all options.)

Table 17.1
Comparison of New Auto Purchase Options

	Charley's Investment Rates of Return			
	0%	5%	8%	15%
	Present Value Costs of Options $			
Lease	$22,532	$20,455	$19,363	$17,115
Pay cash	18,813	18,183	18,183	18,183
Finance	21,400	19,896	19,070	17,329

Figure 17.1
Present Value of New Auto Purchase Options

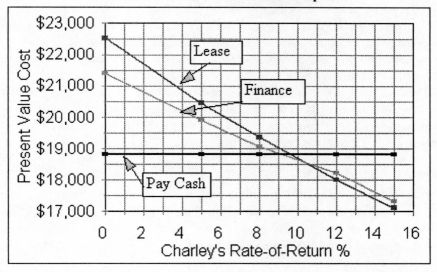

Several interesting conclusions can be drawn from the results shown in Table 17.1 and Figure 17.1:

1. When Charley pays cash, the present value is simply the total sum paid for the auto, and it's value does not change regardless of Charley's investment rate of return. This is because all the money for the auto is paid upon delivery.

2. For the cases where there are time payments made in the future, Charley's investment rates of return strongly influences the present value costs of the auto. If Charley enjoys no return on his invested, the present value cost of each option is the sum of money actually paid for the auto.

3. At 9% ROR on Charley's invested money, all present values are essentially the same. Since the interest rate charged for the loan is also 9%, the finance curve passes exactly through 9%.
4. If Charley's investment rate of return is less than 9%, he is better off by paying cash for the auto. Between 9% to 11% ROR, Charley is better off to finance the auto. Above 11%, leasing and financing are about equal values.

BUY A NEW OR A USED CAR?

Often, at financial seminars you, will be frequently told that it is more economical to buy a two-year-old car than a new one. The rationale here involves the relatively large depreciation in the value of a new auto. This can be a fallacy, however. If you do not sell or trade your new auto early on, there is no cash flow. Depreciation is an accounting term, not a cash flow term.

The decision is, of course, an economic one. It depends on the initial price, how long you keep the your auto, the cost of annual maintenance, and the auto's end-of-life sale value. It may be that you are driving a used car for a cost not too different from that of a new car. Let's look at the process for two autos.

Example 17.2: Buy a New or a Used Auto?

Ben decided to buy an auto. He wanted to analyze the options of whether to buy a new auto or a two-year-old one. He set out to gather the financial data of two autos; Car A and Car B. He took sales data for these cars from his local newspaper and he also estimated the annual costs of operation. (The annual costs do not include gasoline, since both models have equivalent gas mileage.)

When conducting such a trade-off study, you must gather data as it pertains to your particular situation. The cost data Ben gathered are shown in Table 17.2. For each car there are cost data for both the new and used models. Ben assumed that he would own the car whether new or used, for eight years.

Solution:

Ben decided to calculate and compare both the present value and the uniform annual capital costs of owning these autos. He selected an interest rate of 8%. He developed and listed the financial data for each option as shown in Table 17.2.

Table 17.2
Cost Data for New and Used Auto Purchase Options

	Car A		Car B	
	New	Used *	New	Used *
Sale price	$18,700	$13,900	$19,200	$16,300
Annual cost	1,500	1,800	1,200	1,500
Trade in value	4,500	3,000	6,300	4,900

* Two-year-old auto

The next step is to calculate the present value and the uniform annual costs of owner-ship using the data of Table 17.2.

Calculating the Present Value

The total present value cost of each of these cars is determined by calculating the present value of the annual cost, adding this to the initial sale price, and subtracting the present value of the trade-in price.

As a sample, we will calculate the present value of Car A. Recall $n = 8$ years, $i = 8\%$. Initial cost = $18,700

PV of the annual costs of (PMT_e) $1,500 for 8 years is calculated as $8,620.
The present value of the trade-in value (FV) of $4,500 is calculated as $2,430.
The net present value sum of these costs is $18,700 + $8,620 − 2,430 = $24,890.

Calculating the Uniform Annual Costs

Once the present value has been determined for each option, it is used to find the uniform annual cost. We will perform a sample calculation of the uniform annual cost of Auto A. The annual costs of the (PMT_e) sales price of $18,700 for 8 years is $3,250 per year. The uniform annual value of the trade-in-value of $4,500 is $FV = \$4,500$, $i = 8\%$, $n = 8$ years, PV = 0, and the annual credit is calculated as $PMT_e = \$420$. The annual cost is $1,500. The total of each annual payment is $3,250 + $1,500 − $420 = $4,330

The calculated data of the alternatives are shown in Table 17.3.

Table 17.3
Present Value and Uniform Annual Costs for 8 Years of Auto Ownership.

	Car A		Car B	
	New	Used	New	Used
Sale price	$18,700	$13,900	$19,200	$16,300
PV of annual cost	8,620	10,340	6,900	8,620
PV of trade in	2,430	1,620	3,400	2,650
Present value totals	$24,890	$22,620	$22,700	$22,270
Uniform annual cost	$4,330	$3,940	$3,950	$3,880

For eight years of ownership, the cost data Ben gathered show that the more expensive Car B bought new has a capital cost (present value) essentially the same as that of used Car A. Further, he found that the present value and uniform annual costs of new Car B are not significantly different from those of the used Car B. This data show the one can drive new Car B as economical as used Car A. Ben decided to buy the new Car B.

KEEP OR REPLACE THAT INEFFICIENT APPLIANCE?

Appliances frequently come on the market that are more efficient than your existing model. Especially when the older model needs some repair work performed, it is prudent to compare the cost of the new model and its savings in operating costs with the option of keeping and repairing the old model. Even if the old model needs no repair, it may still be economical to replace it due to the savings in operating costs. To conduct this economic comparison, you must calculate the present value of the savings in order to determine how much you should pay for the new model.

Example 17.3: *Keep and Repair the Old Water Softener or Replace it with a New More Efficient Model?*

The Jones have a five-year-old water softener that uses $20 worth of salt per month for regeneration. A new model is on the market that will perform the same service for $10 worth of salt each month. The old model needs a new timer at a cost of $150. Mr. Jones expects to keep the old water softener ten more years, but it will probably need another timer in five years.

The new model costs $900. Mr. Jones also believes that the new softener will need a timer every five years. What are the present value and equivalent uniform annual cost of these alternatives? Is the initial cost of $900 justified by the savings in the cost of salt?

Mr. Jones estimates that the time value of his money is a discount rate of (or interest rate) of 8% per year.

Solution:

Mr. Jones decided to use both the present value and the equivalent uniform annual cost method for this comparison. Mr. Jones decided to do both based on the next ten years of operation. Mr. Jones does not think either of these units will have salvage value at the end of ten years, and newer models will be on the market to warrant another decision. The cost data are itemized in the table.

	Old Water Softener	New Water Softener
Initial cost	$150	$900
Annual operating cost	240	120
Maintenance cost in 5 years	150	150
Future value	0	0

Present Value of Old Water Softener
Initial cost............ ......$150
PV of annual costs 1,739
PV of $150 timer.......... 102
Total PV.............. $1,991

Present Value of New Softener
Initial cost.................$900
PV of annual cost.........869
PV of $150 timer..........102
Total PV......... ... $1,871

To calculate the present value of the annual cost involved values of PMT_b = the annual cost, $n = 10$ years, $i = 8\%$ and $FV = 0$. The present value of the five year cost of the timer involved $FV = \$150$, $n = 5$ years, $PMT_b = 0$, and $i = 8\%$.

Annual Cost of Old Water Softener

PMT_b of initial cost.............$21

Annual cost of operation.....240

Annual cost of timer.............14

Total annual cost...........$275

Annual Cost of New Water Softener

PMT_b of initial cost........$124

Annual cost of operation...120

Annual cost of timer.....   ...14

Total annual cost........ $258

We found the annual cost PMT_b of the initial values by using PV = initial cost, n = 10 years, i = 8% and FV = 0.

There is not a large cost differential between these two alternatives, but the results show a small savings to offsetting the higher initial cost of the new unit. Because of this, the Jones decided that they might as well buy a new unit.

REPLACE YOUR AIR CONDITIONER WITH A NEW, MORE EFFICIENT UNIT?

An organization called The American Council for an Energy Efficient Economy has published a guide that points out that newer home air conditioners are significantly more efficient than most of their predecessors. A seasonal energy efficiency ratio (termed "SEER") is used to define the efficiency. The SEER rating is the ratio of the Btu per hour cooling capacity of the evaporator divided by the power consumption of the compressor and the condenser blower, expressed in watts. The SEER rating forms the basis for comparing the efficiency of the units offered on the market. The Council's guide states that older units typically have SEER ratings of only 7, whereas the new units have SEER ratings of 15. All other things being equal, this means that the new units will operate at the same capacity but at one-half of the operating cost.

Let's apply the present value method to see how this difference affects a decision about whether to keep the existing unit or replace it with a more efficient one.

Example 17.4: *Replace Central Home Air Conditioner with a more Efficient*

New Unit?

Suppose you have a home with a central air conditioner. It has been operating for six years. The unit's cooling capacity is 36,000 Btu per hour. Your existing unit has a SEER rating of 8, and the replacement unit offered by a contractor has a SEER rating of 15. The contractor offers to replace the your existing unit for a cost of $3,500. An air conditioner unit is relatively maintenance-free, but the compressors usually requires replacement once every 12 years at a cost of $800.

Assuming that your rate of return on your invested money is 8%, is it economical to replace your six-year-old unit with a new more efficient one?

Solution:

Gathering the economic data takes a little engineering unless your contractor can supply the facts and make the comparison. It isn't too difficult, so we will do it here. First you need to know the cost of electricity. For the PG & E system in the San Francisco Bay Area the cost is 12 cents per kilowatt-hour (kWh).

Let's assume that you will run your air conditioner for a total of 1,000 hours per season. For a 3-ton unit (36,000 Btu per hour capacity) with a SEER rating of 8, the unit has a power consumption of 4,500 watts or 4.5 kilowatts (kW). This is calculated using the SEER ratio definition:

$$\frac{36,000 \text{ Btu / hr}}{\text{watts}} = 8$$

$$\text{watts} = \frac{36,000}{8} = 4,500 \text{ watts or } 4.5 \text{ kW}$$

A unit with a 15 SEER rating will require 2.4 kW power input. Remembering our unit analysis discussion of Chapter 2, the annual cost of operation is calculated as:

$$\text{Annual cost of new unit's operation} = 2.4 \text{ kW} \times 1,000 \ \frac{\text{hr}}{\text{yr}} \times \frac{\$0.12}{\text{kWh}} = \$288 \text{ per year}$$

$$\text{Annual cost of old unit's operation} = 4.5 \text{ kW} \times 1,000 \ \frac{\text{hr}}{\text{yr}} \times \frac{\$0.12}{\text{kWh}} = \$540 \text{ per year}$$

Since inflation will come into play over the 15-year period we will adjust the values to accommodate it. Assume that the cost of electricity inflates at an annual rate of 2%.

In 15 years, the annual costs of operation will be a factor of 1.34 higher. This is calculated by:

$$(1+0.02)^{15} = 1.34$$

The final year annual cost will be $1.34 \times \$288 = \$386$ for the new unit and $724 for the old one. Averaging the first-year and fifteen-year values we have ($228+386)/2=$337 for the new unit and $632 for the old unit. We now have the cost data tabulated in the table below.

| | Air Conditioners | |
	Old Unit	New Unit
Initial cost	$0	$3,500
Annual cost	$632	$337
Cost of compressor	$900 in 6 yrs	$1,014 in 12 yrs
Life cycle	15 years	15 years

The present value of the new air conditioner is the initial cost of $3,500, plus the present value of the uniform annual cost of $337, plus the present value of replacing the compressor in 12 years. We now calculate the present values for an air conditioner life cycle of 15 years. The present value of the new unit's annual operation cost is: $PMT_e=\$337$, $n = 15$ years, $i = 8\%$, $PV = ?$ Using a calculator, we have $PV =\$2,885$.

Calculating the remaining cost values, we arrive at the comparative values shown in the table below.

| | Air Conditioners | |
	Old Unit	New Unit
Initial cost	$0	$3,500
PV of operation	5,410	2,885
PV of maintenance	567	402
Total PV	$5,977	$6,787

With a present value disadvantage of $810 over 15-years of ownership, there is no incentive to make the change now. You would probably be better advised to wait and reevaluate your options periodically.

Notice, too, that the initial cost of the old air conditioner unit did not enter into the comparison. If the old unit had either a salvage or trade-in value, its present value would have been a credit to the initial cost of the old unit.

A CHOICE OF PAYMENT PLANS

Sometimes you will be presented with a payment plan for a necessary expense. Take the case of an orthodontist. The following example provides the situation.

Example 17.5: An Orthodontist Offers Two Payment Plans

Frank and Jane's ten-year-old daughter needs some orthodontic work. The orthodontist offers treatment for $2,500, payable by two methods:
1. Make an initial payment of $628, followed by 18 monthly payments of $104.
2. Make a single payment now of $2,375 (which turns out to be a 5% discount).

Frank and Jane have their money in CDs that pay an interest rate of 4%. Which of these options would be their choice.

Solution:

The comparison can be made by calculating the present value of the first method and comparing it to the second method. The present value of the first method is $628 plus the present value of 18 monthly payments of $104 at an interest rate of 4%. This is $PMT_e = \$104$, $n = 18$ months, and $i = 0.04/12 = 0.00333$. The calculated present value is $1,814. The total present value of the first option is $628 + $1,814 = $2,442.

Frank and Jane selected the second option.

It is illuminating to see why the second payment is more economical than the first. To do this we must determine what interest rate the orthodontist would realize on the first payment plan. This is determined by the parameters $PV = \$2,375 - \$628 = \$1,747$, $n = 18$ months, and $PMT_e = \$104$ per month. The present value of $1,747 is actually the amount that the orthodontist loans to Frank and Jane. Using the HP-12C, we find the annual nominal interest rate to be 8.85%. The effective interest rate is 9.22%. Since Frank and Jane only realize 4% on their investments, it is obvious that they are at a disadvantage when it comes to financing a loan at 8.85%. Only if they made a return significantly higher than 8.85% would it make sense to choose the first payment plan.

Now It's Your Turn:

1. The basic attributes for conducting trade-off studies involves comparing either the present values or the uniform annual costs of the alternatives.
    a. True
    b. False

2. It is easier to compare the uniform annual costs for trade-off studies in which the alternatives have different life cycles.
    a. True
    b. False

3. The time value of money is only of secondary important for economic trade-off studies.
    a. True
    b. False

4. Alternatives A & B have the following data of the table below:
    Compare the total present value costs of these alternatives for a discount rate of 7% if the annual costs are paid at the end of the year.

	A	B
Initial cost	$1,000	$2,000
Uniform annual cost	$500	$200
Life cycle	10 years	10 years

    a. PV of A = $3,468, PV of B = $5,106
    b. PV of A = $4,512, PV of B = $3,405
    c. PV of A = $3,565, PV of B = $2,592

5. Luxury Auto A costs $40,000 new and has an 18 miles per gallon (MPG) fuel rating. A good but more common Auto B costs $17,000 and is rated at 25 MPG. Mike would like to know the present value cost of driving the luxury auto in comparison to the more economical auto. He intends to keep his auto *eight* years. The sale price of Auto A at that time is $25,000 compared to $4,500 for Auto B. Mike drives 12,000 miles per year and realizes a rate of return of 18% on his investments. The

cost of gasoline is $1.30 per gallon. All other things being equal, what did Mike find the present value costs of these auto to be? Assume that gas money is charged at the beginning of each year.

    a. Auto A's PV = $40,200, Auto B's PV = $22,600

    b. Auto A's PV = $37,500, Auto B's PV = $18,000

6. Mike found that he made an error in estimating his annual rate of return for question 5. The value should have been 6% per year. What are the present values now?

    a. Auto A's PV = $30,000, Auto B's PV = $18,300

    b. Auto A's PV = $42,000, Auto B's PV = $24,500

7. In question 5, Mike decided to compare keeping Auto A for 12-years with Auto B's cost of 8 years. Auto A will sell for $6,000 in 12-years. Compare the annual cost of owning each of these autos. Mike decided that his discount rate should be 10% for the period of time under consideration.

    a. Auto A's PMTb = $5,500, Auto B's PMTb = $4,400

    b. Auto A's PMTb = $5,900, Auto B's PMTb = $3,400

8. Mary heard that newer refrigerators are much more efficient than older units and thus can save considerable money. She called a local appliance store and obtained the data on a new unit. She took data from her 25-cubic-foot refrigerator's manual and aligned all the data in the table. Mary estimates her discount rate to be 8%. What did she find the present value costs of these options to be?

Refrigerator Cost Data	Old Unit	New unit
Initial cost	$0	$1,200
Annual electricity cost *	175	95
Annual maintenance cost	50	10
Salvage value	0	200
Life cycle years	10	10

*@ 0.12 cents per kw hr

a. Old unit PV = $1,510, New unit PV = $1,800

b. Old unit PV = $2,300, New unit PV = $2,100

9. The Johnsons live in Grand Rapids, Michigan. An inspection of their furnace revealed a cracked bonnet. The contractor told them that they could repair the bonnet for $500, or install a new unit for $3,000. The new furnace has a thermal efficiency of 90%, verses 60% for the existing unit. Their current home heating bill is $1,200 per season. The new unit would reduce their annual heating bill to $800 (60/90 × $1,200 = $800). The Johnsons intend to live in this house ten more years, then sell it and retire to Arizona. They believe that a more efficient furnace will help sell their house in the future but do not think it will add to the sales price in ten years. If the present value costs of these alternatives are roughly equal or favor the new unit, they will replace the old unit. Did they replace the old unit? The cost of money to the Johnsons is 9%.

    a. Yes

    b. No

ANSWERS: 1.a, 2.a, 3.b, 4.b, 5.b, 6.a, 7.b, 8.a, 9.a

Consumer Credit and Loans

LEARNING OBJECTIVES:

The government has provided a federal regulation to implement the federal Truth-in-Lending Act (Regulation Z). This Act is intended to promote the informed use of consumer credit. In this chapter we review different types of consumer credit and loans. We show how Regulation Z defines the annual percentage rate (APR) applicable to such loans. The consumer loans discussed in this chapter include:

1. Credit card loans
2. Home equity lines of credit
3. Add-on loans
4. Discounted loans
5. The Rule of 78

Credit is something that virtually everyone will use. In order to make wise choices, it is advantageous to understand and be able to analyze different credit options. In Chapter 3 we stated that some interest calculations applied by the financial community are not pure compound or simple interest methods, but aberrations of these methods. Some Consumer loans also fit this description. Some of these loans are desirable, others are not.

FEDERAL REGULATION Z:
THE TRUTH-IN-LENDING ACT

Regulation Z is issued by the Board of Governors of the Federal Reserve System to implement the federal Truth in Lending and Fair Billings Acts contained in Title I of the Consumer Credit Protection Act. It also implements Title XII, Section 1204 of the Competitive Equality Banking Act of 1987. Regulation Z applies to each individual or business that offers credit. The regulation does not govern charges for consumer credit. The declaration of purpose of this title states, in part:

> The informed use of credit results from an awareness of the cost of credit thereof by consumers. It is the purpose of this title to assure a meaningful disclosure of credit terms so that the consumer will be able to compare more readily the various credit terms available and avoid the uniformed use of credit, and to protect the consumer against inaccurate and unfair billing and credit card practices.

For those who might have a need to further understand Regulation Z, an official commentary on Regulation Z has been prepared by the staff of the Division of Consumer Affairs of the Federal Reserve Board. The commentary can be obtained along with Regulation Z.

For your use we will review how Regulation Z, Truth-in-Lending defines and applies the *annual percentage rate* (APR). This is the crux of determining the cost of credit. The following are some definitions taken from the Regulation Z, SECTION 226.14 — Determination of Annual Percentage Rate.

(a) *General rule.* The annual percentage rate is a measure of the cost of credit, expressed as a yearly rate. An annual percentage rate shall be considered accurate if it is not more than 1/8 of 1 percentage point above or below the annual percentage rate determined in accordance with this section.

(b) *Annual percentage rate for Sections 226.5a and 226.5b disclosures, for initial disclosures and for advertising purposes.* Where one or more periodic rates may be used to compute the finance charge, the annual percentage rate(s) to be disclosed for purposes of sections 226.5a, 226.5b, 226.6, and 226.16 shall be computed by multiplying each periodic rate by the number of periods in a year.

(SECTION 226.2 (14) defines *credit* as the right to defer payment of debt or to incur debt and defer its payment.)

Based on the terminology we have used in this book, you will recognize the annual percentage rate (APR) defined above as the nominal annual compound interest rate derived by multiplying the periodic interest rates by the number of periods in a year.

Regulation Z does not distinguish between simple and compound interest rate transactions. This is a shortcoming that you must circumvent with your knowledge of interest rate fundamentals.

Calculating the APR

Regulation Z defines and shows how finance charges (interest) are calculated. We have observed that the Regulation Z method of determining the annual percentage rate (APR) results in a *nominal* interest rate, not an *effective* interest rate (APY). For instance, on page 84 of Appendix J of the Regulation, an example is offered to explain the solution of a simple transaction. The example shows how to find the annual percentage rate (APR) of a loan of $1,000 repaid by 36 monthly payments of $33.61. It finds the annual percentage rate to be 12.83%. By using the values $PV = \$1,000$, $PMT_e = \$33.61$, and $n = 36$ months to calculate the interest rate i with the HP-12C financial calculator, you will compute 1.069% per month or 12.83% as the nominal rate for monthly compounding. Regulation Z does not point out that, to the lender, this is an effective annual percentage yield (APY) of 13.61%.

Yield is never mentioned in the Regulation. This approach is sufficient as long as you recognize that Regulation Z is written to inform the borrower (consumer). It does not reveal what the lender realizes in the loan transaction. But because the loan example offered by the Regulation stipulates that the borrower is paying monthly rather then annually, the APR is not the actual annual cost to the borrower. Rather, the annual percentage yield (APY) is.

Banks usually quote the APY (effective annual interest rate) when your money is on deposit, whereas the APR is quoted when you borrow money. The latter is in keeping with the terminology and requirements set forth by Regulation Z.

CREDIT CARD REVOLVING LOANS

Examples of credit cards are Visa and MasterCard. It is no secret that credit card borrowing is done at very high interest rates. Rates as high as 18% are normal. However, if you choose to pay the loan balance every month within the grace period, there is no interest charge. This is tantamount to interest-free money. This could appropriately be termed "smart money." For those who do not pay their full monthly balance, lenders calculate the interest charged by the "average daily balance method." In

Regulation Z, Section 226.5a—*Credit and Charge Card Applications and Solicitations* defines this method.

The *average daily balance* method is a hybrid between simple and compound interest. Simple interest is charged daily over the monthly billing period. For example, suppose your unpaid balance was $1,000 at the beginning of the billing cycle month and you charged $100 on the 10th, $50 on the 15th, and $200 on the 20th days of the month. The month is a 30-day month. The lending institution advertises and charges an APR of 16.15%, which is 0.0442% per day. The amount of interest accrued during this month is calculated as follows:

Table 18.1: Average Daily Balance of a Credit Card Loan

Loan Balance	Number of days	Weighted Balance
$1,000	30	$30,000
100	20	2,000
50	15	750
200	10	2,000
$1,350	75	$34,750

The average daily balance is: $\dfrac{\$34{,}750}{30 \text{ days}} = \$1{,}158.33$

The interest charged is: $\$1{,}158.33 \times 0.000442 \times 30 \text{ days} = \$15.36$
This interest is added to the loan balance, so you would be billed:
$\$1{,}350 + \$15.36 = \$1{,}365.36$

The minimum amount you are required to pay at the end of this billing cycle is 2% of the total billing or $0.02 \times \$1{,}350 = \$27$. (The minimum payment is 2 % or $10, whichever is greater.) If you only pay $27, the amount of $\$1{,}365.36 - \$27 = \$1{,}338.33$ is the starting balance for which daily interest is charged during the next month. Although the daily interest is calculated as simple interest, the unpaid interest carried over to the next month again earns interest. This is tantamount to monthly compounding. Although the APR to the borrower is 16.15%, the APY to the lender is 17.40%. The lender thus realizes a four-year doubling time of money.

If you pay the full balance each billing cycle, credit cards can be a very convenient way of handling money and keeping records. Also, you can take advantage of perks such as those offered by major auto manufactures, who will rebate 5% of your charged purchases up to a total credit of $7,000 toward the purchase of a new auto.

What Happens When You Only Pay the Minimum Monthly Amount?

If you pay only the minimum monthly amount on your credit card debt, you could be courting financial disaster. It was reported that consumers have been piling on credit card debt encouraged by the growing convenient of charging such items as groceries, doctor visits, auto down payments, and even college tuition. This resulted in 70% of us having a credit card debt of $3,900. Household debt is rising simply because many people are paying the "2% minimum due" each month, not realizing that such a low payment barely covers the interest charge.

Table 18.2 shows how this debt escalates. Assume the consumer starts the year with a $1,000 debt balance and charges $200 per month on his card. In one year the debt grows to $3,299 and the consumer pays $395 in interest. The 2% minimum payment barely covers the interest charged.

Take this to the extreme. We ran out this scenario on a computer spreadsheet program. If the consumer stopped monthly charges at the end of the first year and decided to make minimum payments, it would take about 36 years to pay off the $3,299 debt. The total interest paid by that time would be on the order of $11,000. We term this "dumb money."

Table 18.2: One-Year Credit Card Minimum Payment for an 18% Annual Interest Rate

Month	Monthly Amount Charged	Debt Balance	Monthly Interest charged	2% of Monthly Balance
0		1,000		20
1	200	1,197	17	24
2	200	1,394	20	28
3	200	1,589	23	32
4	200	1,783	26	36
5	200	1,976	29	40
6	200	2,169	32	43
7	200	2,360	34	47
8	200	2,550	37	51
9	200	2,739	40	55
10	200	2,926	43	59
11	200	3,113	45	62
12	200	3,299	48	66
Totals	$2,400	$3,299	$395	$562

HOME EQUITY LOANS

Banks offer loans secured by the equity in your home. Two type of loans are offered: *equity lines of credit* and *fixed-term loans*. The *fixed-term* loan is the same as your conventional mortgage loan, in which a principal sum of money is lent at an interest rate and is amortized by uniform monthly payments over a fixed term. (See Chapter 14 for a presentation of the fixed term loan.) The *equity line of credit* is a loan that allows you to write checks for funds as needed; you are charged interest only on the outstanding balance.

The interest charged for a home equity loan has the advantage of being income-tax deductible. Since tracing rules do not apply to home equity loans, the funds from these loans can be used for personal purposes (e.g., auto purchases, medical expenses). By making use of the home equity loans, therefore, what would have been nondeductible consumer interest becomes deductible qualified residence interest. You should check with your tax advisors for the specifics of this feature.

Equity Line of Credit Loans

A home equity line of credit is a form of revolving credit. Regulation Z describes a sample home-equity loan with a ten-year draw period followed by a five-year repayment period. During the draw period, it is not necessary to pay down the principal monthly, but all interest charges must be paid monthly. The principal can be paid any time—either as you go or deferred to the end of the ten-year draw period. At the end of the draw period, you must make monthly principal and interest payments. You can elect a repayment period of up to 15 years. No future money can be borrowed during the repayment period. As you will see later, the repayment schedule is not the same as that under a conventional home-mortgage amortization loan.

The bank we contacted offers a variable-interest-rate line of credit. They do not offer a fixed-rate line of credit loan. The variable rate is based on a publicly available index. This bank provided documentation which completely disclosed every thing required by Regulation Z. There are many different plans. Anyone interested in an equity line of credit must evaluate the terms, conditions, and fees. We will walk through the financial arrangements of a typical home-equity line of credit plan.

Determining the Amount of Credit Available.

The credit limit on your home equity is 75% of the equity in your home. Suppose you have a home appraised at $150,000 and a mortgage debt of $50,000. Your available credit would be:

Appraisal of home	$150,000
Percentage	× 75%
Percentage of appraised value	112,500
Less mortgage debt	− 50,000
Potential credit line	$62,500

The Draw Period

Let's suppose you chose to use a lump sum of $15,000 over a draw period of ten years. You elect to pay only the finance charges, and then intend to repay the principal over a 15 year term. (These are the bank's maximum available time durations.) There is an annual fee of $75, but no points and no other charges. Assume that at the start of your loan the stated APR is 9.25% variable, the margin is 3%, the index is 6.25%, and the lifetime rate CAP is 18%. You will be required to pay as a minimum the monthly finance charge of $15,000 × 0.0925/12 = $115.63. If the index changes to 6.00% by the next billing cycle, which is one month, the new APR would be 9.00%, and your monthly finance charge would be $15,000 × 0.090/12 = $112.50. Although you are currently using only $15,000, you could borrow an additional amount of $45,500 during the draw period. If you chose to withdraw additional money and/or pay money mid-monthly during the draw period, the method of determine the monthly finance charge would be the average daily balance method describe above for the credit card revolving line of credit.

The Repayment Period

During the repayment period, the consumer can no longer borrow money. The repayment method is a plan in which the minimum monthly payment changes every month even if the index remains constant. Also, the principal payment remains constant. It works like this. The monthly principal payment is determined by dividing the principal balance by the number of months in the payback period. For our example this would be $15,000/180 months = $83.33. The finance charge is the APR divided by 12 and multiplied by the monthly balance. Table 18.3 shows the minimum payments for the first six months and the last two months, assuming the index does not change. The first monthly interest payment is $15,000 × 0.0925/12 = $115.63. The next month's principal balance is reduced by $83.33. This process goes on for 180 months unless the consumer chooses to make additional monthly payments. The consumer could, in fact, discharge the loan at any time by a balloon payment. The last payment is $83.97 in 180 months if no additional principal payments are made and the index remains the same. The nominal rate of return of this payment series is, of course, 9.25% (except for the $75 annual charge). The APY to the bank is 9.65%.

Table 18.3: Repayment Schedule of a $15,000 Loan at 9.25% APR for a Term of 180 Months.

Month	Principal Balance	Monthly Interest Payment	Monthly Principal Payment	Minimum Monthly Payment
1	$15,000.00	$115.63	$83.33	$198.96
2	14,916.67	114.98	83.33	198.32
3	14,833.33	114.34	83.33	197.67
4	14,750.00	113.70	83.33	197.03
5	14,666.67	113.06	83.33	196.39
6	14,583.33	112.41	83.33	195.75

Observe that the consumer must pay a different amount of money each month. This disadvantage can be offset, however, by authorizing the bank to automatically withdraw the payment from a savings or checking account. Some banks will lower the interest rate charged, on the order of 0.25%, for automatic payment from an account held in that bank.

An overriding advantage of the home-equity line of credit is that it is income-tax deductible. This can be appreciated by examining your equivalent APR finance charge as a function of your marginal tax bracket. Table 18.4 shows these values for a 9.25% APR loan.

Table 18.4 Tax-Deductible Equivalent Annual Percentage Rate

Marginal Tax Bracket %	APR %	Tax-Deductible Equivalent APR %
15	9.25	7.86
28	9.25	6.66
36	9.25	5.92
39	9.25	5.64

For example if you itemize on your 1040 tax form and are in the 36% marginal tax bracket, the deductibility feature reduces cost of this loan to an APR of 5.92%.

THE ADD-ON LOAN

Add-on loans do not appear to be in widespread use currently. One prevalent use in the past has been auto loans. After we explain these loans you will see how hokey they are. It is difficult to believe that anyone would buy into these loans, but apparently many have. Here is an example of how, they work.

Example 18.1: The Add-On Loan

You have cut a deal to buy an auto and will finance $10,000 of the purchase price. The lender offers a 3-year add-on type of loan at 6%. (Not a bad interest rate, is it?) The lender calculates the carrying charges as: $10,000 \times 0.06 \times 3$ years $= \$1,800$. The total amount to be paid is determined by adding the carrying charges to the amount financed: $10,000 + \$1,800 = \$11,800$. The monthly payments are $11,800/36$ months $= \$327.78$. Is this really a 6% loan? What are the nominal and effective rates of this loan?

Solution:

This is not, of course, a 6% loan. If we set $PV = \$10,000$, $n = 36$ months, and $PMT_e = \$327.78$, we find the nominal interest rate to be 11.08%. This is an effective interest rate of 11.66%.

Section 226.22 (2) (c) of Regulation Z requires that the lender disclose the highest annual percentage rate for any such transaction. Thus the APR for the above add-on loan should be disclosed by the lender as 11.08%.

THE DISCOUNTED LOAN

The discounted loan is a loan to avoid if at all possible. For the discounted loan, the consumer must pay the interest charges up front. It is similar to a T-bill in reverse. The total amount of interest is initially discounted from the stated loan value, and the loan value is paid at the end of the term. Regulation Z does not address the discounted loan.

Example 18.2. *The Discounted Loan*

Matt is offered a simple interest discounted loan of $2,000 over a period of two years at an interest rate of 6%. How much interest is charged for this loan, how much money does Matt receive at the start of the loan, and what is the APR?

Solution:

The amount of interest charged is: $2,000 × 0.06 × 2 years = $240. Matt receives $2,000 − $240 = $1,760 at the beginning of the loan, not $2,000. He must pay back $2,000 at the end of two years.

The APR can be calculated as either a simple interest or a compound interest loan. Regulation Z does not provide an example of how a simple interest loan APR is calculated.

Simple interest APR:

For a simple interest loan the APR would be calculated by Formula 3.3 which is $FV = PV(1+i \times n)$.

If we rearrange Formula 3.3 we have $i = (FV/PV - 1)/n$
$PV = \$1,760, FV = \$2,000, n = 2,$
$i = (\$2,000/\$1,750 - 1)/2 = 0.0714$ or 7.14%

Compound interest APR

For a compound interest loan $FV = PV(1+i)^n$

$$i = \left(\frac{FV}{PV}\right)^{1/n} - 1 = (\$2,000/\$1,750)^{1/2} - 1 = 0.0690 \text{ or } 6.90\%$$

It would be interesting to see how lenders quote this loan in order to be in conformance with Regulation Z. It is not a 6.0% APR loan.

THE RULE OF 78: AVOID IT

The so called Rule of 78 is a method used to determine the schedule repaying the interest and principal of a loan. We could not find anyone who knew the origins of this method, Regulation Z does not address the Rule of 78. It appears that this type of interest schedule was resorted to before financial math became known because it is a method of getting more interest from borrowers who repay their loans early. It's not a lot of money, but why pay it? Use the correct financial math when calculating the repayment schedule and you will save money if you should desire to repay a loan early. Moreover, the Rule of 78 is not described in Regulation Z and it does not state the correct APR if the loan is not carried to term. It may not be an entirely legal process.

It is the practice to use the Rule of 78, when financing an auto. You may see a little box on the loan document that is checked, indicating the Rule of 78 will be used to calculate the repayment interest schedule. Avoid this if possible. In fact the Internal Revenue Service does not accept this practice when calculating something like the amount of deductible interest of a home mortgage.

The Rule of 78 is a sum-of-the-digits method. If you add the sum of the digits for the number of monthly payments in one year the result is: $1 + 2 + 3 + 4 + \cdots \cdots + 12 = 78$. Thus the name of the rule. The general equation to determine the sum of the digits (SD) is:

$$\text{Sum of the Digits} = \frac{n\,(n+1)}{2}$$

where n = the total number of payment periods in the term

For a payment period of 24 months, the $SD = \dfrac{24\,(24+1)}{2} = 300$

The amount of interest payable in any given month is the ratio of that month divided by the sum of the digits, multiplied by the total interest charged for the loan.

Example 18.3:

Using the Rule of 78, determine the repayment schedule for a loan of $15,000 over 12 months at an APR of 9.00%, then compare it to a conventional loan repayment schedule. Round all values to the nearest dollar.

Solution:

1. Determine the PMT_e of a loan with PV = $15,000, n = 12 months, and i=0.090/12=0.0075. The calculated PMT_e = $1,312.
2. The total finance charge is (12 × $1,312) – $15,000 = $744.
3. The first month's interest is: 12/78 × $744 = $114.
4. The principal balance at the end of the first month is $15,000 – ($1,312 – $114) = $13,802.

This procedure is repeated until all 12 month's interest has been calculated. The results are shown in Table 18.5. The last column shows the schedule of principal balances for a conventional loan.

Table 18.5: Loan Payment Schedule Comparing the Principal Balance of a Rule of 78 Loan and a Conventional loan

Month	% of Interest Earned		Monthly Payment	Interest payment	Principal * Balance	Principal** Balance
1	12/78	15.38%	$1312	$114	$13,802	$13,800
2	11/78	14.10	1312	105	12,595	12,592
3	10/78	12.82	1312	95	11,378	11,375
4	9/78	11.54	1312	86	10,152	10,149
5	8/78	10.26	1312	76	8,916	8,913
6	7/78	8.97	1312	67	7,671	7,668
7	6/78	7.69	1312	57	6,416	6,414
8	5/78	6.41	1312	48	5,152	5,150
9	4/78	5.13	1312	38	3,878	3,877
10	3/78	3.85	1312	29	2,595	2,594
11	2/78	2.56	1312	19	1,302	1,302
12	2/78	1.28	1312	10	0	0
	78/78	100%	$15,744	$744	$15,000	$15,000

*Principal balance, Rule of 78 loan.   **Principal balance conventional loan.

Notice the higher principal balance you would have to pay if you were to pay off the loan early under the Rule of 78 schedule. Although for this example the difference is not great, it becomes more significant for longer term loans. For example, if you had an auto loan of $18,000 for a term of 48 months, you would pay a penalty of $47 to pay the balance after 15 months. Why pay it? If possible, just refuse to take a loan with the Rule of 78 invoked.

Now It's Your Turn:

1. Regulation Z of the Truth-in-Lending Act informs the consumer about how the cost of credit is determined. It does not regulate the cost of credit.
    a. True
    b. False

2. Regulation Z discloses the methods for calculating both the APR and the APY of a consumer loan.
   a. True
   b. False

3. The APR defined by Regulation Z is actually the nominal annual interest rate charged.
   a. True
   b. False

4. The average daily balance method of calculating finance charges for a credit-card revolving credit type of loan results in a:
   a. A simple interest loan
   b. A compound interest loan
   c. A combination of both

5. Richard's credit card account has a starting balance of $2,570. During the next month, which was September, Richard charged $50 on the 5th, $65 on the 11th, $105 on the 18th, and $255 on the 25th. Using the average daily balance method, how much interest will Richard be charged for the month of September? The APR charged is 18%.
   a. $10.52
   b. $40.50
   c. $50.52

6. For question 5, what was Richard's total billing for September?
   a. $2,630.50
   b. $2,750.20
   c. $3,085.50

7. Stephanie has been offered an add-on loan of 5% over a term of 48 months. She will borrow $10,000 for the purchase of a new car. What is the finance charge for this loan and what will her monthly payments be?
   a. $2,000 and $250.00
   b. $400 and $216.67
   c. $800 and $225.00

8. What APR should the lender quote to Stephanie for the loan of question 7?
    a. 5.00%
    b. 9.24%
    c. 7.73%

9. Jack and Betty have decided to secure a home equity line of credit to buy an auto. They need to borrow $18,000 over a four-year period. The bank offered this credit for an APR of 9.25%. They decided to make interest-only payments for 5 years. What is the required minimum monthly payment for this line of credit?
    a. $238.67
    b. $128.75
    c. $138.75

10. Jack and Betty decided to repay the loan of question 9 over a 5-year repayment period. What will their first month's required minimum principal and interest payments be?
    a. $200 and $138.75
    b.$300 and $138.75
    c. $350 and $152.75

11. If Jack and Betty are in the 28% marginal income tax bracket and they itemize deductions, what would their tax-equivalent APR for the loan of question 9 be?
    a. 6.66%
    b. 9.25%
    c. 7.66%

12. Clarence is offered a discounted type of loan in which he would borrow $3,000 over a period of 3-years. He will receive $2,400 initially and pay $3,000 at the end of 3-years. What would the APR of this loan be if Clarence considered this to be a simple interest loan?
    a. 6.66%
    b.6.00%
    c.8.33%

13. Using the Rule of 78, what would be the sum of the digits for a 36-month term loan?
    a. 666
    b. 300
    c. 444

14. If you took a 36 month loan of $20,000 at an APR of 9.25%, what would the first month's interest and principal payments be for a Rule of 78 type of payback method?
    a. $159.07 and $479.25
    b. $161.06 and $477.26
    c. $171.06 and $467.26

ANSWERS: 1.a, 2.b, 3.a, 4.c, 5.b, 6.c, 7. a, 8.b, 9.c, 10.b, 11.a, 12.c, 13. a, 14.b

Using Computer Spreadsheets for Financial Calculations

LEARNING OBJECTIVES:

Computer spreadsheets are a valuable tool for calculating financial problems. This chapter will help you learn how to:

1. Apply basic worksheet techniques
2. Write and apply mathematical formulas
3. Use built-in preprogrammed financial functions such as the internal rate of return (IRR)
4. Create worksheets for financial applications such as a mortgage amortization schedule

Computer spreadsheet programs are introduced to demonstrate how they can be used to perform the financial analyses presented throughout this book. Computer spreadsheet programs are extremely versatile for calculating anything mathematical. Spreadsheets use a *worksheet program* that replaces a ledger sheet, a pencil, and a calculator. A good example of this application is Table 11.6, "Present Value Calculation of the Carsons' Retirement Income," which was rapidly performed on a worksheet and pasted into the text of Chapter 11.

Spreadsheet programs can be purchased on the open software market. Excel, Lotus 1-2-3, and Quattro Pro are some of the excellent spreadsheet programs available. Regardless of the spreadsheet program selected, the calculational methods and applications are similar throughout.

Spreadsheets have two options for solving mathematical problems. You can either (1) compose a mathematical *formula* from scratch, or (2) select a mathematical *function* that has been preprogrammed and permanently built into the spreadsheet program.

A *formula* combines values and operators into algebraic expressions. An example of a composed formula in spreadsheet format is the familiar future value (*FV*) formula The variables are *PV, i,* and *n,* whereas the operators are *, +, and ^. The operators, which will be explained later, tell the computer what operation is to be performed. Formulas are usually composed for relatively simple operations, such as addition and subtraction of numbers, and for some algebraic expressions such as the above example.

Preprogrammed *functions* are special commands that perform particular calculations and return the results. Functions are built-in commands, and all spreadsheets have them. Most spreadsheet programs offer nine types of built-in functions: mathematical, engineering, statistical, database, financial, logic, date and time, string, and miscellaneous. In the financial category there are some fifty built-in financial functions available in a typical computer spreadsheet program. Some examples are internal rate of return (IRR), net present value (NPV), and uniform payments (*PMT*). In this chapter we concentrate on how to use built-in financial functions.

Preprogrammed functions offer a tremendous advantage. They provide a quick and easy way to calculate the results of very long, complicated expressions. Functions allow you to perform calculations that in some cases are impossible to calculate by a formula only. One of the most valuable functions is the internal rate of return (IRR). Since the IRR requires calculation by trial and error, it can be laborious when done by hand. The computer performs it instantly.

THE WORKSHEET

Mathematical formulas and built-in functions are simple to compose and apply. But first it is necessary to become familiar with the worksheet. The blank worksheet shown in Figure 19.1 below is what you see when you open a file. (Figure 19.1 is only a small section of screen-sized worksheet. A full worksheet can have as many as 4 million grid boxes.)

Figure 19.1: The Worksheet

A1   Data Entry Description

	A	B	C	D
1				
2				
3				
4				
5				

The worksheet is a grid made up of many individual boxes, each grid box is called a *cell*. The worksheet has a numbered row boarder (1, 2, 3, 4, . . .) and a lettered column border (A, B, C, D, . . .), as shown by the shaded vertical and horizontal borders. These identify the address (i.e., the coordinates) of each cell. In Figure 19.1 there is a heavy border around cell A1. This means that cell A1's address has been selected and is active. Its location is further designated by A1, as shown at the top of the row column. A cell must be active before data can be entered (typed) into it. A cell is activated by simply using the mouse to move the arrow pointer (currently shown pointing to cell B1) to the desired cell and then clicking on it and the designated cell will become activated. Only one cell can be active at a time.

Cells can hold either *values* or *labels* (text). The term *labels* is computer nomenclature for text. A *value* can be either a number, a formula, or a function. The labels are text that you use in the worksheet to explain and identify the meaning of the values that are applied. The values can be numbers, formulas, functions, or results that the worksheet calculates.

Entering Values and Labels in a Worksheet

Suppose you want to enter the data and identifying labels of Table 19.1 in a worksheet. The labels are shown in the top row and the data are the numbers in the last three rows.

Table 19.1: Labels and Data

Present Value	Interest Rate	Number of Years
$1,000	10%	10
1,000	10	20
3,000	10	30

Figure 19.2: Labels and Data Entered in a Worksheet

C2   10

	A	B	C
1	Present Value $	Interest Rate %	No. of Years
2	1000	10	10
3			
4			
5			

We typed the labels and first row of numbers of Table 19.1 into the worksheet of Figure 19.2. The specific typed-in entries are:

CELL	ENTRY
A1	Present Value $
B1	Interest Rate %
C1	No. of years
A2	=1000
B2	=10
C2	=10

Notice that the numbers in cells A2, B2, and C2 are typed in by first typing an equals (=) sign in front. This tells the computer that they are numbers (values) rather than labels. Numbers, of course, can also be labels. The border around cell C2 indicates that the cell is active. Only one cell can be active at a time. The address C2 is also shown at the top of the first column and the number 10 is shown by the data-entry indicator. Also notice that in cells A2, B2, and C2 only numbers are entered, because no symbols, such as $ or commas, can be entered. These can be easily inserted later by formatting procedures available with all spreadsheet programs.

WRITING MATHEMATICAL FORMULAS

We explain formula development by using the formula for future value of a single payment. Recall that Formula 4.1 to calculate the future value is $FV = PV(1+i)^n$

To express this in computer spreadsheet format, we must use operators that tell the computer what operations are to be performed. The operator symbols are +, −, *, /, and ^ . The first two are obvious, of course. The asterisk designates that multiplication is to be performed; the forward slash is for division; and the circumflex denotes raising the value to an exponential. Each operation in a formula must be preceded by the appropriate symbol. When we apply the operators the spreadsheet formula becomes: $FV=PV*(1+i/100)^{\wedge n}$

The computer knows how to plan the sequence of events. It first divides i by 100 to convert it to decimal form, adds $1 + i/100$, raises $(1 + i/100)$ to the nth power, then multiplies the results by PV. In is important to note that the formula must have a parentheses about the quantity $1 + i/100$ just as the correct algebraic formula would have. The computer begins its calculational process inside the parentheses and does the others in sequence. Programming is not difficult as long as the parentheses are correctly placed.

As with algebraic formulas, we must substitute values for the variables in order to calculate numerical results. In Figure 19.3 we have put the additional numbers in rows 2 and 3 and have added the label "Future Value $" above the column where the results will appear. We now compose a formula of the future value and place it in cell D2. The formula is composed of the cell addresses of the values. Thus the formula in cell D2 is composed as =A2*(1+B2/100)^C2 where A2, B2 and C2 are the addresses in row 2 of the present value (1000), interest rate (10), and number of years (10), respectively. To place formulas in cells D3 and D4, the formula in cell D3 is simply copied to these cells using a standard copy command. These become =A3*(1+B3/100)^C3 and =A4*(1+B4/100)^C4. Notice that an equals sign precedes each formula. This is necessary to tell the computer that this is a formula rather than a label. Labels do not perform calculations. The resulting values appear immediately in the results cells where the formulas were installed. The heavy outline around cell D2 shows the result and the formula in the currently active cell D2 is shown at the data-entry indicator on top of the figure.

Figure 19.3: Formula Calculations in Column D

D2   = A2*(1+B2/100)^C2   Formula result

	A	B	C	D
1	Present Value $	Interest Rate %	No. of Years	Future Value $
2	1,000	10	10	2,593.74
3	1,000	10	20	6,727.50
4	3,000	10	30	52,348.21
5				

We can also calculate the present value by putting the actual numbers in the formula. The formula in cell D2 would then be =1000*(1+10/100)^10, which also produces the value 2,593.74. Check this by hand calculation.

One advantage of a spreadsheet is its ability to perform numerous calculations easily. You can put values in many cells, compose the first formula using the cell address of the first cell, and then use the copy command to place that formula in all the other cells where you want results. The computer automatically changes the corresponding cell-value designations as the formula is copied to different cells addresses. Also the worksheet can be saved as a file, so that you can call it up later and use it for a new set of value calculations.

Using Parentheses

The art of writing spreadsheet formulas involves the ability to correctly use parentheses. It is necessary to a have an equal number of left and right parentheses in any given formula; otherwise you will be notified that a *syntax error* is present in your formula. For example, the formula (1+0.10)^2)*100 has one left side parentheses and two right. This will not work. It should be ((1+0.10)^2)*100. You cannot go wrong by using many pairs of parentheses, but you get into trouble when you do not use enough.

Computers so you must think for them. For example, if we wanted to find the effective interest rate of 10% compounded monthly, recall that we would use the formula

$$i_E = \left(1+\frac{i_N}{M}\right)^M -1$$ When we substitute the numbers and solve the formula

$$\left(1+\frac{0.10}{12}\right)^{12} -1$$ using a hand-held calculator, we get 0.1047, then change it to percentage by multiplying it by 100, for 10.47%. The correct way to write this in spreadsheet format is to use an additional set of parentheses as =((1+0.10/12)^12 − 1)*100. Also spreadsheet programs have a formatting command that will automatically change values to percent when selected.

From this exercise, you can see that the computer works first within and then outward from the parentheses. Thus if you use a lot of pairs of parentheses it will work just fine.

RELATIVE AND ABSOLUTE CELL ADDRESSING

There are two types of cell addressing, *relative* and *absolute*. These can best be understood by example. In Figure 19.3, we calculated the future value of three sets of data. This is repeated below in Figure 19.4, but which has a slight change: In column E the formulas we wrote for the future value solutions are shown in place of the resulting value (given in Figure 19.3). This is an option available in spreadsheet programs which allows the operator to view the formulas in each cell. To originate these formulas we initially wrote the formula =A2*(1+B2/100)^C2 and inserted it in cell D2. Then we copied it to cells D3 and D4. The computer program automatically changed the cell addresses to the row numbers. The formula then picked up the appropriate numbers in each corresponding row. We did not have to write a new formula in each row. This process is an example of *relative cell addressing*. The cell address changes relative to the cell row to which it is copied.

Figure 19.4: Formula Calculations in Column D

D4   = A4*(1+B4/100)^D4   Formula result

	A	B	C	D
1	Present Value $	Interest Rate %	No. of Years	Future Value $
2	1,000	10	10	=A2*(1+B2/100)^C2
3	1,000	10	20	=A3*(1+B3/100)^C3
4	3,000	10	30	=A4*(1+B4/100)^C4
5				

There will be times when you want to make a permanent reference to a cell that you do not want to change when applying the copy command. This is *absolute cell addressing*. The method is implemented by including a dollar sign $ before both the row and column designators (the $ sign here has nothing to do with money). For example, notice that the interest rate of Table 19.4, column B is always 10%. If we wanted to write the formula to use only the address in cell B2 throughout all calculations, we would write it as:

$$=A2*(1+\$B\$2/100)^C2$$

When we copy this formula to cells D3 and D4, they become = A3*(1+$B$2/100)^D3 and B4*(1+$C$2/100)^D4. Cell address $C$2 never changes, no matter where the formula is moved by copying it.

USING BUILT-IN FINANCIAL FUNCTIONS

A function is defined by its *arguments*. Arguments are the data that a function uses in its calculation. A dictionary definition of an argument is "one of the independent variables upon whose value that of a function depends." An example of a function and its arguments is the internal rate of return, which has the computer format =IRR(*values, guess*). IRR identifies the function which you select and the computer brings up in the cell address you select (i.e., activate). This function returns the internal rate of return based on the arguments *values* and *guess*. The argument *guess* is an estimate of what the discount rate might be and is the number that the computer uses to iterate on. The argument *values* are the cash flows of the problem. Arguments are always enclosed by parentheses and the different arguments are separated by a comma. The equal sign (=) preceding the IRR is used by some programs such as Excel to show the computer the expression is a function. (Note: Arguments in the functions of various spreadsheet programs are the same, but sometimes appear in a different order.)

A function designation is an abbreviation of a much more involved preprogrammed mathematical operation. Notice that there are no operational symbols such as *, +, or −, involved in a function format. This differs from a formula which must include symbols for each operation to be performed. Let's demonstrate the use of a function.

Example 16.1: Using the IRR Function

For this example let's select Example 6.8 and the cash flow data shown in Table 6.6 from Chapter 6. The cash flow portion of that table is repeated here for convenience:

Year end	Paid $	Received $
0	− 2,500	
1	− 2,000	
2	− 1,500	
3		1,000
4		6,800

In the spreadsheet of Figure 19.5 we typed identifying labels in cells B1 and A7. The cash flow values (arguments) are typed in cells B2 through B6. The IRR function =IRR(0.10, B2..B6) is then typed in cell B7, complete with the range where the arguments are located, and a value of 0.10 is typed in as the guess. The range of cash flow is covered by typing in B2..B6 with a period between the first and last cell location. No matter how many values are contained in a column of numbers, the designation of the whole is defined by the first and last cell designation.

Figure 19.5: Internal Rate of Return

B7   =IRR(0.10, B2..B6)

	A	B	C	D
1		Cash Flow $		
2		−2500		
3		−2000		
4		−1500		
5		1000		
6		6800		
7	IRR =	8.95 %		
8				

The results appear in cell B7, while the function that was typed in B7 is shown at the top of the worksheet and its location is shown as B7. Remember that numbers entered in a cell are typed in only as numbers: no commas or dollar sign, etc. are included, although minus signs are typed to indicate negative numbers. Numbers typed without a negative sign are assume to be positive .

Recall that in Chapter 6 we laboriously calculated the IRR of Example 6.8 as 9.00% using a trial-and-error method. The accurate value by the computer is 8.95%, and its solution takes only the time required to type in the function and its arguments and. As long as we do not make an error in typing, the computer always provides accurate answers.

The Summation Function

To add a column of numbers a very simple function is available. Suppose we have a column of numbers as shown in column C below. We simple write =SUM(C1..C4), place it anywhere in the worksheet, and get the results as shown. In this example we selected cell C5 for the address of the results.

C5   =SUM(C1..C4)

	A	B	C	D
1			1000	
2			500	
3			25	
4			350	
5			1,875	

Understanding Financial Functions in a Spreadsheet Program

It is quite simple to identify and use financial functions as long as you understand the application of the math behind what you are seeking. The "*Help*" section of a spreadsheet program describes functions very clearly and offers examples. Let's see how one works. When you click on the "Help" section, then on "Contents" and then choose "Financial Functions," you will see all the available functions. Choose FVAL and this is what appears:

FVAL = Future Value of Investment

Format :   *FVAL(Rate, Nper, Pmt, <Pv>, <Type>)*

Rate = a numeric value > - 1, representing the periodic interest rate per compounding period (the fixed interest rate per compounding period).

Nper = number of periods, which should be an integer > 0.

Pmt   = a numeric value representing the amount of the periodic payment.

Pv   = a numeric value representing the current value of an investment (present value).

Type = an optional numeric value that indicates whether payments or cash flows occur at the beginning (1) or the end (0) of the period; default =0.

Notice: The last two arguments Pv and Type are optional.

Example:

Assume you want to set aside $500 at the start of each year in a savings account plan that earns 15% annually. To determine what the account will be worth at the end of six years, starting with a present value of $340, enter this formula:

$$FVAL\ (0.15,\ 6,\ -500,\ -340,\ 1)$$
The result is $5,819.84

Notice that the payment and present value are out of your pocket so you enter a negative sign. If either is omitted they are assume to be zero.

CREATING A WORKSHEET WITH FORMULAS AND BUILT-IN FUNCTIONS

Let's create an amortization worksheet for this demonstration. Figure 14.1 in Chapter 14 is such a schedule. Assume that a home mortgage has a borrowed principal of $100,000, an interest rate of 7.50%, and a term of 30 years. Figure 19.6 below shows the first 12 months of the amortization schedule for this loan. The general procedure is to first type in the labels. Then the following calculations are inserted:

(1) Monthly payments are calculated in cell C6 using the input data as arguments in the function (after Excel) "PMT(*rate, nper, pv, fv, type*)," which calculates Formula 5 of Chapter 5. The result is $699.21

(2) The principal is typed into cell D11, and the first month's interest is calculated in cell B12 as 0.075/12 × $100,00 = $625.00.

(3) The monthly principal is calculated by subtracting the monthly interest payment from the monthly payment. This is $ 699.21 − $625.00 = $74.21.

(4) The principal remaining is calculated by subtracting the principal from the starting loan principal. That is $100,000 − $74.21 = $99,925 79.

(5) The formulas in columns B12, C12, and D12 are rapidly copied down their respective columns ending in cells B371, C371, and D371, and the entire 360 month schedule is complete. This spreadsheet should not take more than 20 minutes to accomplish once you are familiar with worksheet operations.

Figure 19.6: A Home Mortgage Schedule

	A	B	C	D
1	AMORTIZATION SCHEDULE			
2	Home Mortgage			
3	Principal		$100,000	
4	Interest		7.50%	
5	Term		360	Months
6	Payments		$699.21	Per Month
7				
8		Interest	Principal	Principal
9	Month	Payment	Payment	Remaining
10				
11				$100,000.00
12	1	$625.00	$74.21	99,925.79
13	2	624.54	74.68	99,851.11
14	3	624.07	75.15	99,775.96
15	4	623.60	75.61	99,700.35
16	5	623.13	76.09	99,624.26
17	6	622.65	76.56	99,547.70
18	7	622.17	77.04	99,470.66
19	8	621.69	77.52	99,393.13
20	9	621.21	78.01	99,315.13
21	10	620.72	78.49	99,236.63
22	11	620.23	78.99	99,157.64
23	12	619.74	79.48	99,078.17

After the labels are typed in, the specific input values are typed into the spreadsheet as follows:

CELL	ENTRY	COMMENTS
A12	=A1 + 1	Adds 1 to cell A1 and use the copy command to fill the A column down to cell A371.
C3	= 100000	Data input
C4	= 0.0750	Data input
C5	= 360	Data input
D11	= C3	Places starting principal's value
C6	=PMT (C4, C5, C3, 0, 0)	Calculates payment of a fixed-rate loan. PMT(*rate, nper, pv, fv, type*) The *fv* = 0, and the *type* is 0 for end of period payments.
B12	= ($C$4/12)*D11	Calculates first months interest
C12	= $C$6 − B12	Calculates pay back of principal
D12	= C11 − C12	Calculates principal remaining

Notice that absolute cell addressing was used in the creation of the mortgage schedule in cells B12 and C12. In these applications the interest rate in cell C4 and the monthly payment in cell C6 are constants.

After the formulas are placed in cells B12, C12, and D12, they are copied and pasted down their respective columns through cells B371, C371, and D371, respectively. This completes the 360-monthly payments schedule. The values appear in the corresponding cells as soon as the formulas are copied. The loan would be paid off the last month so cell D371 reads "0" principal remaining.

Remember that we type the numbers as 100000, 0750, and 360 in cells C3, C4, and C5, respectively. Only numbers are typed into cells, but the cell is formatted to add the $ signs and commas to the numbers (values) as they appear in their cells. Formatting the worksheet is a simple procedure for spreadsheet programs and so is not addressed here.

This worksheet can be handy for making advanced payments, as described in Chapter 14, as well as keeping track of the annual interest paid as an income tax deduction. Once you have created the worksheet, you can save it to a disc and reuse it to calculate monthly payment, the schedule of interest payments, principal payments, and the remaining principal for whatever you might finance.

Now It's Your Turn:

In these exercises write all spreadsheet formulas in a form that uses the operators. In this set of questions we do not use a multiple choice format but provide the answers at the end of the problem set.

1. Write a spreadsheet formula to solve $y=x^n$, where $x = 100$ and $n = 2$.
2. Suppose you want to calculate the effective interest rate given a nominal interest rate of 10% compounded daily. Recall that the algebraic formula to convert a nominal interest rate to an effective interest rate is Formula 4.2: $i_E = \left(1 + \dfrac{i_N}{M}\right)^M - 1$

    Express the answer in percent.
3. Write the formula for the payments of an ordinary annuity, which is:

$$PMT_e = PV \left[\frac{i(1+i)^n}{(1+i)^n - 1} \right]$$

    Use $PV = 100000$, $i = 6\%$ compounded monthly, and for a term of 30 years.
4. Suppose we have the information of problem 3 in a worksheet and want to calculate the PMT_e for three different interest rates, as shown in column B below. If we want to hold the interest rate and number of months constant, write the formula that you would place in cell D2 to be copied to cells E3 and E4.

D2   Formula?

	A	B	C	D
	Present Value $	Interest Rate %	No. of Months	PMT_e
1				
2	100000	6	360	
3		7		
4		8		

5. The function for payments for the Quattro Pro spreadsheet is PMT(*Pv,Rate,Nper*). The *Nper* is the number of compounding periods. Contrast this with the formula developed for problem 4 above. Which is easiest to use?

Answers:

1. $=100^2$ $y = 10{,}000$
2. $= ((1+0.10/365)^{365} - 1)*100$ $i_E = 10.52\%$
3. $=100000*((0.06/12)*(1+0.06/12)^{360})/((1+0.06/12)^{360} - 1)$
    $PMT_e = 599.55$
4. $= \$B\$2*(C2/100/12)*(1+C2/100/12)^{\$D\$2}/((1+C2/100/12)^{\$D\$2} - 1)$
    $PMT_e = 599.55$
5. $=PMT(Pv, Rate, Term)$, which is $=PMT(\$B\$2, C2/100/12, \$D\$2)$
    $PMT_e = 599.55$

The function is obviously easier to apply. Notice that absolute cell addressing can also be used in function arguments.

Appendix: Compendium of Formulas

Formula 2.1: Percentage Difference

$$\frac{\text{Final Value - Base Value}}{\text{Base Value}} \times 100 = \% \text{ Difference}$$

Cash Flow Diagrams

Four-year timeline

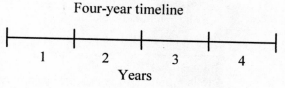

Years

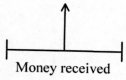

Money received

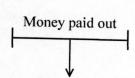

Money paid out

Formula 3.1
Calculation of Interest

$$INT = PV \times i \times n$$

Where:
  INT = interest earned
  PV = present value of
      money (principal)
  i = the interest rate per
      time period
  n = number of interest
      time periods

Formula 3.2
Periodic Interest Rates

$$i = \frac{\text{Annual Rate}}{\text{Period}} = \text{Periodic Rate}$$

Formula 3.3
Future Value of a Simple Interest Loan

$$FV = PV(1 + i \times n)$$

Where

PV = present value (principal starting amount)

FV = future value (total sum of money) payable at the end of the term.

i = interest rate per interest period.

n = number of periods.

Formula 3.4: The Rule of 72
(The doubling time of money)

$$\frac{72}{\text{Interest Rate}} = \text{Years to Double}$$

Interest rate is annual and is expressed in percent.

Formula 4.1: Future Value of a Present Value Amount
(The power formula)

$$FV = PV(1+i)^n$$

Where

FV = *Future Value* of a compounded amount of money at the end of n periods

PV = *Present Value* of money at beginning of the first period

i = *Interest rate* per compounding period

n = *Number* of compound periods.

Formula 4.2: Calculating Effective Interest Rate

$$i_E = \left(1 + \frac{i_N}{M}\right)^M - 1$$

Where

i_N = nominal interest rate

i_E = effective interest rate

M = number of compounding periods per year

Figure 5.1: Cash Flow Diagrams of Annuity Payment Modes

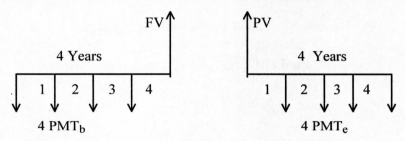

Annuity Due	Ordinary Annuity
(Beginning-of-period payments)	(Amortization end-of-period payments)

PMT_b = the uniform *beginning* of each year payment

PMT_e = the uniform *end* of each year payment

Formula 5.1: Future Value of Beginning-of-Period Uniform Payments (Annuity Due)

Find FV, given PMT_b, i, and n.

$$FV = PMT_b (1 + i)\left[\frac{(1+i)^n - 1}{i}\right]$$

Where

FV = present value of the uniform series of future cash flows

PMT_b = the uniform *beginning* of periodic payments

i = the interest rate per compound period

n = the number of compound periods

Formula 5.2: Present Value of a Uniform Series of End of Period Payments

Find PV, Given PMT_e, i, and n.

(Ordinary annuity)

$$PV = PMT_e \left(\frac{(1+i)^n - 1}{i(1+i)^n}\right)$$

The symbols are the same as those of Formula 5.1 except for the end of period uniform payments:

$$PMT_e = \textit{End}\text{-of-period payments}$$

Formula 5.3: End-of-Period Uniform Payments
(Ordinary Annuity-Amortization)
Find PMT_e, given PV, i, and n.

$$PMT_e = PV \left[\frac{i(1+i)^n}{(1+i)^n - 1} \right]$$

Formula 5.4: Present Value of Beginning-of-Period Uniform Payments.
(Annuity Due)
Find PV, given PMT_b, i, and n.

$$PV = PMT_b\,(1+i)\left(\frac{(1+i)^n - 1}{i(1+i)^n} \right)$$

Formula 5.6: Generalized Compound Interest Formula

$$0 = PV + (1+iS)\ PMT \left[\frac{1-(1+i)^{-n}}{i} \right] + FV(1+i)^{-n}$$

Where:
n = number of compounding periods
i = interest rate per compounding period
PV = present value
FV = future value
PMT = periodic payment

S = payment mode factor (0 or 1). $S = 0$ for payments made at *end* of period (ordinary annuity), $S = 1$ for payments made at the *beginning* of period (annuity due). Thus for PMT_b, $S = 1$; and for PMT_e, $S = 0$.

Formula 6.1: Present Value of a Single Sum

$$PV = \frac{FV}{(1+i)^n}$$

Formula 6.2: Capitalization of Costs

$$\text{Captalized Costs} = \frac{\text{Annual cost}}{\text{Interest Rate}}$$

Formula 10.1: Calculating Income Tax Savings Due to Deductions

Tax Savings = Value of Tax Deduction × Marginal Tax Rate

Formula: 10.2: Calculating the Effective State Tax Rate

Effective State Tax Rate = State Rate × (1 − Federal Rate)

Formula 10.3: Combined Effective Marginal Income Tax Rates

Combined Marginal Tax Rate = Effective State Rate + Federal Marginal Tax Rate

Formula 10.4a: Calculating Tax-Equivalent Yields

$$\frac{\text{Tax Free - Yield}}{(1 - \text{Marginal Tax Rate})} = \text{Tax - Equivalent Yield}$$

Formula 10.4b: Converting Tax-Free Income to Equivalent Taxable Income

$$\frac{\text{Tax - Free Income}}{(1 - \text{Marginal Tax Rate})} = \text{Equivalent Taxable Income}$$

Formula 10.4c: Before-Tax Equivalent Yield

$$\frac{\text{After - Tax Equivalent Yield}}{(1 - \text{Marginal Tax Rate})} = \text{Before - Tax Yield}$$

Formula 12.1: Current Yield of a Bond

$$\text{Current Yield} = \frac{\text{Annual Interest}}{\text{Current Price}}$$

Formula 12.2: Bond Yield to Maturity (YTM) by the Approximate Method

(First calculation)

$$\frac{\text{Par Value} \times \text{Coupon Rate} + \dfrac{\text{Par Value} - \text{Price}}{\text{Years to Maturity}}}{\text{Price}}$$

(Second calculation)

$$\frac{\text{Par Value} \times \text{Coupon Rate} + \dfrac{\text{Par Value} - \text{Price}}{\text{Years to Maturity}}}{\text{Par Value} - \dfrac{\text{Par Value} - \text{Price}}{\text{Years to Maturity}}}$$

Formula 13.1: T-Bill Discount Yield of T-Bills

$$\text{Discount Yield} = \frac{F - P}{F} \times \frac{360}{N}$$

Where:

F = face value (FV) of the bill at maturity
P = current market price (PV)
N = number of days to maturity
y = yield of T-Bills

Bid Price:

$$P_{\text{Bid}} = F - y_{Bid} \times F \times \frac{N}{360}$$

Asked Price:

$$P_{\text{Asked}} = F - y_{Asked} \times F \times \frac{N}{360}$$

Formula 13.2: Effective Yield of T-Bills

$$\text{Effective Yield} = \left(1 + \frac{F - P}{P}\right)^{365/N} - 1$$

Formula 13.3: Coupon-Equivalent Yield of T-Bills

$$\text{Coupon - Equivalent Yield} = \frac{F - P}{P} \times \frac{365}{N}$$

Formula 15.1: Tax-Deferred Annuity Exclusion Amount

$$\frac{\text{Investment}}{\text{Expected Return}} \times \text{Annuity Payment} = \text{Exclusion Amount}$$

Glossary

add-on loan A loan in which annual interest is calculated for each year of the loan term, then summed and added to the principal. The monthly payments are determined by dividing the total interest and principal by the total number of months of the loan. The annual percentage rate, as calculated by accurate compound-interest mathematics, is higher by about a factor of two than the stated interest rate of the add-on loan.

adjustable rate mortgage (ARM) A mortgage interest rate that is adjusted at specified intervals to follow the changes of some index, such as the interest rates of U.S. Treasury bills. In return for the risk of fluctuating market interest rates, borrowers usually get a lower starting interest rate in an ARM.

amortization Retiring a debt by making ordinary annuity type of payments. Each payment consists of the sum of an interest and a principal component. The principal amount of each payment retires part of the loan's principal balance. As the loan progresses, the amount of the principal payment increases and the amount of the interest payment decreases.

annual percentage rate (APR) The stated nominal interest rate—the cost of credit that consumers pay, expressed as an annual percentage rate. According to the federal Truth in Lending Law, every consumer loan agreement must disclose its APR.

annual percentage yield (APY) The effective annual yield of an investment, computed from the nominal annual interest rate and the specified number of compounding periods in a year.

annuitant The person on whose life monthly insurance payments depend.

annuitize To contract with an insurance company to begin receiving annuity payments. The payments received are based on the value of the annuitant's holdings, the interest rate the company chooses to pay, and the annuitant's expected lifetime. Once annuitized, the action is irrevocable and the annuitant can no longer change cash-withdrawal options.

annuity The generic term for cash flow (payment or receipt) of an equal amount of money disbursed at equal intervals. A cash flow of $100 each month for 120 months is an example of an annuity. Insurance companies have adopted this term in cases where they contract to pay regular payments to a policyholder.

annuity due   An annuity in which the payments (or receipts) of money are made at the beginning of each compounding period.

asked price   The price at which a dealer offers to sell a security.

average income tax rate   The amount of income tax paid in a given year divided by the total amount of taxable income.

average rate of return   The return obtained by dividing the sum of the annual returns by the number of years of the transaction. The average rate of return is not a compound annual rate of return, nor is it comparable to the annual percentage yield.

balloon payment   The amount of payment necessary to retire an amortized loan that has not yet been paid to completion. For example, a "30 in 5 year loan" means that monthly payments will be made for 5 years and then the loan balance must be paid off by a balloon payment equal to the remaining principal balance of the loan.

basis points   The term used to describe the amount of change in yield of a security. One hundred basis points equals a 1% change. For example, an increase from 2% to 2.10% is a 10 basis point change ($2.10\% - 2.00\% = 0.10\%$ change, and $0.10 \times 100 = 10$ basis points).

bear market   A prolonged period of falling stock prices.

Beneficiary   The person who receives the proceeds in the event of the policy holders death.

bid price   The price at which a dealer offers to buy a security.

biweekly payment mortgage   A home mortgage in which the normal payments of a 30 year mortgage are divided by a factor of 2 and are made every two weeks instead of monthly. This allows the mortgagee to make 26 annual payments a year in place of twelve. This results in paying more principal during each year so the mortgage that is paid off in about 21 years instead of 30 years.

bond   A debt security that obligates the issuer to pay the bond holder a specified amount of money at specific intervals, usually semiannually, and to repay the principal at maturity.

bull market   A prolonged period of rising stock prices.

callable bonds   A provision of a bond contract in which the issuer retains the right to retire the bond prior to the maturity date. When called, the issuer usually pays a premium over and above the face value of the bond for this privilege.

capital gain   The difference between an asset's purchase price and its selling price when the selling price is higher than the purchase price. The percentage gain is this difference divided by the purchase price and then converted to percent.

capitalization   The present value of a perpetual annuity, computed by dividing the annual annuity payment by the annual interest rate. For example, an annual payment of $1,000 at an interest rate of 10% is capitalized by a present value of $1,000 ÷ 0.10 = $10,000.

cash flow diagram   A diagram that shows the magnitude of each cash payment and each cash receipt on a time line scale.

cash surrender value   The amount of cash available upon voluntary termination of an insurance policy prior to the death of the insured.

cash-on-cash return   The rate of return on an investment calculated on a year-by-year basis, rather than the compound annual rate of return of a complete life-cycle investment. For example, a cash investment of $10,000 that returns $1,000 the first year has a cash-on-cash rate of return of 10% for that year only.

certificate of deposit (CD)   A "time deposit" in a bank that earns interest at a specified rate and matures on a specific date stipulated by a certificate. Bank usually compound the money daily.

compound interest   A reinvestment method in which interest earned during each compounding period is added to the previous principal and the new principal sum again earns interest during the next compounding period.

constant dollar   The buying power of a dollar that is constant—not adjusted for inflation over time. It is the dollar of a base year when performing inflation studies.

coupon   The promise to pay interest at a specified rate based on the face value of a bond.

coupon-equivalent yield   The yield of a T-bill equivalent to the coupon yield of a bond.

cumulative total return   The gain of an asset over a given period of time. (See capital gain.)

current yield   The annual amount of interest earned on a bond, as defined by the coupon, divided by the current market price of that bond, converted to percent.

death-benefit rate of return   The computed internal rate of return (IRR) of the future value of a death benefit (when received at the time of death) and the annual premiums paid to maintain the life insurance policy.

discount rate   The interest rate used when conducting present value calculations.

discount yield   The yield computed for a T-bill, based on the difference between the face value, purchase price, and maturity date. The discount yield understates the yield of T-bills because of the erroneous way it is calculated, based on the results of the Treasury Department's weekly auctions of T-bills.

discounted annuity   The present value of an annuity stream of cash flows calculated with a given discount rate.

discounted bond   A bond whose current market price is less than its face value

discounted cash flow   The present value of expected future net cash flows using a given discount rate (interest rate).

dividend   A payment declared by a corporation's board of directors. Dividends are usually paid quarterly to holders of the security.

effective interest rate   The annual interest rate computed from the nominal interest rate (or APR) and the number of compounding periods in a year (which is defined in association with the nominal interest rate). In order to compare investment alternatives on an equal basis their effective interest rates that must be computed. Nominal interest rates are not comparable.

exclusion amount   The calculated amount allowed as nontaxable return of principal in the cash flow stream of annuity payments. An exclusion amount is allowed for insurance annuities but not for mutual funds or other types of investments.

face value   The value of a bond, note, or other security as specified by the certificate. For bonds, the face value is usually $1,000.

Federal Reserve Board (FRB)   The governing board of the Federal Reserve System.

fixed annuity   An annuity contract in which the insurance company guarantees to disburse fixed payments to the annuitant, either for life or for a specified period of time.

future value   The total amount of all compounded money at a given date in the future.

GNMA   The Government National Mortgage Association, known as "Ginnie Mae" for short. This is a government agency, carrying the full faith and credit of the U.S. government, that purchases mortgages from the original lenders and then sells them to brokers who in turn sell them to investors. The money paid by the home owners each month is passed through to the buyers of the GNMA certificates.

home equity line of credit   A bank loan backed by the equity in a home. A form of revolving credit in which the borrower can either write checks for money as needed or take a lump sum. The amount available credit is based on a percentage of the borrower's equity in the home. The borrower must pay the monthly interest incurred but can defer paying the principal.

income-tax avoidance   The use of legal measures allowed by the U.S. tax laws, such as deduction of home mortgage interest, to reduce the amount of one's total federal income tax.

individual retirement account (IRA)   A personal tax-deferred retirement account set up with the custodian of a qualified plan. An working investor can deposit $2,000 per year ($4,000 for a married couple) of earned income. Income invested in the plan is usually tax-deductible. The money can be withdrawn when the investor reaches age 59 ½ years. Before that age the investor is subject to a 10% penalty on the withdrawn money. Upon withdrawal the money is taxed.

inflation   The rise in the cost of goods and services over time. Two U.S. indicators of inflation are the Consumer Price Index (CPI) and the Producer Price Index (PPI).

initial public offering (IPO)   The first offering for sale to the public of a new stock or a bond issue.

installment loans   Loans that are repaid by a series of fixed payments.

interest rate   The ratio between the interest chargeable or payable at the end of a period of time, usually a year or less, and the money owed at the beginning of that period.

internal rate of return (IRR)   The interest rate that renders the present value of the net discounted cash flows equal to zero. The IRR is a method of discounted cash flow analysis.

joint and survivor annuity   An annuity that provides monthly payments during the lifetime of the annuitant and a designated second person.

leveraging   The use of borrowed money to invest in securities in the hope that the rate of return of the securities will exceed the cost of borrowing. This practice increases the rate of return of investments in a bull market but causes greater losses in a bear market.

life annuity   An annuity that provides monthly payments during the lifetime of the annuitant. No payments are made after the annuitant dies.

marginal income tax rate   The federal tax rate paid on the next dollar of taxable income earned. This is usually referred to as the "income tax bracket." Currently there are five marginal rates, 15%, 28%, 31%, 36%, and 39.6%. A taxpayer's rate depends on the magnitude of the his or her taxable income.

maturity date   The termination or due date on which a debt must be paid in full.

mortgage   A debt in which the borrower (mortgagor) gives the lender a lien on the real property as collateral for the loan.

municipal bonds   Bonds issued by state or local governments. The interest earned from these bonds is usually free of state and federal income taxes.

mutual fund   An open-ended investment in which a mutual fund company pools investor's money into a portfolio of various securities to provide professional management and diversification.

negative amortization   A mortgage in which the interest rate charged by a mortgage is lower than the contract interest rate, so that the borrower's monthly payments can not cover the interest charged. Thus the loan principal balance must increase to make up the deficiency. A negative amortization loan can never be paid off. It can occur when the interest rate is adjusted upward causing a higher monthly payment, but the borrower does not what to pay the increased payment amount. So to maintain the monthly payments constant they are willing to accept negative amortization.

net present value (NPV)   A method of evaluating investments by calculating the present value of all cash flows, both inflows and outflows, using a given discount rate. If the NPV is positive, the investment returns a rate to the investor that is greater than the discount rate; if the NPV is negative, it returns a rate of return lower than the discount rate.

nominal interest rate   See annual percentage rate (APR).

ordinary annuity   An annuity in which the periodic payments are disbursed (or received) at the end of each compounding period. Amortization of a home mortgage is an example of an ordinary annuity. The lender pays off the loan and then begins to receive the first payment at the end of the first monthly compounding period.

par value   The face value of a security. A bond selling at par means that it is worth the price (typically $1,000) at which it was issued, provided it was not a discounted bond.

payments for a designated period   Annuity payments made for a defined period, as opposed to lifetime payments made as long as the annuitant lives.

premium bond   A bond whose current market price is greater than its the face value.

premiums   The periodic payments made to maintain an insurance policy.

present value   The value of money in hand today plus all future amounts of money discounted to today at a given interest rate (which is termed the "discount rate").

price volatility   Relatively large swings in the prices of securities over time.

principal   The original amount of money on which interest is earned or paid. The balance of a debt, not including any interest earned.

principle of equivalence   The principle that all values of a dollar are equivalent over time. Invested at an interest rate of 10%, one dollar at the beginning (year 0) is equivalent to $2.69 (future value) in ten years. Similarly, a dollar received ten years from now is equivalent to having 39 cents today (present value). These statements are true only if the interest rate realized on the invested or borrowed money is 10%. At a different interest rate, the time value of money changes accordingly.

qualified plan   An employee retirement plan that qualifies for favorable tax benefits under the U.S. tax law. There are two types of plans, (1) defined benefit and (2) defined contributions. A pure pension plan is a defined benefit plan and a 401(k) plan is a defined contribution plan.

rate of return (ROR)   The general term for the annual compound interest rate realized on any investment. The ROR is calculated by compound interest mathematics.

real dollar   The buying power of a dollar over time, adjusted to account for inflation. For example, at an annual inflation rate of 4%, the buying power of $10 today will buy only $6.76 worth of goods in ten years. The real value of a dollar in ten years is thus 67.6% of one of today's dollars.

reverse annuity mortgage (RAM)   A mortgage in which a home owner at least 62 year of age, contracts to receive income payments based on the value of their house. The payee organization agrees to make payments until the owner(s) are deceased or sell the house. Upon sale of the house, the payee recoups the future value of the money paid at an agreed-on interest rate, while the heirs receive the balance. Some contracts are written so that the payee organization receives the entire value of the home when the owner(s) die.

salary reduction plan 401(k)   An employee retirement plan in which employers and employees contribute pre-taxed money; the earnings and capital gains of this investment then grow, tax-deferred, until they are distributed at retirement.

securities   A general term for stocks, bonds, and other investment instruments.

simple interest   Interest calculated only on the original principal. Once earned, the interest is never added to the principal to earn interest again, regardless of the length of the loan term. For simple interest transactions, no payments are made at any time until the loan matures. The difference between simple and compound interest is often misunderstood. Because compound interest is calculated for each compounding period, it is often thought to be a simple interest transaction when it is not, since the interest from the previous compounding period *is* added to the next compounding period to earn interest again.

sinking fund   Money paid at regular intervals to a dedicated account to secure a future amount of money to pay for the replacement of worn-out equipment, or to repay bonds when they mature. This concept is a good strategy, but the sinking fund formula used to calculate the future value of the accumulated money is flawed. The future value of an annuity due is the correct formula to use.

Standard and Poor's 500 index   The composite index of 500 stocks identified by the Standard and Poor's corporation, a subsidiary of McGraw-Hill, Inc. The companies selected for the 500 index includes 400 industrial, 20 transportation, 40 utilities, and 40 financial firms.

tax-deferred investment   An investment whose accumulated earnings and capital gains are free from taxation until the investor takes distribution.

tax-equivalent yield   For a given marginal income tax rate, the yield of annual interest from a taxable security, after paying the income taxes, is the same as the yield realized from a tax-exempt security (such as a municipal bond).

tax-exempt security   A security whose interest earned is exempt from taxation by federal, state, and local governments. One class of these securities is called municipal bonds, or "Muni bonds" for short.

term   The duration of time between the starting date and the maturity date of a loan or other types of financial instruments such as bonds.

the Rule of 72   A rule that estimates the compound doubling time of invested money. Dividing the number 72 by the interest rate in percentage form provides an estimate of the number of years it takes to double invested money. Money invested at 10% annual interest doubles in $72 \div 10\% = 7.2$ years.

the Rule of 78   A sum-of-the-digits method of determining the schedule for repaying the interest and principal of a loan. Under this rule the borrower pays a greater amount of interest if he or she pays off the loan before the term expires.

total rate of return   The rate of return on an investment that takes into account all cash components, such as dividends, interest payments, and capital gains. Conversely, the customarily quoted yield of a stock consists of only the declared dividends, not the capital gains.

trade-off study   A decision-making process utilizing a time-value-of-money comparative analysis of economically driven alternatives, such as buying a new refrigerator versus repairing an old one.

Treasury bill   A debt security of the U.S. Treasury that is issued in maturities of 3, 6, and 12 months and sold at a discount. T-bills are initially sold to an investor in $10,000 minimum denominations, and in $5,000 increments thereafter. A one-year maturity, $10,000 face value T-bill at a quoted discount rate of 5.00% would cost the investor $9,500.

Treasury bond   A debt security of the U.S. Treasury that is sold with maturities greater than 10 years. These bonds pay semiannual interest. The 30-year maturity bond is referred to by the financial community as the "long bond."

Treasury notes   A debt security of the U.S. Treasury that is sold with maturities of 1 to 10 years. These bonds pay semiannual interest.

the Truth-in-Lending Law   A federal law stipulating that lenders must state the terms, conditions, and annual percentage rates of loans offered to consumers.

uniform series of payments   A series of equal-value payments made at equal intervals of time. The generic term for this is "annuity."

variable annuity   A contract with an insurance company, sometimes allied with a mutual fund company, in which the investor selects a variety of subaccount investments—i.e., bonds, stocks, mutual funds—whose values fluctuate according to their market performance. The investments grow tax-deferred. The rate of return of the underlying securities is not guaranteed by the insurance company, but depends on their performance in the market. The investor can, after the age of 59 ½, either annuitize the plan to receive monthly income from the insurance company , or take monthly periodic or lump sum payments by selling securities in the subaccount.

yield   In general yield is the rate of return from any investment; more specifically yield is calculated and quoted for the rate of return of fixed investments and for such income as stock dividends.

yield curve   A graph of the current yield and yield-to-maturity values of bonds versus maturity dates from the present day to 30 years in the future. A yield plot shows the relationship between long-and short-term bond yields. If short-term yields are less than long-term yields, the curve is a positive yield; the converse produces a negative-yield curve.

yield to call   The same as the yield to maturity, except that the time span of the term ends with the date on which the bond is callable.

yield to maturity   The yield realized on a bond determined by a compound interest rate calculation that considers the initial price paid, the coupon yield payments, and the face value returned at the end of the term.

zero-coupon bond   A government debt security that is sold at a discount from its face value. No cash distributions are made until maturity when the face value is paid. The imputed interest is not-tax-deferred and the bond holder must pay income taxes on the imputed annual income even though no money is received until the bonds mature. Zero-coupon bonds are usually held in tax-deferred accounts to avoid annual payment of the imputed interest.

9 781583 483787